THE PEDDLER'S PREROGATIVE

A guide for your bag carrying, door banging, dialing for dollars, shoot the moon, when in doubt panic and accelerate, kind of sales folk

THE **PEDDLER'S PREROGATIVE**

A guide for your bag carrying, door banging, dialing for dollars,
shoot the moon, when in doubt panic and accelerate, kind of sales folk

DENNIS FORD

Next Phase Business Development
15 Parker Point Road
Hopkinton, MA 01748
Web Site: www.nextphasebizdev.com

Printed in the United States of America.

ISBN-13: 978-0-9793172-0-0
ISBN-10: 0-9793172-0-7

First Edition 10 9 8 7 6 5 4 3 2 1

The publisher offers quantity discounts on this book. For information, contact Dennis Ford at Next Phase Business Development: Dennis@nextphasebizdev.com.

Publishing Consultant: Neuhaus Publishing (www.neuhauspublishing.com)
Cover Design: Red Door Media (www.reddoormedia.com)
Interior Design/Composition: Marian Hartsough Associates
(www.marianhartsoughassociates.com)
Cartoonist: Ryan Hannus (ryanhannus@aol.com)

This book is dedicated
to my daughter, Caitlin, and my son, Patrick.

CONTENTS

INTRODUCTION

*It was one against a million . . . and they all agreed that
you were the toughest peddler they had ever met!*

Being a good peddler is all about being the grand leader of an army
of one. You get to wake up every day and say, "roll 'em!" You are the
primary driver of your deals—who you're going to call, what products you're going to pitch, how you're going to position them, and
how you're going to move your deals on down the pipe.

Got to, got to, got to get *it* going. (Think James Brown or George
Clinton funky.) Got to get on up! Got to find some blue sky and fly
like a mother trucker!

In other words, the most important ingredient of being a great peddler is you: your attitude, your desire, your personality, your integrity,
your sixth sense for peddling, and the magic you create. These are the
main things that make up your success.

You should feel pretty good about that. Now, I'll let you in on a
little secret. That scares the bejesus out of your manager and everyone else at corporate. Why? Because most of what accounts for your
success can't be measured. And we all know managers like to do
nothing more than measure, write a report, and send the data up the
chain. In fact, many folks are under the impression that the more
things they measure, the more you'll sell!

If there are any corporate drones reading, listen up! Measuring the minutia of everyday sales activity isn't the way to sell more. Let's all stop pretending here. It's a waste of time, not to mention just plain silliness to spend all of your time measuring the things that make up such a small part of a peddler's success.

Ya, there are a million and one ways to set up and execute better, and as many books and consultants willing to tell peddlers how. But I would like to put forth that there's something missing from these approaches. Something basic and ultimately more important than organizing your To Do lists, working your database with a zeal that should be reserved for Red Sox games or belting out your favorite show tunes, or diligently writing up your weekly sales plans.

That something is a peddler's philosophy. I've cobbled mine together over the past 25 years. I have my lists and my databases, but it's my philosophy that I rely on most, day in and day out. It's a simple approach to peddling that boils down to this: You know what's right and you know what's wrong, so call 'em as you see 'em and act accordingly.

This brings us to our first Peddler's Prerogative—one of many "peddlerisms" that pop up throughout this book. They identify some of the common themes and issues of peddling, help you see them for what they are, and suggest the proper course of action, as well as provide a set of guidelines, rules, and dictums that give you the courage to pursue the right peddler strategy.

PEDDLER'S PREROGATIVE #1

You know what's right and you know what's wrong, so call 'em as you see 'em and act accordingly.

My philosophy has served me in good times and in bad, through all kinds of wild situations, and all types of crazy deals. It's my way of thinking about me, my company, and my customers, which essentially is what sales is all about. And it's a way to be successful (before you're measured to death).

My first of many epiphanies was this: A peddler is an army of one. You're it! So you better know where you're going and what you're doing. It has its ups and downs, but the ride is one that you don't want to miss.

Lucky for you, getting the lay of the land is easy. No matter where you go—no matter what company you join or what product you peddle—the landscape is roughly the same. It's comprised of your fellow peddlers (your band of brothers and sisters), your technical support (dead without them), your sales management (everybody's got one), the product managers and marketing 'bots (I mean professionals . . . OK, no, I really mean 'bots), the executive group with their radar screens (where you want your deals to be), and your customers.

Lining up Allies

Even luckier for you, because the terrain's the same so, too, are the everyday sales dynamics. Everyone pretty much has a role and acts true to type. Nevertheless, an army of one can't be everywhere at once, so line up your allies.

As all good peddlers know, you want the support of your company and all its players. When you and your company are aligned, you are strong. But as any veteran peddler can tell you, the company does not revolve around you. So your first tactical initiative is to hard-wire your connections inside the company. By doing this, you have the whole company working for you (just don't tell them that).

STORY TIME

I am working my first peddling gig at a Fortune 500 computer manufacturer. I am there a week when my manager sends me and a bunch of other new reps off to sales training, where the instructor explains in painstaking detail all the processes and procedures put in place to make the selling and delivery of products efficient. Several times during his presentation he notes that improperly completed forms will delay products from getting out the door.

(continued)

"Considering you are paid your commissions when your products ship," he warns, "it is in every peddler's best interest to fill out the forms properly." We all take note.

It takes me a couple months, but eventually I realize The Corporate Way has its pros and cons, and that if I am going to make some bucks, I need another way to get things out the door.

Spring rolls around and one day I'm talking to my twin brother who works on the manufacturing floor of Building 5 testing machines one last time before they ship. He's telling me about the company softball league:

"It's really competitive. You should try out for our team. We could use some good players."

I played a lot of ball when I was younger, so I try out and make Building 5's team. Every game I play hard and gladly spend some of my commission dollars at the bar afterwards.

Several weeks go by when I land a big order 48 hours before the quarter closes. This sale is important to me, but I know it isn't going to make the end-of-quarter's Must Ship List from the executive office. So I call up my brother and my softball buddies and ask them to make sure it isn't delayed in the end-of-quarter bottleneck.

Sure enough, my order ships. When the area manager posts the list of peddlers who are the Booked and Shipped leaders for the New York and New England turfs, my name is at the top of the list. Everyone's amazed. No one can figure out how my order made it out the door when I brought it in only two days before the end of the quarter. "It must be the luck of the Irish," I joke. But it's then that I realize there is another way—The Peddler Way.

That night after the game, I tell my buddies how great it was that they wired my deal through the line. They all grin and say, "We take care of our own first."

"Our own first." Does this happen in every corporation? Yes! Would I have gotten in serious trouble if anyone found out about it? Yes! Was it the way to play the corporate game? Well, now, that depends on what kind of peddler you are. I developed an edge and then worked that edge to help myself and my customers. So goes the way of the peddler.

The net-net is this: A good peddler finds an advantage and uses it. And many times, it is a good, old-fashioned, who-you-know-not-what-you-know connection. You need to make enough connections between you and others in the company to give your one-person army great maneuverability and awesome firepower—despite all of the policies and procedures put in place to prevent you from doing just that.

There are two kinds of peddlers: those who follow policies and procedures, and those who really do try and then go around them (beep beep). My view is when policies and procedures work for me, I follow them and am the poster child for compliance. When they don't I create my own, which usually gets me listed on the company's Ten Most Wanted poster. Let's face it, it's not always easy. Some days you get the bear and other days the bear gets you. Some days you're the windshield and some days you're the bug. Smile for the camera.

This brings us to our second Peddler's Prerogative. This one gives you a green light to go about your business as you see fit.

PEDDLER'S PREROGATIVE #2

It is the peddler's prerogative to follow corporate processes and policies if they keep the deal moving forward. If corporate policies and procedures impede business, it is the peddler's prerogative to do whatever is necessary by any means possible to get the business. (You will be rewarded either with compassion or a new job.)

XIV   THE PEDDLER'S PREROGATIVE

Understanding the Nature of Business

I am a big believer in working my Boston-Irish arse off. I am a big believer in being the first one in the game every morning and the last one off the field every night. As a matter of fact, I basically keep a work task going in my brain 24/7. That's the nature of business as I see it. It's part of my commitment to my company and my customers. They get it free of charge.

Many companies, on the other hand, are committed to the bottom line. That is their singular focus, and many have become combative and predatory in their relentless pursuit of quarter-to-quarter growth, profits, and market share.

Think I exaggerate? Next week, count the number of times someone uses lingo or metaphors more suitable for war than peddling. You may think it's a jungle out there, but I have news for you and your army of one: the higher-ups see a battlefield.

Now, if anything can mess with your peddler head, this can. You're putting it on the line day after day, doing your best, giving your all, building something from nothing, moving your deals along and, wham!, they 86 a division, discontinue a product, consolidate an office, move in a manager, merge or shut down. The corporate dictum from on high is, "Nothing personal, boys and girls, just business as usual."

Nothing personal? Ya, it sucks being part of this Business Is Business culture. But that's the way it is. So, my friend, don't let it boggle your mind, get you down, or slow you down. The peddler's philosophy is for times like these. It will help you keep the right perspective on trials and tribulations, which is just as important as closing a big deal.

The right perspective is this: Nothing really matters except your family, friends, and other important people in your orbit; business is what you do to earn money. It's just a job for Pete's sake! A job should never run your reality. If you take a job too seriously, you may end up so stressed out you won't know if it's Tuesday or January.

Recognize that business is business and deal with it. Never kid yourself or be fooled into thinking business is anything other than business. Trust me on that one. Take out your yellow highlighter, mark that sentence, and then bend this page, as you might need to be reminded, oh, let's see, 20 or 30 times a day.

Once you got that down, then focus on making business work for you.

PEDDLER'S PREROGATIVE #3

If business is business, it's the peddler's prerogative to understand intimately how the business runs, and then figure out how to make it work for him.

Mapping Your Reality

Here's a notion for your peddler head. If you really want to be a great peddler, you need to get yourself in tune with all the folks on your path. Whether they're inside your company, outside, or anywhere in between, you better be boppin' to their beat.

Don't be fool enough to expect them to try to get in tune with you. After all, has anyone ever greeted you by saying, "Please, have a seat. Peddling is such a tough job. I really admire you for doing it. How can I help you today?"

I didn't think so. It's up to you to clue into them without expecting them to do the same. Accept it and move on.

Now, you know peddling is a crazy, unpredictable job based on complex and ever-changing relationships and circumstances. It's why we do it. It's what makes it fun and interesting. What you might not know is that this is a direct contrast to most corporate jobs. Where your reality constantly changes, most other workers' remains fixed. Where your job is to create something out of nothing, their task is to keep things together and moving nicely along.

In addition, companies have spent decades streamlining and compartmentalizing all the business processes they could get their hands on. The net-net is that a lot of the challenge and fun has been wrung out of the corporate environment.

Keep this in mind next time you're cold calling a prospect, talking with a customer, or trying to get something through the pipeline at your company. You need to take the time to see the world from their perspective, and then entice them into yours.

STORY TIME

I am a social worker and helping people who, for one reason or another, have gotten the short end of the stick. The work I do deeply affects their lives and is very satisfying. After five years, however, the allure of being young with a meaningful job begins to wear thin. With a wife, a child, and a small house, it's becoming apparent that having enough money at the end of the week to go out for pizza and beer isn't cutting it anymore.

About this time, I have an epiphany (funny how that happens just when you need it): The people who make the most money are the people who sell things and get a piece of the action. I decide to shave my beard, cut my hair, buy a suit, and become a peddler. While I am doing this, I have a second epiphany (such is the luck of the Irish): The bigger the item, the bigger the piece I keep. I think to myself, "What are big ticket items? Cars? Think bigger. How about boats? Getting there. Planes? Ya, those are big tickets! Ah, I got it, satellites! That's what I need to sell, freakin' satellites."

Off I march to Grumman and a few other companies in the satellite space and quickly realize that my experience as a social worker isn't going to get me a job as a satellite salesman. Rejected, I regroup. "What about computers?" I think to myself. "After all, every major computer company on the planet is in Massachusetts and they are all hiring. (It's the late '70s.) I'll get myself in the door and work my way up to being a sales guy."

Off to the "Help Wanted" section of the *The Boston Globe* I go. "Hmmm . . . ya, computers, need a job in 'puters." After weeks and weeks of writing letters and explaining I am a social worker, but . . . I am roundly rejected. Not a single interview.

Nevertheless, when Sunday rolls around, I'm back at it. I see an ad for E.C.O. Coordinator of the Test Equipment Design (T.E.D.) department. This person works with different departments getting Engineering Change Orders (edits to hardware designs) incorporated. I decide to apply. Since letters aren't working, however, I decide to find the dude in charge.

First thing Monday morning I call the Human Resources depart-

(continued)

ment of this Fortune 500 company, where I get a crash course in why I cannot and never ever will talk to the guy who wrote the ad (the hiring manager). Plus, I am told that I am unqualified for every job that computer company will ever have.

Ah, a bureaucracy! Being a social worker, I can spot one a mile away. I know how to play this game: Get to the right bureaucrat, get him in a corner, and beg for three minutes of his time. Plead your case fast and eloquently, and have a solution that he has the power to give you the nod on.

Using the only lead I have, I call up and ask to speak to the Test Equipment Design Department. "One moment please," the operator answers and puts me through. Then I hear, "T.E.D. How may I help you?" "Um, er, gee, um, could I talk to the manager of your group?" "One moment please." Two seconds later, "Hi, this is Tony." (OH MY GOD!)

"Hey, Tony, this is Dennis. I know I am not supposed to call you, but I am really interested in the job you advertised in the *Globe*. I've been a social worker for the last five years and am trying to break into high tech. I'm looking for a place to get my foot in the door. (Deep breath.) Could you take a minute and help me out? Can you tell me a bit about the job and what you're looking for?"

"Your right, you shouldn't be calling me," says Tony, "but I have a minute and will tell you a bit about it."

Tony then launches into a long list of problems he is having within his division. After a while, I ask him about the personalities involved and the group dynamics (my expertise), and quickly realize that the department heads aren't working together. They are supposed to be working toward a common goal: testing computers before they are released to manufacturing, and quickly enough so as not to hold up the assembly line. Instead, each department has its own functions and personalities, and acts as if it were autonomous.

After talking for 15 minutes I say, "No offense, Tony, but it sounds like you need a social worker." I explain to him that I have a lot of experience working with groups and getting folks to cooperate, and he invites me in for an interview.

This story illustrates a few things, but mostly it's about mapping your reality. That is, figuring out what you want to do, finding a way that works for you to get what you want done, and then getting the rest of the folks not only to buy off on your idea but to embrace it. I could have been a shoe salesman and told Tony his folks weren't getting along because their feet hurt—that he needed a guy who understands people's feet. He probably would have been so amused that he would have given me 15 minutes to make my case.

OK, by now you have a feel for what awaits you—or not. Either way, it's time to read on my friend, and acquire a high sense of value for the peddling profession and appreciation of your fellow brothers and sisters.

THE STORY OF STONE SOUP

Three soldiers trudged down a road in a strange country. They were on their way home from the war. Besides being tired, they were hungry. In fact, they had eaten nothing for two days.

"How I would like a good dinner tonight," said the first. "And a bed to sleep in," added the second. "But that is impossible," said the third.

On they marched, until suddenly, ahead of them, they saw the lights of a village. "Maybe we'll find a bite to eat and a bed to sleep in after all," they thought.

Now the peasants of the village feared strangers. When they heard that three soldiers were coming down the road, they talked among themselves. "Here come three soldiers," they said. "Soldiers are always hungry. But we have so little for ourselves." So they hurried to hide their food. They hid the barley in hay lofts, carrots under quilts, and buckets of milk down the wells. They hid all they had to eat. Then they waited.

The soldiers stopped at the first house. "Good evening to you," they said. "Could you spare a bit of food for three hungry soldiers?" "We have no food for ourselves," the residents lied. "It has been a poor harvest."

The soldiers went to the next house. "Could you spare a bit of food?" they asked. "And do you have a corner where we could sleep for the night?" "Oh, no," the man said. "We gave all we could spare to the soldiers who came before you." "And our beds are full," lied the woman.

At each house, the response was the same—no one had food or a place for the soldiers to stay. The villagers stood in the street and sighed. They looked as hungry as they could.

The soldiers talked together. The first soldier called out, "Good people! We are three hungry soldiers in a strange land. We have asked you for food and you have no food. Well, we will have to make stone soup." The peasants stared.

The soldiers asked for a big iron pot, water to fill it, and a fire to heat it. "And now, if you please, three round smooth stones." The soldiers dropped the stones into the pot.

"Any soup needs salt and pepper," the first soldier said, so children ran to fetch salt and pepper.

"Stones make good soup, but carrots would make it so much better," the second soldier added. One woman said, "Why, I think I have a carrot or two!" She ran to get the carrots.

"A good stone soup should have some cabbage, but no use asking for what we don't have!" said the third soldier. Another woman said, "I think I can probably find some cabbage," and off she scurried.

"If only we had a bit of beef and some potatoes, this soup would be fit for a rich man's table." The peasants thought it over, and then ran to fetch what they had hidden in their cellars. A rich man's soup, and all from a few stones! It seemed like magic!

The soldiers said, "If only we had a bit of barley and some milk, this soup would be fit for a king!" And so the peasants managed to retrieve some barley and milk.

"The soup is ready," said the cooks, "and all will taste it, but first we need to set the tables." Tables and torches were set up in the square, and all sat down to eat. Some of the peasants said, "Such a great soup would be better with bread and cider," so they brought forth the last two items and the banquet was enjoyed by all. Never had there been such a feast. Never had the peasants tasted such delicious soup, and all made from stones! They ate and drank and danced well into the night. In the morning, the villagers gathered to say goodbye.

"Many thanks to you," the people said, "for we shall never go hungry now that you have taught us how to make soup from stones!"

PART ONE

YOU

CHAPTER 1

YOU AND
YOUR ATTITUDE

Weakness of attitude becomes weakness of character.
—Albert Einstein

This might sound a bit corny and a tad smarmy, but to be a good peddler you need to have the right 'tude, baby. If you have a good one, it's a lovely day. If you have a bad one, the world sucks. It's pretty much that simple. Think about it.

Anyone with the right attitude can sell. Not because that's all they need, but because they can learn everything else. They can learn the sales process, they can learn the product, they can learn how to build relationships with prospects and customers. But the wrong attitude, well, that can kill you from the get-go!

PEDDLER'S PREROGATIVE #4

It is a peddler's prerogative to wake up every single morning knowing that a good attitude will change the world and a bad attitude will really kill your quarter.

Before we go any further, drum this into your peddler head: We convey our attitudes by our actions and behavior. Do you say hello to coworkers and ask them how they are, or do you grunt and hurry past or ignore them completely? You are probably known as having

a friendly attitude if you do the former and an unfriendly attitude if you do the latter.

Each of us develops attitudes about most things in our lives, from holidays to Hip Hop and everything in between. In this chapter, when I talk about attitude, I mean your attitude toward peddling. Do you love it? Do you hate it? Do you know the answers to these questions?

I'm not going to sugarcoat this: If you don't love selling, if your heart isn't in it, there is no way in hell you are going to be a great peddler. That, my friend, is the long and the short of it.

Coming Straight from the Heart

Go ahead. Right now. Ask yourself: Is my heart in this peddling gig? When you do, what you are really asking yourself is: Do I have a passion to sell? Do I have a passion for the peddling life?

Passion is what pulls us through the difficult times. If you have a passion for your work, you can do what you need to do, day in and day out, no matter how hard it is. You see hurdles as par for the course and roadblocks as gateways to opportunities. Nothing gets you down (well, not for more than a day or so) or deters you from your goal.

What many folks don't realize is that selling is hard work, so you have to have a passion for it. You are an army of one, out in the field, living by your wits. You gotta love it or leave it.

So sit yourself down for a friendly but honest chat, and figure out where your passion lies today. Perhaps you did love selling, but lately find your enthusiasm waning. It happens. But now you must ask yourself why, and if there's something you can change to get back in the groove. If so, do it! If not, move on. Do something you are passionate about for criminy's sake!

On the other hand, maybe you never loved selling and are doing it for the wrong reasons, the most common one being money. Money can be a great motivator—but usually, only for so long. Ask yourself this: If you were not making a lot of money would you still be selling? If the answer is no, you are in the wrong profession. Now that we got that out in the open, accept it and follow your heart.

Your heart is the most difficult thing for you to control. Almost all attempts are frivolous. The primal forces in your heart are much stronger than the thoughts in your head. I don't want to get into a philosophical debate of the power of the head versus the power of the heart, or logic versus emotion, but to me the ultimate confrontation is man's basic nature versus his intellect. I think of the heart as nature and the head as intellect. We think we can tame nature, we think we can control nature. But when nature exercises its true power, intellect is but a leaf in the wind. As Mr. Tom Waits (the famous songwriter) says, "You can drive out nature with a pitch fork, but it always comes roaring back again."

This is why you must find out if your heart is in selling. If it's not, it will thwart your success at every turn. If it is, you are unstoppable. Some forces can't be reckoned with. There is no stopping a great attitude fueled by a strong passion.

The cool thing about asking your heart a question is it doesn't lie. It always gives you a straight-up answer. This is unlike the head, which can spin you silly. The head will effortlessly concoct a rational for us to carry out whatever folly we are considering.

Some of us listen to the head, because we believe the rationale it dishes out. We think the head knows better than the heart. "If my head is telling me I can do this, I can do it." Wrong! First, check your heart. If it's in the game, then check your head.

Head in the Game

There are a few peddlers who can truly sell anything. Sneakers, satellites, sailboats—you name it, they can sell it. These folks are rare birds.

Most peddlers should sell products that are related to their interests, education, or experience, and for which they have an aptitude. Products that they can wrap their minds around. Products that they find compelling. The reason is that when a product engages us, we are willing to take the time to learn all the ins and outs of how it works, who buys it, and why. We see its great features and benefits, and we find workarounds for its shortcomings. We are willing to spend the time showing others how it can help them.

I call this having your head in the game. If you can't do this, if you can't take a product and make it yours, you don't have a prayer. You may even get hurt.

STORY TIME

"OK, guys, let's keep our heads in the game!"

I have heard this for as long as I can remember. My father yelled it at the Red Sox on TV. My coaches screamed it at me and my teammates. But I was about eight before I figured out what it really meant.

It's a warm summer night and I'm playing baseball on a Little League team. I'm scanning the bases when I notice that my buddy over in center field is off in la la land, ignoring the game, watching the world go by. Before I can get his attention, the batter hits a fly ball to center field.

Like any good left fielder should do, I run my tail off to back him up. I'm hoping to prevent an inside-the-park home run when I see the ball sail within an inch of his head. As I grab the ball, I think, "Whoa! That could have been ugly! I need to get my buddy to focus on every pitch. He needs to anticipate his next move if the batter hits the ball to him. He needs to get his head in the game." At that instant, the meaning became crystal clear.

It also became clear that not having your head in the game can result in needless errors, if not serious injuries!

If your product doesn't grab you and hold your attention, if you can't grasp how it works, if you can't for the life of you understand why anyone would buy it, you won't be able to keep your head in the game. You won't be able to stay focused on your deals, laying the groundwork, anticipating prospects' objections, providing answers, and moving your deal to the next step.

The net-net is this: To have a great attitude, your head has to be in it, too. So if your heart says, "Hell, yes! I'm in!" then check your head to figure out what you should be selling.

Heart versus Head

There is an epic battle that rages daily on any given topic between your heart's primal emotions and your head's logical thinking that can confuse the hell out of you. When it comes to peddling, it often goes something like this:

Head: You can sell.

Heart: I'm not so sure about that.

Head: Yes you can. You know the product backwards and forwards. You know who needs it. You're good with customers. You can sell!

Heart: Talking with people who already have the product—that's one thing. Talking people into buying the product—that's a whole other kettle of fish.

Head: Hey, it's no big deal. The worse they can say is no.

Heart: Exactly!

Head: It's nothing personal!

Heart: It is when you work really hard on a deal, do everything right, go the extra mile and, in the end, the prospect just says no.

Head: Think of the money you'll make.

Heart: Yeah, WHEN a deal goes through, which makes it doubly hard when a customer says no. I've got a mortgage to pay and two kids to put through college.

When your heart and your head start wrestling for control, it's often difficult to know which to listen to. Here's a tip: Don't listen to your head. Find something that really floats your boat, that makes your heart sing. Don't worry, I'll send you a refund. Hey, wait a minute! I just helped you change your life. You should pay me! Twenty-five smackers, please. Ya, that's the ticket! My heart almost got in the way of my head for a minute.

Behavior and Actions

I am not a pop-shrink, counterculture, shaman dude, but I can tell you this: If you choose to sell, you better have done some deep thinking about where your heart is and where your head is. If you choose to be a peddler without having done some righteous thinking, it will be obvious through your behavior and actions.

PEDDLER'S PREROGATIVE #5

It is a peddler's prerogative to make it obvious through behavior and actions that he or she loves peddling and enjoys all things sales. Joy is contagious and makes everything better.

Peddlers whose hearts and heads are into selling tend to do all the right things. They treat customers and coworkers with respect. They put their customers first. They help customers solve problems rather than sell customers products. They find a way to do what's right for their customers and their companies. And that's just for starters. Such behavior and actions convey an attitude that creates some pretty irresistible vibes.

Behavior and actions do not automatically follow the lead of the heart and the head, however. Such is the case when we let ourselves be distracted by life's temptations. We stay up late, sleep in, and roll into work long after we should. We spend time shooting the breeze or surfing the Internet when we should be making calls. We do minimal prep for meetings, wing presentations, and let follow-up calls slide so we can be out by 5:00.

There are a load of bad behaviors and actions that convey the wrong attitude. You need to guard against them.

STORY TIME

I am consulting for a start-up, assessing its business strategy and tactics. As I sit in on meetings, learn about the company's products and markets, and analyze the sales process, I start to bump heads with a senior sales guy who seems to have a cavalier attitude.

Now, I'm a big fan of taking life's ups and downs in stride, and I have learned that it doesn't pay to sweat the small stuff. But this company has serious issues to deal with and the clock is ticking. Yet, nothing seems to faze this guy despite his being a stockholder. It is frustrating everyone, but especially me.

I decide to talk with him about the deals we're doing, why they are not good for the company, and how that's causing delivery problems.

"My job is to sell the product," he tells me, "not deliver it."

"But we can't deliver on the type of deals you're doing. We don't have the resources."

"That isn't my problem."

"It is if you want to keep these customers. If we don't deliver, do you think you're going to get another order from them?"

"Do I look like I have trouble selling these products? I'm one of the top reps. I can always find customers."

I can see my attitude and his attitude are on a collision course and I try to head it off.

Over the next couple of weeks, I engage him in several conversations. I explain that it is not just about him making money, it is about building a reputable company—a company that customers buy from again and again, that honors its commitments and makes a profit, that has a long list of happy customers to call for references. And on and on. His responses range from a laugh to a shrug, and I leave even more frustrated.

Then, one day, we are in a meeting discussing our perennial problems of overextended resources and an underwhelming fore-

(continued)

cast. There is no solution in sight when, out of the blue, this peddler makes an impassioned, cogent, lucid summary of what he sees as the issues and problems. I mean, he is loud, strong, confident, and serious. And his insights and suggestions are right on the money.

As he speaks, everyone listens and nods in agreement, especially me. I am extremely proud, because finally he is putting a stake in the ground. He is saying what is on his mind and in his heart. He is taking what he does seriously.

Then, in the weeks that follow, he begins to change his behavior and actions—how he sells to prospects and customers, ensuring the company does the right thing—and goes on to lead the company out of a serious sales jam.

The moral: It's not enough to have a passion for selling and a product you can call your own. You must also behave and act as a good peddler would.

The Reflection of You

Here is a big surprise for all of you hyped-up, trumped-up, megalomaniac peddlers out there: It is the reflection of your attitude that is stored inside the little cubbyhole each person creates for everyone they meet. It is not your can-do approach. It is not how much you know. What is forever etched inside their consciousnesses is how your attitude made them feel. Whoa!

Let me give you a little example. It's 8:45 A.M. and our peddler is in high gear having been in the office since 7:00. It's her only day in the office this week and she has a lot to do and many people to see, starting with Bill.

Peddler: I'm here to see Bill.

Assistant: He's on the phone. Why don't you have a seat and . . .

Peddler: I can't wait. I set up an appointment to see him at 8:45. I need to see him now. You'll have to interrupt him.

Assistant: I'm sorry, but I can't do that.

Bill's assistant could probably help our peddler, but when she came in on the attack, the assistant went on the defense. If the peddler had stopped, taken a deep breath, and then approached the assistant, the exchange may have gone something like this:

Peddler: Good Morning. How are you today? Sorry to bother you, but can you help me? I have to go into a meeting in 15 minutes, and I have to see Bill before I do or I'm not going to have what I need. I told him I'd stop by about 8:45 this morning. Can you do me a favor and see if he's free for a moment?

Assistant: He's on the phone, but I'll interrupt him.

Peddler: Thanks. I really appreciate it. I owe ya one!

Even more important, the next time this peddler shows up, the assistant will be inclined to help again, because she was treated with respect rather than as a barrier to be moved aside.

This is nothing new to many of us peddlers, but we get so caught up in our daily battles that we slide right out of human mode and into 800-pound gorilla mode. We start our day running up hills, dodging bullets, lobbing hand grenades, and attacking machine-gun nests. Barging in and making demands seems perfectly fitting.

Only the folks we meet have no notion of our struggles and assume we should go about our day much as they go about theirs. In this environment, a hard-charging, aggressive attitude can wreak mayhem and destruction. (Oh, geesh, do I know that!)

PEDDLER'S PREROGATIVE #6

Not everyone is wired to leave the safety of their foxholes, join the charge, and take the hill. It is your prerogative to shield your scary, Rambo peddler side from animals, children, and the elderly.

Consciously moderating our behavior and actions to reflect the right attitude to all those we meet—coworkers, prospects, customers—is something peddlers must work on everyday until it becomes rote. Read on, my friend.

CHAPTER 2

AUGMENTING YOUR 'TUDE

The fight is won or lost far away from witnesses—behind the lines, in the gym, and out there on the road, long before I dance under those lights.

—Muhammad Ali

All peddlers have their busy times and their slow times. It is easy to behave and act as a good peddler should when the phone is ringing, e-mails are flying, deals are rolling, and the world is whirring around you. But when you are in slow mo, peddling can suck. This is the time when it's easy to get distracted. Here's a tip: Commitment to your process is what gets you through.

I have been around the block a few times and from what I've seen, no matter what you are peddling, for the most part it is tedious and mundane, and your hard work goes pretty much unnoticed. In addition, despite that success is possible only with compelling products that fit customers' needs, great dialogue, and relationships that are human2human, sales is also a numbers game. (Just one of the many paradoxes of peddling.)

To wade your way through the long hours of hard work, you have to create a process—a game plan and a schedule—and then you have to stick to it. Unlike a lot of other books, this one is not about to prescribe one; you probably have a good one already. But I will tell you this: Part of a superior peddler attitude is adhering to your process and not getting derailed. Some peddlers act like puppy dogs, chasing whatever ball comes rolling by. Don't let this be you—if you want to be a great peddler, that is.

The great peddlers are creatures of habit. They are focused and disciplined. They are like selling machines. At the end of each day, they set goals for the next one, such as making a certain number of calls, finding a decent prospect, or moving a deal down the pipeline. The next day, they come in, buckle down, get into their zone, and they go and they go. They are like the Energizer Bunny!

No matter what you are selling, you should be able to make daily goals you can reach.

PEDDLER'S PREROGATIVE #7

It is your prerogative to take the time and figure out a selling process that works, that is nice and cozy. Then stay with your process when great things are happening and when thing are in slow mo. It is adhering to your process that will get you through the selling doldrums.

I have a saying that if a person is the first one in the office and the last one out, he or she will always—and I mean *always*—be one of the top reps in the office if not *the* top rep. Why? Because after you understand your product and how to pitch it, peddling is truly a numbers game. The peddler who adheres to his or her process makes the most calls, and the peddler who makes the most calls gets the most deals.

Now for the caveat: As with most things sales, corporate folks think nothing of imposing a process on you even though most of them have never carried a bag. It comes in the form of productivity software and it works like this: You log every blessed thing you say and do and the software tells your manager and corporate if you are worthy to serve.

They won't admit that, of course. They will say that the software is to make your life easier, to help you sell more. What a bunch of hooey! Corporate is bent on making every process modular and repeatable, and nothing is exempt. Things that you thought could (should!) be done only face-to-face, that depend on human dialogue, are suddenly automated. It's all in an effort to control everyone and every aspect of their environment. Once you remove the human element, they don't need you; any nonthinking, unskilled person will do.

Unfortunately, you can't avoid it. Productivity software will be thrust upon you whether you want it or not. My advice is to spend time learning it, understand what it REALLY does, and figure out how to use it minimally and for your benefit. You are a freethinking human who is capable of creating your own process. You are a responsible adult who knows when you're working your process and when you're slacking off. You don't need to be monitored and measured by a machine!

Now, whether it's their own process or someone else's, some peddlers hop on the bandwagon and proceed to get so bogged down in minutia that they can't claw their way back out. Don't get lost in the detail! Keep your plan and schedule simple. Keep it general. Don't take the act of self-help and turn it into self-mutilation.

PEDDLER'S PREROGATIVE #8

It is a peddler's prerogative to create a solid process that works. It is also your prerogative to be careful when you hop on the process bandwagon and not let an act of self-help turn into self-mutilation.

Other peddlers think they can keep it together flying by the seat of their pants, and for the most part this is folly. I must admit I have seen some pretty gosh darn good jugglers (myself included), but in the end, the bear always gets you.

You must find a process that works for you and then stick with it. Get in the groove, find your zone, and practice it every day. If you are the type of person who can figure out how to find the time to work out regularly and stay in shape, your discipline gene is turned on, so point it at your sales day as well.

As a matter of fact, if you are not on a physical workout program three to five times a week, you should by all means and at any cost get on one. It should be part of your process so you maintain the right 'tude, baby!

The Creative You

I'm going to go out on a limb here: Creativity is more important than product knowledge in the peddler world. That's not to say that you don't need a deep understanding of your product. You do. But it is more important to be creative.

Join a company and you will learn all about its product: what it does, how it works, how it's sold, how the deals go, and so on. Now, you could simply take this information and keep building the same types of deals. Or, you could be creative with these product elements and find new markets and new customers, and build new deals.

Take heed: Being creative is something you probably have to do on your own. It is unlikely that you will receive any support from your company or manager. The reason is, once again, the corporate cookie-cutter mentality: Let's create a pitch, teach it to the sales folks, and have them execute it without deviation.

Puhleeze! If these brilliant folks had ever spent some time in the field they would know that this is unrealistic. Selling is dynamic. A peddler must be able to react to prospects. To expect peddlers to stick to a script is laughable, especially because the corporate presentations and selling scenarios that the marketing folks cook up never match the prospects' needs. They don't cut it! Making peddlers into automatons shows how truly warped and silly the corporate view of selling is.

Ya, we all need a process, but as a guide not a dictator. A good process is one that encourages peddlers to be creative. If you want a good laugh, bring that up at a sales meeting, then sit back and watch. The thought of relinquishing control and allowing fresh thought is sure to make the marketers' heads explode.

Creativity is what differentiates great peddlers from good peddlers. To be creative, you must be willing to think outside normal confines, think about the same old things in new ways, let your imagination roam. Folks who are creative ask a lot of questions, three of the more important ones being: what if, tell me why not, and, my personal favorite, what does that mean (remember to squint and cock your head back when you say it).

To be creative, you also have to be willing to fail. In this way, it's no different from peddling. Statistically speaking, on average, a peddler must call a hundred leads to get 10 prospects, and out of those 10 prospects, one will become a customer. You can look at that in one of two ways: You can get wrapped up in the failure (90 leads and 9 prospects say no!), or you can focus on your successes (10 leads and one customer say yes!). Is the glass half empty or half full?

Similarly, a lot of questions don't lead to anything. And it can be scary when you are the lone voice relentlessly asking questions. But I can tell you, it's definitely worth it to witness the moment of rapture when one of your questions hits, and eyes pop, mouths drop, and everyone utters in unison, "Holy shit! That just might work! What a great freakin' idea!"

STORY TIME

I am on the road making calls with my buddy Ed. Ed is the V.P. of Customer Support and a great guy. A hellion. A riot. And really smart to boot. A lot of the time we spend on planes, in bars, and in restaurants is spent talking shop.

On this particular day, I tell Ed about an idea that I have—that if we were to implement our technology in a certain way, we might be able to snag some additional functionality. With those features, we could position it differently in the marketplace.

Ed dismisses my idea right out of the box, and we spend the next three hours on a plane arguing, during which time he tells me not only is it a stupid idea, but that I am stupid and silly as well.

Being the persistent peddler that I am, however, I don't give up. As we travel around the U.S. over the next nine months working on major opportunities, I keep bringing it up.

"Hey, come on. One more time. Tell me why my idea won't work."

(continued)

After several months, this request is hardly out of my mouth before he starts raving about how fed up he is and how stubborn I am for not getting it.

One night, Ed and I are at a restaurant with one of his top techies. When Ed heads to the men's room, I explain my idea to the techie. Bracing myself, I say, "OK, now you can tell me why it won't work."

The techie looks at me and says, "What a great idea!"

Just then Ed approaches the table and sees me with an ear-to-ear grin, practically laughing out loud.

"What's up?" he asks.

"Here's someone who relates on my level," I say, motioning to the techie. "He GOT IT."

"Dennis, you better not be wasting my techie's time with that hair-brain idea of yours."

"NO, NO, Ed, Dennis is right!" and the techie shows him a diagram on a napkin.

Over the next 15 minutes, Ed is nodding his head one minute and shaking his head the next. Finally, he has his gadzooks moment.

"You were right, you son of a bitch. That is a great freakin' idea."

"Oh, geesh, that's great," I say. "It only took nine freakin' months before you'd listen."

I pretend to be annoyed, but in truth, I am thoroughly enjoying the moment and the look on Ed's face.

Anyone can be creative, they just have to ask questions. To start, remove the filter between your head and your mouth, and then let the questions fly. No one remembers the bad questions (not for too long, anyway), but someone always remembers who came up with the idea that succeeded—even if it is only the person who steals it.

Corporate America is like rock 'n' roll: full of beggars, thieves, and pirates. When you come up with a great idea, you should expect others to take the credit, for they most assuredly will. Take it as the ultimate compliment and let it go. After all, you have a million questions streamin' from your noggin, so more creative ideas will come. Plus, a good peddler's mantra is: Pays me, don't praise me.

Humor

OK, let's get funny! It has been a heavy chapter, so let's talk about humor and your attitude. Humor *must* be a part of your repertoire to convey the right attitude. It's your passport to anywhere. Why do we all have the ability to smile, grin, giggle, and laugh? In case a peddler says something funny! Ba da boom!

As you might have already figured out, I like to think of myself as a pretty funny bunny.

PEDDLER'S PREROGATIVE #9

You better be a funny bastard if you want to be a good peddler. It is your prerogative to figure out how funny you want to be. Be as funny as you should be, less isn't enough, more is too much. It's all a riddle anyway!

Most folks who sell have a pretty good sense of humor. I guess it's because it beats the alternative. Ba da boom!

Humor shows that you are human, that you have insight into the human condition. To understand humor is to understand people. In the next chapter, "They Must Like You," I talk about knowing the folks in your universe.

Think about what happens when you smile at someone. Usually, they smile back. It is human nature. Most good peddlers understand this and use it as an intricate part of their repertoire.

Humor warms the coldest of hearts. If you can get a grin or a giggle from someone, you have found common ground. It's all downhill from there, baby. Ba da bing! Ba da boom!

Being a humorous person telegraphs a lot about you to the folks you meet. If you get a chuckle for one zany reason or another, that says they are inclined to like you. If they like you (and they like your products and services), there is a good chance you can close a sale. More on this in the next chapter.

If you are one of those peddlers who take everything seriously, then you are an incredible candidate to start a humor campaign. Start by looking at everything you do and seeing how funny it is. Learn to chuckle at yourself.

If you can't find a thing to laugh at, find the funniest sales guy you know and ask him to help you. Ask him to make fun of you for a few minutes. Listen to what he says and see if you grin a time or two. He will probably start with your clothes. Just a guess! Ba da boom!

You can find humor everywhere and in everything, you just have to be open to it. Often when serious people decide to be funny, they are really hilarious. Who knew?

If you do decide to climb aboard the humor train remember, it is OK to tell a funny story. It is OK to make fun of yourself. But never be stupid, callous, or gross. Leave that for your sales manager. Drum roll, TA DA!

All right. Here are a few clutch jokes if you need them.

It's trash day and I'm running late for a sales meeting. Just as I get out the door, the garbage truck pulls away. I run after it, briefcase and garbage bag in hand.

"Hold on!" I yell. "Wait a second!"

The trashman sees me and stops. "Thanks," I say. "Am I too late for the trash?"

He eyes me up and down. "Nope, hop in!"

Ba da boom!

… … … … … … … …

I'm on my way into a bar and I see a duck in the gutter. I pick up the duck and walk in.

"Hey, Joe, I'll have a shot of Jamison and a Bud."

Joe looks over and asks, "Where did you get that pig?"

I look at the duck and say, "Joe! It's not a pig, it's a duck."

Joe smiles and says, "I was talking to the duck."

Ba da bing! Ba da boom!

… … … … … … … …

A peddler friend and I are hiking in the woods when we see a bear. Trying not to make a sound, my friend crouches down, unzips his backpack, and takes out his sneakers.

"What are you doing?" I ask him.

"Putting on my sneakers," he whispers.

"Why? You can't outrun a bear!"

"I don't have to. I just have to outrun you."

Ba da boom!

This Is Dedicated to . . .

Getting your attitude right requires deep thought, followed by the proper behavior and actions, and topped off with dedication. The funny thing is, it's hard work to be dedicated! To do everything you know you should do day after day isn't easy. In fact, it can burn you out.

If you find yourself in the doldrums, it might be time for a Budweiser or a break. I recommend as many as needed. (I mean breaks . . . no, Buds . . . no, breaks.) It is important to ditch and chill when you feel the strain. I am a big fan of taking a break, recharging, and coming back swinging (as opposed to going down swinging). Even the best peddlers need to take a break, or they won't be the best for long.

PEDDLER'S PREROGATIVE #10

It is your peddler's prerogative to take a break guiltlessly. Rest, recharge, and come back swinging. It is essential not to let anyone but you determine when you need a breather and when you should take it.

No one can prescribe how hard you should work or how much you should rest. You need to figure out the right balance for you to be 100% in the race. If you're not firing on all cylinders, those who are will beat you every time. They will spot opportunities before you do and blow their numbers out the door. They will make the most money and become the most successful member of the team.

Here's another reason: You're not the only one with skin in the game. Unless you're at your best, companies don't want you on the field. They know that peddlers have to be at the top of their game to make the big plays, close the big deals, and do what's needed to win. They want to make their numbers just like you.

So, if you feel your energy waning and your concentration failing, take some time and recharge. At the same time, ask yourself, do I want to be in this league? Am I willing to put it all on the line and go for it? Am I willing to ratchet up to 110%?

Many peddlers have the talent, ability, creativity, and smarts to be a great peddler, but something holds them back. Maybe they are intimidated by other peddlers, or believe they'll never measure up, or think that they don't deserve such success.

Hey! We all encounter doubts. What matters is what you do about them. Are you going to let them stop you, or are you going to say, "I'm not going to be intimidated, I'm going to work harder, I'm going to earn my success. I am going for it! Deal with it people of planet Earth."

It's not easy, but it's either that or sitting around years from now saying, if you only knew then what you know now, if you only followed your gut. Ya, you know, the shoulda woulda coulda stories!

So, what'll it be, boys and girls? Time's a wastin'! Are you going to throw caution to the wind and go for it?

The Jerks Amongst Us

We have been chatting about attitude and what it is, what it is made of, and how to have a good one. I have met my fair share of peddlers with great attitudes. I also have found that there are some pretty clueless folks carrying a bag and schlepping products. I never cease to be amazed how many of these characters fall into the net of peddlery.

Me, Me, Me

I find that people generally look at the world through one of two constructs. The first is the *me* construct, which is that the world revolves around the wonderful me. Think Miss Piggy. Unfortunately, there are a lot of peddlers who are stuck in the me mode.

Ya, I know that you have to value yourself and love yourself and all that good stuff. But let's face it, there are a lot of people who take it to the extreme. These are the folks who look at the world and all they see are objects—objects to be used and manipulated to get what they want. The problem is that many of these objects are people, and PEOPLE DON'T WANT TO BE USED AND MANIPULATED!

The me folks are a very weird group. They really think that they are the center of the universe. If you are one of them, you probably don't know it, as you cannot possibly see yourself other than as a dazzling life force of wonderfulness.

Narcissism isn't a new phenomenon in the sales arena, and you need a pinch of it to survive, but corporate tends to cultivate the "it's all about me" formula for success to an excessive degree. So you had better get this straight: How you view people and treat them will determine if you become a great peddler or not. It is one of those fundamentals that make you or break you in the long run.

Then, there is the *us* construct, as in "all of us are in this together." These are the folks who value the members of their team, who realize it takes a village to close a deal, who understand that they can accomplish far more with the help and support of others than they can on their own!

I am one of the us folks. I am always grateful when someone is kind enough to lend me a helping hand and I am always on the look out to see if I can do the same. It might be those clannish Irish genes or having played a lot of team sports. Either way, I am an us person. If you are in the "it's all about me" contingent, here's a news flash: There are others in your universe of one—mainly the rest of us! So move over, Rover!

Other Peoples' Attitudes

It is bad enough being sucked into your own negative vortex; you don't want to be pulled into someone else's. So how do you deal with folks whose attitudes are toxic? You have two choices. (I love making everything as binary as I can.)

First, you can love bomb them, like the Krishnas do, which is acting so positive that you smother their negativity with your good vibes. Of course, me being me, I always try to go for this approach. It is really nothing more than recognizing that the person you are dealing with is in a funk. I have a third eye and when I see this, I say, "Hey, so what's with you? Are you feeling OK? I am seeing that things are not great."

There's no downside here. If the person says, "Ya, you are right. It's not a good day for me," you can start a dialogue, find out what is wrong, and learn more about them in the process. If they say, "Ya, you are right. Can we meet another time?" rescheduling the meeting shows you're cool and you care.

There is always a contagious goodwill that exudes from you when all is right with your world. You are in a state of selling grace and you just pass out the goodness. When you are on that kind of roll, it's hard for anyone to duck out of the way. Great peddlers always seem happy to be just who they are: good, happy humans!

The second thing you can do to ward off any negative vibes is call up the deflector shields and let them bounce off. When you meet folks with negative attitudes, recognize them, acknowledge them, thank them for their input, and proceed to ignore them verily. If you engage folks with negative 'tudes, you will be sucked under the train. They will weaken you. Remember, you have to stay focused and strong. So when someone shows up who can derail you, SHUN THEM.

PEDDLER'S PREROGATIVE #11

When you meet folks with bad 'tudes, make no mistake, THEY WILL WEAKEN YOU! It is absolutely your prerogative to remove them from your reality. SHUN THEM!

Tune Your 'tude

Listen up! It's easy to talk about having the right attitude and extremely hard to implement. But ya gotta try. Ya gotta wake up every single day and have the right attitude. Why? Because folks do business with folks they like.

CHAPTER 3

THEY MUST LIKE YOU

> *There are people who in spite of their merit disgust us*
> *and others who please us in spite of their faults.*
>
> —François de La Rochefoucauld

In Chapter 1, we talked about having your heart and your head in the game, which has to do with passion and commitment, which you need in order to have the right attitude.

But a good attitude alone doesn't guarantee that prospects and customers will like you. Some peddlers have a great attitude, but no one likes them. Others have a lousy attitude and everyone likes them. Go figure!

Here's what I can tell you for certain: If you want to sell, folks must like you. For folks to like you, you must be a caring and sincere individual. A good person.

A Day in Your Life

As a peddler roaming through life, you probably interact with more people in a year than most folks do in a lifetime. How you relate to the folks you meet is a reflection of the type of person you are and how you generally see the world. How they react to you is an indication of whether they feel your good vibes and see you as real.

Capisci? OK, let's say you start out your day meeting with a prospect. You have a great call. In fact, you wind up spending all day there. It's mostly a techie meeting, but you stick around because Mr. Big, the decision maker, is participating.

As you chat up Mr. Big over lunch, you learn that you both live in the same town, have kids the same ages, fish the same lake, the whole bit. As the day winds down and it is agreed that more discussion should take place at your offices the next day, Mr. Big comes over to you: "Hey, peddler, can I hop a ride with you in the morning? My wife needs my car."

The next day you pick up Mr. Big and stop for gas. As you pull in to the station, you are greeted with a smile from Ahmed, the attendant.

"Hello, my brother peddler, how are you doing today?"

"Ahmed, my friend, all is great. I'm taking my new friend, Mr. Big, into work today."

You introduce them: "Ahmed, this is Mr. Big. Mr. Big, this is Ahmed."

You chitchat about last night's Sox game, make a few desperate comments about how we are always in the soup after the All-Star break, everyone laughs at the sad truth, and you head off for some java.

Into the coffee shop you bop and the same thing happens.

"Mornin' Betty. What's rockin'? The usual for me and what would you like, Mr. Big?"

More introductions: "Betty, this is Mr. Big. Mr. Big, meet Betty. Best java and breakfast in town."

A few more jokes about the Sox's pitching, and everybody smiles and says so long. Onto the highway you fly, stopping at the tollbooth.

"Hey, peddler, why did God invent guns?" the attendant asks.

"So we can shoot the Sox's pitching staff?" Everybody laughs.

Soon you are entering the parking garage. Jimmy is at the entrance.

"Good morning, peddler, good to see you."

"Same here, Jimmy, how goes the morning?"

"Same old, same old, peddler."

Into the building you go, saying hello to the receptionist and feeling like you own the place, like you are the mayor of the city. In the office, everyone smiles, greetings and introductions all around.

The next sales meeting hasn't even begun, but Mr. Big is starting to get a picture of you and your outlook. You're friendly, caring, sincere. You know the names of the folks you see every day. You look at them, greet them, and notice how they're doing. You exchange some light banter. Not a lot of pomp and circumstance, just a real human.

"Um, excuse me, Mr. King of Sales Leprechauns and Fairies," you say, "How does knowing everyone's name and exchanging pleasantries prove you are friendly, caring, and sincere? I know peddlers who do this and they are anything but."

'Tis true. Some peddlers are posers, actors, or just plain jerks. They try to engage others not because they're interested in them, but because it makes them feel good, or because they're trying to impress someone—usually themselves!

Folks have a sixth sense, however. They know if someone is genuinely interested in them or not. They don't engage (at least not willingly) with jerks. They avoid eye contact, force a smile, and give short answers, all the while wishing he be gone. If they detect an honest human interest, however, they smile and trade small talk. This is why it is equally important to notice people's reactions, which is what our illustrious prospect is doing.

As you go about your morning, Mr. Big is not only watching you, but also how these folks respond to you. They smile, they're glad to see you. They laugh at your jokes and crack one themselves. They ask how you're doing and remember your usual. It's not long before Mr. Big decides he likes you, too.

It's pretty much all downhill from here, boys and girls. You can come up with a million other reasons why people buy from you, but when all else is equal—when your product is as good as the next company's, your price is the same, your installation as quick, and on and on—they must like you. I will grant you that sometimes folks buy from peddlers they dislike, but they do it begrudgingly. If they have a choice, people buy from people they like.

Miss this point and you will be an OK, mediocre, run-of-the-mill sales rep. Get it straight and you're on the road to great peddlery.

Putting Your Best Foot Forward

By and large, we peddlers are friendly, caring, and sincere folks. It's a matter of learning how to display our good nature to the world, and then remembering to do it. All good peddlers give off good vibes. (If you're wondering how I know all this, well, through good old trial and error. I've screwed up enough that the errors of my ways were clear—even to a thick mick like me.) Here are a few important skills to get you started.

The Name Game

A good peddler always gets the name protocol straight. As you greet someone with a strong handshake (this includes you gals—no wimpy shakes), always say your name unless you're 110% sure that the other person knows it cold. To cover that issue from the get-go is the considerate thing to do.

Get their name as well, and repeat it when you hear it. This will imprint it on your brain. There is nothing worse than not knowing or mispronouncing a prospect's or customer's name. It's one of those details that can make or break you. However, don't be presumptuous with a person's name.

> *Peddler:*   Hi, I'm Mike.
>
> *Prospect:* Good to meet you, Mike. I'm Thomas.
>
> *Peddler:*   You know, my best friend's name is Thomas. You look just like him. I call him Tommy. Do you mind if I call you Tommy? So, Tommy, what I was saying was . . .

Oy! Some peddlers think that the more intimate they are with a prospect or customer, the easier it is for him or her to buy from them. They twist their names to act like they are their best buddies. If you are one of these misguided peddlers, here's some news: They will buy from you if they like you. But they won't like you if you do perverted things with their names!

Here's another don't. For the love of Pete, don't use a prospect's or customer's name in an overbearing manner or as a weapon.

> So, Dennis, we were going to talk about your insurance policy. Dennis, why is it that your current policy only covers you? Dennis, don't you want make sure your kids have everything they need? Dennis . . .

Stop already! Repeating someone's name over and over is beyond irritating; it makes folks feel as if it's being used against them. Hey! It's their NAME. Be cool. Respect the person, respect their name.

Here's a good rule of thumb: Repeat a person's name when you hear it. Use it once or twice during your conversation, and when you say thank you and goodbye. That's three or four times, total. That's enough. Don't be a meathead and blow the name game.

The Eyes Have It

Peddlers often don't take the time to observe and assess the folks they are meeting. They charge in, assume control, pull out a presentation, and launch into their spiel.

Don't do this. Take a moment to notice your prospects or customers. Do they look like they're having a good or bad day? Do they look like they're ready for you? Of course, when you learn to read folks, you should adjust accordingly: "Do you need a few minutes? No problem. I'll be in the reception area."

Whenever you speak with folks, looking them in the eye is critical. This doesn't mean freaking them out with a power glare. Rather, it's a friendly, caring look. You know, human2human. Never stare in an overly-aggressive manner, never get into a staring contest. Simply look at them when you're speaking to them and when they're speaking to you. This will tell you if you are getting any hits, and it will tell them that you are truly interested in them.

Listen Up!

One of the best ways to show that you are a caring, sincere peddler is to listen to prospects and customers. I mean really listen. Actively listen. While they are speaking, nod and confirm you understand with an affirming, "Yup . . . I see . . . OK . . ." When they are finished, echo back what you heard: "So, if I understand you, Ms. Prospect, your problem is . . . Your goals are . . . Your project schedule is . . ." Listen so closely that you catch the subtleties: "Ms. Prospect, earlier you said this. Now you mention that. Are you saying . . ."

Nothing gives prospects and customers more confidence in you than when you can reiterate what they said to their satisfaction. Nothing makes them feel better as individuals than your having listened so closely that you can echo back what they said. Nothing increases your chances for success more than reiterating the issues, plans, concerns, solutions, and so on, and getting everyone to agree.

Be Engaging

For all you knuckleheads who are lost when the conversation isn't revolving around the magnificent you, here's a two-second primer on how to be engaging: Be enthusiastic, be positive. Let them know that you are psyched to be a peddler and completely into selling your wares. Smile.

A simple, happy, glad to see ya, it's a joy to be here smile as you look a prospect or customer in the eye can get—and keep—a meeting on the right track. Get that ear-to-ear grin going. Throw your best ham-and-egger smile as wide as a mile. Let your enthusiasm and happiness dazzle through those pearly whites. Come in smiling, stay smiling, and leave smiling. Never underestimate the value of a smile! It is the most potent weapon in your peddler arsenal.

Here's a one-second primer: Focus on them. Selling isn't about you. It's about the prospect, customer, or whomever you are pitching. Minimize the focus on you; shift it to the other person by asking them questions. We discuss what questions to ask in Chapters 13 (Finding), 14 (Selling), and 15 (Closing). For the moment, suffice it to say that you should 86 yes/no questions and ask open-ended questions. Query, query, and query some more.

Prospects and customers have questions, too, and you have to answer them and carry on a meaningful dialogue. Modulate your voice. Choose your words. Be articulate. This is a good way to demonstrate that you are confident and comfortable, and it makes folks want to engage with you. A good way to bring a meeting to a premature close is to mumble or talk fast. Take some deep breaths. Compose yourself. Ready? Set? You're on!

All of us know peddlers who do all the right things effortlessly. We wish we were them but resign ourselves to our lot in life. Do not kid yourself. Very few peddlers are naturals. Their secret is that they practice, practice, practice. The more they practice, the more comfortable they are and the easier it gets. If you want to be like them, PRACTICE!

STORY TIME

I am the U.S. and European sales manager for a mid-sized company, which means every week I'm strapping a jet to my butt, and flying all over God's creation to help my sales reps open new accounts and close deals.

On this particular Monday, I pull into San Francisco to meet a new peddler. We spend a couple hours reviewing the itinerary and the deals in progress. The next day we're on the road early, making call after call. We don't stop for lunch, pounding the pavement until dinner when we meet a prospect, share some drinks and a nice meal, and try to move that deal on down the line.

After our guest goes on her merry way, I suggest we pick a place to have a drink. This is my time with the peddler to review what we did and didn't do right. It's also time for a little fun, which we have, enjoying the night life and slamming back quite a few beers before we crash.

The next morning, I'm up early and the first one at our breakfast meeting. I'm joking with the waiter and in high gear by the time my bleary-eyed, hung-over peddler drags himself in looking like he just got hit by a truck. Now, any peddler that's worked with me just shakes his or her head and sits down. This new peddler, however, is not sure what to make of this scene. After a few sips of black coffee he finally says, "I feel like I've been through the wringer and you look like you didn't even go out. What gives?"

At which point, I lower my glasses, look him in the eye, and say, "PRACTICE! Pass the O.J."

Knock, Knock, It's Me!

OK, peddlers, ready for some controversy? There are two lines of thought regarding interacting with prospects and customers. The first is to be strictly professional; keep the human you separate from the business you.

This is how most folks in corporate want you to be, because then you'd be just like them. Automatons. Freaking robots! It's a phenomenon that probably originated with the analytics and the measurers, who are not really human anyway.

The corporate folks would like nothing more than to say to all peddlers, "Here is the sales profile. Here is the pitch. Here is what to say if someone raises objections. Here is the competitive analysis. NOW SELL!"

The second school of thought is to be professional but with a human touch. If you've read up to this point, you know which camp I'm in. I'm always trying to bring the human side to the business side, because I believe that ultimately, it's your personal relationships that make you and your business a success.

STORY TIME

I'm working for a Fortune 500 computer company as a new business account rep. One day, a lead comes in from a Regional Bell Operating Company (RBOC). Now, this is around the time that a judge by the name of Green is in the process of breaking up a company called AT&T, so I'm surprised when everyone ignores it. I decide to ask about it.

"Anyone going to follow up on this lead?"

"That guy's a crazy New Yorker," someone tells me. "He's impossible to deal with and he talks a mile a minute. You can't understand a word he says!"

"OK, if no one wants it, I'll take it." I say.

It takes me a few weeks, but I hook up with Warren, a new business analyst and strategist. He is one hyper dude who does, in fact, talk a blue streak. He seems smart, and he's one funny bunny—just like me!

In our first few conversations, we lay our cards on the table. I tell Warren that I don't know anything about the phone business, but I know computers. Warren tells me that he understands computer architecture and knows telecom inside and out. His job is to

(continued)

come up with new products. He seems straightforward. My kind of prospect.

I tell him that I'm looking for a partner. "By teaming up," I tell him, "I think we could make a lot of money for our companies and get a little career boost for ourselves."

"I like the way you're thinking, Dennis. Let's see how far we can take this."

Over the next several months, we get to know each other. We realize that we're both fast thinkers and fast movers who take a radical, damn the torpedoes, when in doubt panic and accelerate approach to life. As we teach each other our respective businesses and brainstorm about potential products, we gain a respect for each other's thought process, ideas, and ability to work through the requisite corporate channels. We develop a trust when we realize that we are both determined to make something happen. It's not long before there is a strong bond between us.

Eventually, we come up with a novel idea that combines our technologies. The executives at Warren's company like it because it broadens their product line. It thrills my executives because we get to sell the RBOC the equipment to produce it.

Warren and I work our companies to keep the deal moving forward, and work our executive teams to break the logjams along the way. We are on the phone with each other eight hours a day, plus two or three hours at night, for a year.

The deal becomes so complex that our companies form a SWAT team with executives, architects, product managers, and systems folk from each side. Warren and I sit in the middle with all the trials and tribulations of two people who are trying to do something new and big. Really big. $65 million big.

It is a nerve-racking time. Not only is there a lot of money at stake, but we are highly visible to all the folks up and down the corporate chain. Any mistake would be supremely embarrassing. We pull together and become even closer, looking out for each other and our deal. It takes a year to close the business because of the AT&T breakup and resulting RBOC reorganization, but Warren and I hang in there and have one hell of a ride.

Doing this deal taught me a lot. First, a peddler can't do a big deal alone. You need someone on the other side of the table who has as much desire as you. He or she may be the navigator, recommender, or evaluator, but I see this person as a kindred spirit—the one who, like me, owns the deal in his or her heart.

Second, when you click with someone, it's to everyone's benefit. He's taking your calls and you're happily taking his. He's anticipating the bumps in the road and guiding you through his corporate maze, and you're returning the favor. Like minds, like goals. This is the way to get business done. When I see a big deal taking shape, I start looking for my counterpart, because I know I'm not going to get far without him.

Third, a strong bond with your counterpart keeps the vultures at bay. It's a fact of life: When a big deal surfaces, everyone wants to own it and the politics begins. Smart execs who respect and trust relationship selling are quick to look for a bond and back off if it exists. They know a solid relationship helps bring a ship in, and that they should be happy to be associated with the deal and help move it along. I was lucky to be surrounded by great sales management during this deal who did this. That's not to say I didn't scare the heck out of them and cause a gray hair or two by the time it was over. Of course I did!

Lastly, well, it's just more fun to work with folks you're in tune with.

This leads to two big questions: How do you act like a professional with a human side? And, how human can ya get?

These calls are hard to make, but the first rule is go with your gut—until you've gathered enough data and can follow the second rule, which is, do what works.

One way to get past the professional-to-professional hurdle is to engage in a personal conversation. You or your customer or prospect discloses something personal that has absolutely nothing to do with your companies or your reason for meeting, but may (or may not be) something you have in common.

You walk into a prospect's office and see a picture of him or her holding a 36-inch stripped bass. Revealing that you are a crazed fisherman is a beginning. If the other person listens and shares more, a personal relationship starts. When you start trading your latest fishing stories and e-mailing each other pictures of your latest catch, then the relationship is getting meaningful and fun.

Sharing the nonprofessional you with prospects and customers can lead to expressing more private feelings and emotions. But be forewarned: It's usually a gradual progression from brief acquaintances to good acquaintances to almost friends to friends to good friends to best friends. Sometimes you get lucky and hit it off with another instantly. That is always a great thing. More often, relationships grow slowly. Sometimes they take years, sometimes a lifetime.

PEDDLER'S PREROGATIVE #12

Being a peddler is a career that often expands across decades. It takes years to develop close acquaintances and solid friendships. It is the peddler's prerogative to take the time to cultivate meaningful professional relationships, as they will carry you through the down times and happily share your success in the good times.

Whenever you reach out, there's always a chance that the other person won't respond. Or that a relationship progresses to a certain point (for example, to almost friends) and then stops. If this happens, don't take it personally. As a matter of fact, be careful how you take things in general. You are a peddler. You should take everything with a grain of salt!

You Must Like Them

I don't know why some of us don't mesh. I have thought about it and decided it's just the way it is. So it's important to have a strategy for handling personality conflicts in your life. Let's face it, even if you are an angel, there will always be some devil you just can't stand.

After years of peddling, I know fairly quickly who I can work with and who I have a better than 50% chance of pissing off. Once you know this, then you have to decide what to do about it. When I meet prospects or customers who set off my alarm, I know to stay calm and mosey on down the line the first chance I get. Often times, a fellow peddler or one of my own sales reps will say, "Hey, I think the guy's fine." At this point I'll say, "Lovely, then, he's all yours," (grumble, grumble).

Other times, there's no way to get out of a relationship and you have to deal with it, eat your share of dirt, and grovel as best you can. For the most part, I can keep cool and stay loose. But every so often I can't resist unleashing my inner imp and siccing him on a particularly irritating prospect or customer just to cause a merry riot. It's like being told, "Don't press that button!" and you can't help but push it as you ask, "This one?" KAPOW! Needless to say, you can't do this too often if you want to keep your job.

PEDDLER'S PREROGATIVE #13

A right of passage for any great peddler is being formally stripped of an account, thrown out of an account, or quitting an account verily. Good for you. Bravo!

The net-net is, if I'm going to close a lot of business, I have to like the prospect or customer as well. It's a two-way street. Once you acknowledge this, your selling days will be at least palatable, and perhaps even fun.

Ladies and Gentlemen, Your Attention Please

One of the best things about being a peddler is that folks you didn't know yesterday can become your friends today. All it takes is being attentive, considerate, caring, and sincere with the folks in your orbit.

Unfortunately, peddlers get so caught up in the day-to-day minutia, pressures, and general insanity of their realities that they forget to do this. They succumb to schedules, to-do lists, goals, and quotas. This chapter is a reminder not to do that. Rather, connect with others, recognize when there's chemistry, and take the time to create a bond. Because once a bond forms, then the all-important rapport clicks in. And when the rapport is cooking, a genuine relationship can be cultivated, which is what being a good peddler is all about.

CHAPTER 4

REJECTION

There are no facts, only interpretations.

—Friedrich Nietzsche

Now that we have established the premise that they must like you, it's time for the fun part: REJECTION!

"You're a salesperson? How do you deal with all that rejection?"

I get asked this question all the time. A lot of sales folks put on the bravado and reply, "Well, ya gotta be thick skinned!" Or, "I just let it roll off my back. It never bothers me!" Or, better still, "To me, a no means they are getting warmed up to say yes." What a bunch of malarkey!

Other peddlers take each no to heart, feeling as if they were personally rejected by the prospect or customer. I'm not going to mince words here. It's impossible to do that and peddle a product at the same time. If this is you, you need to get another gig.

Then there's my personal favorite: the peddler who never hears the word no. Ever! He can be thrown under a train, lit on fire, be told in no uncertain terms to leave the premises, and when asked how it's going, he says, "Great. I'm very close now." These peddlers are eternal optimists and entirely clueless about the reality of a situation. It makes ya love 'em, but it also drives ya nuts. Eventually, they always get canned.

So here's the real deal: No matter how long you've been a peddler, hearing a hard core no thank you, can't help you, don't need it, wrong person, wrong number, try another dimension, or a string of epithets puts a downer on your day.

But peddlers who have been around the block know not to take any of this personally. It's true that prospects and customers must like you to buy from you. But the converse is *not* true. If prospects or customers say no that doesn't mean they don't like you. It also doesn't mean you've done something wrong. When prospects and customers say no (drum roll, please) it usually means there isn't a fit!

So what's a fit? A fit is when a company has a real need for your product (roger wilco, check); when your product meets the company's requirements (check); when the timing is right (check); and when the company has the money to pay for it (check). When any one of these things doesn't fall into place, it's not a fit. And when something's not a fit, the logical response is no thanks.

How often have you done something like this? You're out shopping and you see a coat that you like. You've been needing a new one, so you try it on. Too big. As you're searching the rack for a smaller size, a salesperson comes over.

"Can I help you find something?"

"I like this coat, but as you can see, it's too big. Do you have it in a smaller size?"

He searches the rack. No luck. "Let me check in the back. There's a lot of stuff we haven't put out yet."

A couple of minutes later the salesperson returns. "I'm sorry, but we don't have a smaller size," he says.

"It sure is a nice coat, but I'm not going to take it. It doesn't fit. Thanks anyway."

We all do this all the time. We need an item, but the size is wrong. Or the size is right, but the price is too high. Or, the price is right, but we don't really need it right now, at this very moment; we'll get it another time.

Remember this the next time a prospect or customer says no to you. More often than not, the reason is that your product isn't a fit. That's the long and the short of it. No hard feelings. A fit is a fit! Don't make a mountain out of a molehill. Accept it and move on.

Of course, it's always important to see if there's a way to make your product fit the prospect's or customer's needs. Some peddlers hear no, and they pack up and bolt for the door. Don't do that! Stay right where you are and ask some questions.

There are a lot of reasons why a product might not fit. You want to find out why it isn't a fit for this person. You won't be able to overcome a prospect's or customer's objection and make it fit every time, but you need to ask every time because it's rare that an issue crops up just once. Rather, you'll find a pattern, which you can use to go back to your company and plead your case.

Peddler: We really need to order more of this coat in smaller sizes.

Buyer: This late in the season? We'll just be marking them down come January!

Peddler: It's very popular and it's only October. I've lost five sales this week alone because we didn't have the right size.

Manager: Five? It's a very expensive coat. Are you sure?

Peddler: Yup.

Manager: OK. Order a few more.

Remember, you never know until you find out! So do your field research. Ask prospects and customers why your product isn't a fit. Look at it this way. You've put in a fair amount of time and work to get in front of a prospect or customer. Don't leave empty handed; have something to show for your efforts. Find out why they're not buying. Then, commit that all important information to your brain. You may not snag this prospect or customer, but you'll leave with something valuable that you can use to win others down the road.

The one thing you cannot do is force a fit. Forcing a fit always creates pandemonium. If you find yourself in the middle of a forced fit, move on down the road, pronto! Forced fits usually come from a peddler's overactive imagination, a manager trying to save his butt, or someone very stupid thinking they are very smart.

Peddler's Prerogative #14

It is your peddler's prerogative to bail on a forced fit. Whenever you see one coming, quickly parse it. It is usually an overactive imagination, desperation, or stupidity. Whatever it is, you have to throw the flag and make the call. Sit the peddler down and bring them back to reality.

OK, back to demystifying the big NO. One way to reduce how often you hear it is by asking open-ended rather than yes/no questions: Who is in charge of this project? (Rather than, are you in charge of this project?) What type of problem are you having? (Not, are you having this problem?) What's the best way to meet the folks in this department? (Instead of, can I meet the folks in this department?) The bottom line, however, is that to some degree you are going to have to learn to deal with the word no—and no cycles.

For one cosmic reason or another, peddlers wind up in no cycles—weeks or months when you seem to hear nothing but no, no matter what you do. This can send the psyches of good peddlers spinning out of control. Don't let it get to you. Remind yourself that it's just a cycle; it, too, will end.

Receiving no response also can get you down. You call and call, and the person never answers. You leave voice mail, and they don't call back. You send an e-mail, and they don't reply. You call their assistant only to hear, "I really can't say."

A few nos, a few nonresponsive prospects and customers—sometimes that's all it takes before you're feeling rejected. Go through a no cycle and you may start believing there's some worldwide conspiracy against you.

But if you think about it, it's not all that unreasonable. Whether you are dialing for dollars or pounding the pavement, you are calling and bothering strangers who you have decided you need to get to know. Their resistance is natural. Some days it comes as a door in the face or a shot to the head. Other days it's a full body slam to the pavement.

Whatever you do, don't take it personally. That's how the feeling of rejection starts—BY TAKING THINGS PERSONALLY. Then it spreads by feeding on any doubts you have about life in general (we all got 'em). Many peddlers have some bouts of self-doubt, or don't believe that selling is as valuable as being, well, almost anything else! And being thrown out of an office or berated on the phone seems to confirm it.

Hey! Don't read anything into it. It happens. Just pick yourself up, dust yourself off, and remember that selling takes you up mountains and down into some pretty low valleys.

Peddler's Prerogative #15

It is your prerogative not to take anything that happens in the sales process PERSONALLY. When bad stuff happens, it is your prerogative to pick yourself up, dust yourself off, and straighten your clothes (doing your best Charlie Chaplin, of course). Proceed to go about your day.

The key is recognizing when the dark clouds start movin' in and reminding yourself that chasing deals is hard, mother-trucking, tedious work. It takes keeping your head down and your nose to the grindstone. It also helps to have a few stories, pieces of prose, or, as I do, prayers, that inspire you, calm you, console you, or make you laugh (Was it something I said?).

When You're Weary, Feeling Low . . .

Listen up! Every good peddler knows that some days you need something more than yourself to lean on. And let's face it, it's not going to be your manager!

I have two prayers for such occasions. One is the Hail Mary, which my mother used to beg me to say at least once before I opened my mouth and talked with anyone. I say continuous Hail Mary's before I take off in a plane but, strangely, never on landing (go figure). Please note that I am not preaching prayer or proselytizing for Jesus. But I do think that every peddler should have something—a poem, a prayer, a motto (mine is, "When in doubt, panic and accelerate."), a funny story—in his or her arsenal.

My second one is the Prayer of St. Francis. A lot of you probably know or have heard the Hail Mary (if not, ask a Catholic friend), but I've included the Prayer of Saint Francis for your enjoyment; it's a truly wonderful prayer.

The Prayer of Saint Francis

Lord, make me an instrument of Your peace,
Where there is hatred, let me sow love,
Where there is injury, pardon,
Where there is despair, hope,
Where there is darkness, light,
Where there is sadness, joy.

O divine master, grant that I may not
So much seek to be consoled, as to console,
To be understood, as to understand,
To be loved, as to love,
For it is in giving that we receive,
It is in pardoning that we are pardoned,
And it is dying that we are born to eternal life.

Don't be such a chump that you think you can't use some inspiration now and again. Also, remember that you are a chump, *period* (just like everyone else).

Understanding Your Job

If I haven't lost you with the prayers and you're still reading, hopefully you are grokking my peddler creed, including if you're an army of one, you better have some kind of divine channel to tap into other than Budweiser, though it has been pretty damn inspirational as well as consoling throughout my sales career.

You also better have a good understanding of what you do. You sell stuff. There I said it!

Companies produce products and hire peddlers to go out and sell them for money. Sure, many products do great things, such as help people accomplish difficult tasks, and deliver high ROIs. But it's really all about making money, and that's where you come in. It's your job to bring in the cash that will keep the lights on, create more products, and pay the staff. It's a vital function. Companies can't survive without it—without us!

I stress this point, because some peddlers try to hide the fact that they are a peddler. I love to uncover the frauds who pretend they are not selling when they really are, who come on high and mighty with a holier than thou attitude. I'm not a low-life peddler, I'm in business development. (Gimme a break!) I'm not a sales guy, I'm really an engineer who sells. (Ya, right!) I'm not here to sell you; I'm an executive, here to help you. (What door did you come in?) I'm not a peddler, I'm a consultant; you don't have to worry about that sleazy sales stuff with me. (Ya, you only charge for a week and work a day!) Let's face it, shenanigans like these give peddlers a bad rep.

Promises, Promises

Peddlers are famous for their promises, particularly for making ones they can't keep. They are on a call. They are in the spotlight. For some insane reason, they feel like they have to make the big play, hit a home run, catch the Hail Mary pass. They thrash about, come up with nothing and, out of desperation, promise the world and then throw in the sun, moon, and stars for good measure.

Some peddlers will do anything to preempt rejection or create a spectacular moment (that instant where, with a flash of inspiration, they change a deal for the better or miraculously get it to close). Making promises is usually a last-ditch effort to do one or the other.

News flash: Everyone on both sides of the table is watching you commit. Everyone will remember if you come through. Only make promises you can keep, and then, for Pete's sake, keep them! Time after time I see peddlers set up expectations, get some momentum going, and then not follow through. What a waste of everyone's time, not to mention how really inept peddlers look to the folks who have been waiting for the promised goods.

Rather than promises, I take the "Try me!" approach. Throw down a benign gauntlet that helps show you are willing to go the extra mile, and ask the prospect to let you prove how good you are. I love telling prospects, "Let us do a little work for you on our nickel so you can see how good the product fits and how hard we work to make sure your needs are met. No cost, no obligation."

Most folks bite if you offer up a scenario that has no downside for them. For you, it's a low risk way to get more data and prove your concept. I firmly believe that if you want to get a leg up on the competition, you must work harder and do more. Putting some corporate skin in the game can work wonders.

Delivering on a promise, proving you deserve the business—now that's a spectacular moment in the eyes of a prospect or customer. It's also a surefire way to avoid rejection. They will count on you down the road, because you've shown you can pull the necessary strings to make stuff happen for them. Prospects and customers will remember: This peddler delivers!

PEDDLER'S PREROGATIVE #16

It is your prerogative to forget the spotlight and focus on the details of the deal. It is your prerogative to realize that that's the way to preempt rejection, and that your spectacular moment is when you have cashed your commission check and are buying pizza and beer!

Help Me! I'm Sinking!

Let's get something straight. Your job is to come up with ideas for selling your product, get everyone working together, and guide your deals down the pike. To do this, you must be willing to ask the tough questions and make the right calls. You also must be adroit to avoid some major sinkholes.

STORY TIME

A start-up hires me to find out why its peddlers aren't having much luck selling its product. After all, it's a good product, it's reasonably priced, and it has a market. Yet sales are abysmal.

The first week, I plan to sit in on various calls and meetings to get the lay of the land. Unfortunately, it doesn't even take that long to figure out that the reason these peddlers are not closing deals is because they don't have the foggiest notion why their

(continued)

prospects and customers are buying the product. They also refuse to ask.

The next week, the peddler, his manager, and I are on a conference call. They're trying to push a deal along when I pipe up.

"So, why do you guys want to buy our product?" I ask. The peddler and his manager nearly fall off their chairs.

"Well, we're not really sure yet," the prospect responds.

"What else are you looking at?"

"Well, as I've mentioned before, we like your product because it's flexible, but there's this other product that's very similar and it fits really well with what we already have in-house. Our support folks already know how to use it, it integrates seamlessly with our current software, and there's no licensing fee."

As the prospect goes on, I realize that we can't compete—the other product is a perfect fit. But the peddler and his manager don't hear that, and after we get off the call the salesperson turns to me and says, "I can't believe you lost my deal. I can't believe we're paying you for sales consulting!"

"Lost your deal?" I say, "There was no deal to lose!"

There was no earthly reason for this peddler to be courting this company. Yet, that's what he had been doing. And his manager as well! It was a bad idea to have pitched this company. It was a bad strategy to hang in there. It was a fool's errand, but neither one wanted to see it. Or, if they saw it, no one wanted to be the person to call it. They were desperate. They just wanted to do the deal, so they had their happy ears on—they were only hearing what they wanted to hear, which was that our product was still being considered.

When the writing is on the wall, pay attention. This is the kind of stuff that feeds a feeling of rejection when, as is inevitable, the prospect says, "Thanks, but no thanks." Don't let it happen to you. Validate your ideas and strategies with others. Ya, go with your gut, let your creativity and imagination run wild, but always have some checks and balances in place—just in case having a stripper deliver your proposal after jumping out of a cake is a bit much for the local library you're trying to close.

Accept It!

In the corporate realm, there are many people who seem to have high self-esteem. So peddlers believe they need a hefty dose of it, too. Forget it! Playing the corporate ego game inch-for-inch, pound-for-pound is a waste of time. First of all, a lot of corporate types just put on the jive and pretend they are in control. They act confident, but don't let their bluster fool you. Underneath they are trying to hide in the weeds, hoping against all hope that no one comes around and bothers to notice them, causes any conflict, or discovers that they're really human after all.

Second, it is far more important to have self-acceptance than self-esteem. Accepting ourselves facilitates the acceptance of others. Accepting your own limitations and quirks allows us to be more compassionate of others. Accepting what you do for a living makes you a better peddler.

PEDDLER'S PREROGATIVE #17

Repeat after me: It is OK to be a peddler. It is OK to sell for a living. It is OK to tell prospects and customers that you want to sell them your product for cash. It is OK to ask for an order. And, above all, it is OK to treat your prospects and customers right and be true. It is all OK. (Psst! You can fire your psychiatrist now. It's all okey-dokey!)

It is your prerogative to make sure from the get-go that a prospect or customer knows you are meeting with them to sell them your product, that it's your job, and that you are OK with selling for a living. They should be aware that you are there to move the relationship along from a sales perspective. It's what you do. It's what you're all about. Capisci?

What is not OK is creating fancy names and putting up smoke screens to hide the fact that you are selling stuff for money! Don't get me wrong here—titles are good and can help you get a foot in the door. But once you're in, don't give the prospect or customer some bullshit about why you're there and what you want. And don't put down your peddler profession. If you don't accept who you are, your prospects and customers won't either.

There are a million and one names for a salesperson. I happen to like peddler because it evokes an image of a person roving about, selling his or her wares, which is what I do—I go around peddling stuff. I am proud of that, and so must you be if you're going to succeed.

Ya, I know, if you had it your way, you'd be glad to tell everyone you're a peddler. But some peddlers have spoiled it for the rest of us. We can only imagine what happened to the person who first said, "He would sell his mother for a nickel," or "Count your fingers after you shake his hand."

There are stigmas associated with peddlers. No doubt about it. But you perpetuate the bad vibes when you're less than up front about what you do. And if you continue, it's only going to get worse. You need to step up to the plate. You need to make sure you don't act like some of those before you. You have to put it squarely to your prospects and customers: "I understand you're hesitant, so let me gain your trust. Give me a chance to prove myself to you."

It is unfortunate that not everyone in the profession is honorable, but every profession is haunted by those who detract from it. Lawyers are derided for being ambulance chasers, doctors for thinking they are God. So don't get hung up on it. Prove that you are different and don't add to the common misperceptions about peddlers.

PEDDLER'S PREROGATIVE #18

You have chosen to be a peddler and it's your prerogative to enhance or detract from the general world view of your chosen profession. It is under your control, so don't be a featherhead.

Win Some, Lose Some

Everybody does. I have even won them, lost them, won them again, and lost them again. It goes with the turf, boys and girls. You can fight the good fight, do your best, and still lose out on a deal. So don't handicap yourself by worrying that someone might say no. Focus on finding companies that are a potential fit. Then when you meet with them, ask the tough questions so you can decide whether to continue to pitch or ditch. If they say no, consider it a favor, because you are never going to sell anything to the wrong company or the wrong person at the wrong time. You can explain your product 'til you're blue in the face, but a sale ain't ever gonna happen!

PEDDLER'S PREROGATIVE #19

It is your peddler's prerogative to realize that you are never going to sell anything to the wrong company or the wrong person at the wrong time. It ain't ever gonna happen!

So put down the blindfold and the cigarette, and send the soldiers back to their quarters. Pull yourself together and go find a fit. It's no biggie. It happens to all of us. You can't let it drag you down. Are you ready? Good. Now, get your butt in gear!

CHAPTER 5

TRUTH AND DOING THE RIGHT THING

If you tell the truth, you don't have to remember anything.
—Mark Twain

One of the keys to being a good peddler is an impeccable understanding of two concepts, truth and doing what's right. Truth is your best friend, because it is really hard to argue with truth! Telling the truth, being true—it all starts with being aware of the truth. What your product does and doesn't do. What your company will and won't do. What your prospects and customers can and can't do.

It sounds simple, but it isn't—mostly because you can't trust a freakin' thing you're told! Let's face it. Everyone has an agenda today: engineering, marketing, accounting, executives, prospects, customers—you name it. They each have their own goals and priorities—the first one being to convince everyone else that they are in the know and speak the truth. They turn up the knobs and dials and incite a raucous chatter until it seems like everyone's thinking and spouting the same thing, which amazingly can get most everyone to think the same thing. "It seems like everyone thinks it's true, so it must be true, right?"

WRONG!

This is such folly! Groupthink is never a guide to truth. To find out what's true, you must observe keenly with all your senses and only believe what you validate for yourself. When marketing proclaims a new feature is light years ahead of the competition, check it out. When engineering says a customization is impossible, find out why. When executives brag about having the best pricing, verify it. When a customer says your product doesn't solve his problem, do your homework.

Ya, all this takes time, but there's no way around it. There are two rules of thumb that can help you, however. The first one is the age-old adage: If something sounds too good to be true, it probably is. The second one is from my own experience: When something is true, it usually makes sense. I say usually because people and companies do stupid things. A competitor underbids you even though it will lose money on a deal or put its commitments to all its other customers at risk. Such is the way of the world. It happens. But, hey, that doesn't mean you should do the same and be as frivolous.

Rather, once you find the truth amid the jumble, then you should do the right thing for you, your company, and your prospects and customers.

The Peddler's Biggest Challenge

OK, let's deal with your fears first. If you do the right thing, could you lose the deal? (Yup.) Could the prospect or customer get upset? (Definitely.) Could your management get tense and willful? (Bet on it.) Could you lose your job? (It's happened before.)

There are no two ways about it. When you look for the truth and do the right thing, you are putting everything on the line. This is why many peddlers find it hard to do the right thing. It's understandable, but it's no excuse.

Is it OK to commit to a ship date when you know that you will never make it? Is it OK to tell a prospect or customer that they'll receive next-generation functionality when you know it'll never happen? Is it OK to promise to customize the product when you know the engineering staff can't do it? The answer to all three questions is, absolutely not. You must tell the prospect or customer that while you would love to book the deal and you really need the business, you have to let him know that his requirements aren't in line with what you can deliver. You know the truth. Be up front and honest!

See No Evil, Hear No Evil, Speak No Evil

Some peddlers try to get around doing the right thing by not looking for the truth. They don't ask about product plans, manufacturing updates, or delivery schedules. They don't want to see any evil. They figure that what they don't know they don't have to tell their prospects or customers.

Get this through your peddler brain: Sooner or later it will become apparent that you did not know what the heck you were talking about when you were doing the deal. When things start going awry—dates start slipping, features don't show up—your prospects and customers are going to start asking questions. Ya, you can honestly say that you didn't know. In which case the prospects or customers may not see you as the slippery peddler that you are. They'll just see you as INCOMPETENT!

Prospects and customers don't deal with incompetent peddlers for long. They want peddlers they can rely on. Peddlers who look out for them, anticipate problems, and work to avoid them. Make it your business to know the score or you can kiss your accounts goodbye.

PEDDLER'S PREROGATIVE #20

It is your prerogative to be a peddler who prospects and customers can rely on to look out for them and their interests. Make it your business to know the score.

Other peddlers avoid doing the right thing by not engaging in an effective dialogue. They don't really hear what a prospect or customer is saying, and they don't draw them out to gain a better understanding of their needs. Or, if they hear and understand them, they don't address their issues. They hold back information. Rather than clarifying what will surely become a major issue down the road, they let it slide, perhaps even steering the conversation to other things, hoping that the prospect or customer forgets to pin them down.

Actually, it's not just peddlers. Sales managers and corporate types also take this hear no evil, speak no evil approach. And it always turns into a nightmare for everyone involved. Things go south. The customer gets riled. Payments are withheld. A new round of negotiations begins. And the company debooks some amount of the sale. All this could have been avoided if you had been honest and up front. If you had just done the right thing!

Ya, I know, it's a dog-eat-dog, bottom-line world. If you don't close a deal, not only could you miss your quota, but the company could miss its numbers.

I'll let you in on a little secret: There are other ways—LEGITIMATE ways—to win business.

Creating a Sense of Urgency

So you live in a world that doesn't really give a damn about anything but your numbers: How many calls did you make? How many appointments did you get? How many proposals have you done? How much business did you close? All that anyone seems to care about is whether you are going to meet your monthly or quarterly goals.

Constantly being hounded about your numbers is a tough row to hoe, but it's the name of the game, my friend. Peddlers are expected to bring in as much business as possible as fast as possible. The way to do this without veering from the path of truth and doing the right thing is by creating a sense of URGENCY.

First let's discuss what creating a sense of urgency is NOT. It is not causing every living soul around you to get their knickers in a twist. It is not acting like Chicken Little, warning that the sky is falling and scaring the bejesus out of everyone. If this is you, take a moment to see what an idjit you look like running about, fretting and whining, and holding your head. Straighten up and give the rest of us a break.

Creating a sense of urgency isn't about freaking out yourself and those around you. On the contrary. It's about calmly and deliberately finding a reason for your company and your prospect or customer to want to move a deal along. Here's a hint: It must be a compelling reason. Ya, COMPELLING! A compelling offer, a compelling discount, a compelling solution to a problem—maybe even a meeting with some compelling folks who can help get the issues on the table.

There are two ways to find out what is compelling to prospects or customers. The first is trial and error. You think of something, run it by them, they say no. You think of something else, they say no. You think of something else. . . . You get the idea. This is not only tedious for you and your prospects or customers, but it's slow.

The better way is to call up a prospect or customer and simply ask: "Mr. Prospect, what would be a compelling reason for you to move the deal along more quickly?"

Most times, prospects or customers tell you that the deal is going to go at the pace it's going and when it gets done, then it will be done. In which case, you acquiesce—but just for the time being. I always reserve the right to check back with my prospects or customers again. There may be nothing I can do to get a deal moving faster today, but who knows? Down the road the planets may align and I might be able to move a deal up a week or even a day, which can count big time when that day is the last day of the quarter. Obviously, you can't be a nag or a hound, but you shouldn't hesitate to ping prospects or customers with a quick query every so often to find out if now's the time.

There are other times, however, that the prospect or customer pipes up and tells you exactly what is needed to move the deal up a few weeks or a month. Then it's up to you to do a reality check and see what's possible. Off you go, bouncing into corporate to get things cooking.

The Ethical Imperative

Now, here's the thing. It's important to deal honestly with the minutia that pervades a peddler's daily existence, but it's not enough. You need to make doing the right thing part of your peddler's philosophy, the way you do business. As any good peddler can tell you, you must have an ethical imperative deep inside you. Anything less isn't going to cut it.

You are only one part of the sales dynamic. The other two parts are your company and your prospects and customers. That's a lot of folks to do right by—a lot of hyped up corporate folks with big egos and even bigger agendas. You gotta have a solid philosophy and the ability to pinpoint what's right and true, or in very short order you won't know which end is up.

You also must have the willingness to articulate what's right and wrong, and the commitment to act on it. A good place to start is with yourself.

STORY TIME

I'm working for a bleeding-edge technology company. I need to ramp up sales fast by hiring a bunch of peddlers who are able to grok this whacky stuff. I call a few of my posse of peddlers, one of whom mentions another fine peddler named Pete.

I know Pete. He's a peddler through and through. He likes the peddling life and always produces. I give him a call and he comes in for a round of interviews. At the end of the day, he pulls me aside.

"Brother, I have no idea what the heck anyone was talking about all day! I mean, I'm clueless!"

"Not to worry," I say. "It's just a bunch of jargon. It's not that hard. You'll pick it up in no time."

Over the next few days, I continue to assure him that all will be fine and cool. Finally, I talk him into joining the company.

At the end of the first day, I stop by and check on him. "This stuff is sooooo bending my head," he tells me. I sit down and spend some time explaining the technology and answering his questions. Soon he's back on track. I do this for the next three days.

On Friday, after a week on the job, he comes into my office and closes the door. "Forget it!" he says. "I'm done! Not gonna do it. Can't

(continued)

do it!" Then he starts laughing. "I AM NOT TECHNICAL! I don't understand a thing that's going on. This will never work. I have to quit."

"OK, OK." I say. "Quit if you want. No one's going to stop you. But I will tell you that it's not that hard. Yes, it will take some time. But it's not that tough."

"Yeah, maybe for you and the other guys, but I'm not into technology. I can't wrap my mind around this leading-edge stuff. You and the rest of the guys have a techie background, but I don't and I can't get into it. So I am gone."

I can tell he's serious. "No problem," I say. "It's your call. I'm sorry it didn't work out."

Pete was a good peddler. He was not the kind to take a job and quit after one week, but he knew what he could and couldn't do. He also had an ethical imperative to do right. And he knew the way to start setting things right was to get the heck out of that job. Pete and I still laugh about it today. "I can't believe I was in that whacky company for a week," he'll say. "It was like talking to Martians. Glad I got off that alien planet!"

Listen up! You must do right by yourself, or you are not doing right—cannot do right—by your company, and your prospects and customers.

Is He Kidding Me?

You may be acting good and true, you may be in control of yourself, but you have no control over the other folks in your orbit. Most of the time, the internal corporate folks are pretty reasonable, and you can wade through the muck and mire. But there are times when they are out of control. Then it's up to you to be the conscience of your company, speak up, and take the lead.

The general perception is that peddlers don't care; they'll do anything for business. After 25 years of selling, it takes me all of a nanosecond to get on my soapbox when I see a discussion is heading down this

path. I don't care who's in the room—colleagues, department heads, or company executives. I will tell them that all we have is our integrity, and if we blow that, we might as well all go home.

I do this to shocked, horrified, and confused looks. It's very disconcerting when an over-the-top, gun-slinging peddler starts preaching about truth, integrity, and doing the right thing. Usually, someone who knows me steps in and tells them I'm not kidding. I then go on to explain what the proposed bullshit will do to our prospects and customers.

The fact is, the world of the peddler is an ongoing morality play. We are encouraged to take decisive action and rewarded when we succeed, with thin regard paid to the repercussions. For this, you need to have a crisp understanding of where the lines are drawn. Then you must choose to be either a champion of the good side or the dark side. As my father used to say, "Right is right."

PEDDLER'S PREROGATIVE #21

The world of the peddler is an ongoing morality play and you are either a champion of the good side or the dark side. It's your prerogative to choose to champion the good. Remember, right is right!

A Spade Is a Spade

Your company isn't the only one that may cross the line. Your prospects and customers can as well. As the King of Sales Leprechauns and Fairies, I insist that my sales folk learn to call a spade a spade. When a prospect or customer is not doing right by you or your company, you must summon your integrity and strength, and call it as you see it. So many sales horror stories could be avoided if someone would just call the foul, blow the whistle, or put their foot down.

STORY TIME

As is usually the case every few years or so, I'm looking for a job and checking in with everyone I know, including my buddy, Dan. Dan and I go back a long time. We grew up in the same town, and went through all of junior high, high school, and some college together. We are good friends and can talk about anything with each other. Whenever one of us spills our guts, the other laughs, chides, or pokes fun mercilessly before empathizing and helping out. A typical guy relationship.

(continued)

True to form, when I reach Dan and tell him I need work, he proceeds to tell me that I have a major personality disorder, which has gotten me removed from yet another company, and that I'm a miserable failure. Then, he proceeds to set up interviews with his company. Twenty-four hours later, I'm meeting with the executive team and three founders. Within weeks, I'm General Manager of Europe, reporting to Dan who oversees international sales.

My first task is to familiarize myself with all the existing partnerships. As I'm sifting through a pile of reseller contracts, I come across one with a German distributor that gives it a five-year exclusive deal for all of Germany and German-speaking regions of Europe. I'm surprised. This essentially ties our hands in a territory that amounts to 5% of our world market. As I continue to read, it gets worse: If we sell the company within the five-year period, the distributor gets a percentage. To add insult to injury, their revenue commitment is small. There's nothing about this deal that makes sense.

Now, I know that this kind of thing happens a lot in small startups and that hindsight is 20/20. Still, I couldn't resist needling my buddy: "Jesus, Mary, and Joseph, Dan! What were you guys smokin' when ya did this freakin' deal?"

Dan agrees that it is not a good situation and should be fixed. "It was negotiated early on," he warns, "so let's first talk to Don, my boss, and get the facts. He owned worldwide sales and negotiated the deal."

Off we go to see Don. "It was our first big deal in Europe," he tells us. "We were anxious to get it done."

In other words, it was the typical start-up scenario: Get the deal done today, figure out the ramifications tomorrow.

I decide to lay low while we figure out a plan to fix the situation. As a day stretches into a week, however, I begin to get antsy. The new CEO is waiting to meet with me; I was to review all of the existing European deals and give him my assessment, ASAP. I know it's not going to be long before he tracks me down.

Sure enough, one night Dan and I are sitting in his office and in pops the CEO: "You two aren't going anywhere tonight until I look at Europe. I want to get up to speed, NOW."

(continued)

Dan shrugs and gives me one of those don't-screw-it-up looks as I head up to the white board. I outline the status of the deals and the strategy I think we should follow. Like a heat-seeking missile, the CEO zeros in on the German distributor. Dan and I play it as low key as we can, but the CEO is one smart dude. He looks at me and says, "Fix it fast. And if you can't, get the Managing Director over here to meet with me. I don't want to sit on this. I want it fixed."

I schedule a trip to Europe with the CTO, one of the founders, to meet with Mike, the Managing Director. After the introductions, I tell him why we are here, and he informs me that his company has just been bought by a large German car manufacturer. He also says that as far as he is concerned, the contract is a done deal and will not be renegotiated until it terminates. Mike is a meticulous, by-the-book German who knows he has us over a barrel. He tells me he will set up a meeting at corporate headquarters for tomorrow.

The next day, he picks us up at our hotel (in his new BMW), and we arrive at headquarters in record time (via the autobahn). We take the elevator to the top floor of this magnificent glass building and walk into a room the size of Rhode Island with a table half the size of a football field. My buddy Mike has four lawyers there, waiting for us. As we exchange business cards, I notice that one is the Chief Counsel of this large car manufacturer. (Ruh roh!)

"My company has just purchased Mike's company," the Chief Counsel begins. "They are now part of our family. We are a big bear and his company is one of our cubs. We will do anything to protect our cubs. You negotiated a deal and you must live by the terms of that deal." (This is really what he said, with a heavy German accent, of course.)

I look over at the CTO. He has lost all color in his face and is sweating bullets despite the fact that it can't be more than 50 degrees in the room. He's a techie and hasn't had a lot of experience negotiating with humongous corporations. That the Chief Counsel is directing all conversation to him is really freaking him out. Just when he looks like he's going to pass out I butt in.

"Excuse me. We've been sent here by the CEO of our company to get this relationship on track. Mike and his team negotiated a

(continued)

good deal for your company and a bad deal for ours. The CEO and I are new to this company, but we are both experienced in software sales and know how the reseller channel works. So we are either going to fix this deal or blow it up."

I then take my open book and shut it as if I am expecting to leave in a moment or two. "I want to fix this deal," I continue, "and am willing to concede some terms—more than we would normally—as a good-faith gesture."

The Chief Counsel doesn't say anything; he just starts shaking his head. I stand up and say to the CTO, "This isn't going to happen. Let's go."

The CTO looks so astonished that I almost start to grin. Hands shaking, he gets his stuff together and gets up. His shirt is soaked through with sweat. As we're about to walk away from the table, the Chief Counsel pipes up.

"OK, here is what we are willing to do."

He offers so little that it isn't even worth talking about. I thank him for his time and ask Mike if he would be so kind as to come to the States and explain his position to the CEO of my company, as it is now out of my hands.

Fast-forward two weeks. I am back in Boston with Mike, Dan, and Don waiting to meet with the CEO. We're chitchatting when the CEO walks in. He sits down, looks Mike in the eye and says, "I am not mincing words. We are changing this deal around or you can take me to court."

"I am sorry you feel that way," says Mike, "but that is not the way I see it. Your company signed a contract and you need to stand by it." Without another word, the CEO gets up and walks out of the room.

Ticked off, Mike gets up and grabs his stuff. Before he gets to the door I jump up (with hopes of preventing World War III), and ask him to stay and work out a deal. Don and Dan chime in and, soon, we are able to settle Mike down. Over the next two hours, we hammer out an agreement. We gave them a slightly larger discount, they relented on taking a percentage if we were to sell the company. They also made some revenue and purchase commitments. All in all, it wasn't great, but it wasn't bad either.

The moral of the story is, you must call a spade a spade and have a deep-seated need to act ethically—even when that means pointing out to a prospect or customer what's right and true. When I run into folks who think a good deal is one that is great for them and lousy for me, I have no problem telling them that I consider a good deal to be when both parties give a little and get a little and, in the end, are generally happy with the deal. I tell them that that is how I do business!

In the course of your career, it's highly likely that you will peddle many products for many companies. There's little to take from one gig to the next besides your knowledge, your relationships, and your integrity. Lose your integrity and you will lose your relationships. Lose your relationships and what you know doesn't matter one iota.

A few days later, I was walking by the CTO's office and overheard him recounting our visit to Germany. He had obviously learned a whole lot about deals, truth, and doing the right thing on that trip. He had learned to call a spade a spade and was proud of it. For months afterward, he would tell that story over and over again to anyone who would listen until it took on a life of its own.

You and Your Army of One

You're finding the truth, doing the right thing, and acting as the conscience of your company, your prospects, and your customers. It's a lot of work. You look around your company thinking, "Couldn't I get just a little bit of help here?"

Don't bet on it. If your company is like most, its priority is keeping shareholders happy. Go to any business school and you'll learn that a company serves its stockholders. And therein lies the rub. While you're figuring out the right thing to do, the company is doing whatever it takes. The net-net is, most of the time, you are on your own, baby!

Some companies have struggled to find a way to do both, and have broken through because of bold, visionary leadership. I have walked into corporations and immediately felt a sense of spirit and community. They have good people doing good work. They strive to be fine inhabitants of the planet earth as well as model corporate citizens, and they find a way to treat everyone right, be they prospects, customers, employees, investors—even the wandering peddler.

I have walked into other companies and been greeted as if I was carrying a disease, only to find myself in meetings with some hard-core "businessmen" who huff and puff, and act like playground bullies. Oddly enough, these are always the companies that have their pious corporate values prominently displayed.

What gives? It's simple. Some corporate leaders have an ethical imperative in addition to a profit imperative. Others simply kowtow to Wall Street or the Board of Directors and their demands for more profit quarter after quarter. They implement all sorts of systems designed to measure performance, often beginning with a Management by Objectives (MBO) plan or some other type of bonus and incentive program, and going from there. The idea is to get everyone to continually beat last quarter's accomplishments, which they do by pressuring and squeezing everyone in the food chain below them to meet their numbers. It's a more-is-better mentality in which everyone wrings out employees, colleagues, customers—anyone and everyone in their span of control.

Granted, I have seen companies driven by a profit imperative occasionally wire in some touchy-feely, love-bomb-the-customer stuff. Admittedly, I also have benefited immensely from these profit-driven plans, blowing all expectations out of the water and taking home fat cash prizes. I'm not advocating getting rid of them. Peddlers need incentives. We like incentives. We want incentives! But business should find ways to use these plans to achieve more than just meeting the next quota. They should use them to encourage peddlers to develop close, meaningful, real relationships with customers, to find creative solutions to prospects' and customers' problems, to doing a deal right—not just closing it by the end of the quarter.

Business today threatens our relationship with ourselves. Its practices, policies, and processes—while created by humans for humans, amazingly—are either devoid of all human qualities (although they are great at faking them) or intent on embracing the worst ones. It's a sad state of affairs, and it pits the individual against himself or herself.

If your company is like this, you have two choices. You can hit the road, or you can stay and try to make it better. Many peddlers opt out and get another gig, only to find themselves in the same situation. It's not surprising. The number of arrogant, greedy, selfish corporations is greater than the humble, generous, and nurturing ones.

Some peddlers jump ship only to find themselves in a worse situation: working for a company that encourages unscrupulous, immoral, or corrupt behavior. This is a no-win situation. When you see it, get out fast. Recognize it for what it is and ditch. Avoid the dance of death.

Peddler's Prerogative #22

It is always a peddler's prerogative to avoid the dance of death. If you are associated with a company that is unscrupulous, immoral, or corrupt, DITCH!

Assuming you are with what unfortunately has become a normal company, then it's your duty to lead the charge. As peddlers, we see first hand how our companies have made the customer corporate enemy #1. We see that you have to be either a monster or a robot to succeed in corporate (everyday is Halloween in some companies). The only way to counteract this is to examine your corporate life and decide how to go about making it a good and just life—good for you and good for everyone around you. Then call up your army of one and start marching down the road. I'll even lend you a drum and flute!

The best way to get folks to change is to lead by example, show-casing the best human traits we have to offer. Some will follow, others won't. What can I say? One person at a time, one mountain a day. Simple, right? Good. It's now your responsibility to seek truth and do the right thing. Glad we solved that one!

For all of you corporate types who are reading this, maybe you could see your way clear to admit that what you're doing IS NOT WORKING. Why don't you nix the old corporate rhetoric, take the initiative, and establish an ethical imperative as the foundation of your business principles and practices? Why can't you figure out a way to make conscience and compassion part of your corporate incentive programs? Try bringing some milk and cookies to your next meeting and changing the world.

But I digress. Onto our last chapter in this part, "The Mysticism of Peddlery."

CHAPTER 6

THE MYSTICISM OF PEDDLERY

All mystics speak the same language, for they come from the same country.

—Louis Claude de Saint-Martin

Buckle up, boys and girls! You are about to glimpse the mystical dimension of peddlery. A realm where intuition, vision, belief, energy, and magical power rule the day. A space where peddlers transcend the concrete world of dialing for dollars, making presentations, and slamming deals together to another, higher level, where what you can't see and can't measure reign.

Have I lost you? OK, let me ask you a few questions. Have you ever made anything happen by sheer desire? Have you ever made anything happen by force of will? Has a solution to a problem ever come to you in a dream? Have you ever conjured up a scenario and then breathed life into it? Do you believe that great things will happen to you and that peddling is your destiny? Do you believe there are unseen forces that impact what you do? Do you believe you can tap into those metaphysical forces?

If you didn't answer yes to most of these questions, WHY THE HELL NOT? What's wrong with you? Get with the program, for the love of Pete! You need to feel the force Mr. or Ms. Skywalker! Where the material and metaphysical worlds intersect is where the great peddler stands.

Peddlers fall into one of two camps: those who believe in the wellspring of magic and their power to tap it, and those who don't. You need to know which camp you are in. Do you accept that other dimensions exist, or is there only the hard-core reality of the everyday present? Are there spirits, angels, and mystical forces that help and guide you? Can you channel that energy into all you do?

I believe I can. I believe all great peddlers do. The great peddlers are the mystics of the corporate world.

PEDDLER'S PREROGATIVE #23

It is your peddler's prerogative to be a mystic of the corporate world!

Unknown Knowing

If you stick with peddling, eventually you develop a sixth sense for people and situations. It just comes with the territory. You get tons of experience and, all of a sudden, you are sizing things up in a nanosecond. You are reading people and situations like nobody's business. You walk in to a room and, WHAM!, you get this hit. You sit in front of a person and, BLAM!, you got 'em. You immediately know who's cool and who's not; who's going to help you and who's going to get in the way; who's a future friend, a bureaucrat or, God forbid, a fiend:

"This person's evil. I'm in front of the devil!" Somehow you know. You just freakin' know! You are hyperaware, hyperintuitive.

The first time this happens, it's pretty amusing. Then, you get comfortable with it. Then, you start to use it. You're in a meeting, hyperaware of everything around you, tuned in to everyone. Folks are making presentations, asking questions, going through the motions, when you have clarity. You see it: the straightest line to the goal. You look around. Blank faces, every one. Not an ounce of recognition. You decide to take the bold stroke, make the bold statement.

You: "Excuse me. Are we focusing on the right issue? Processing a huge number of requests, and doing it in real-time, 24/7 — those are tactical issues. Our product and all our competitors' products routinely handle them."

Them: "Right?"

You: "It seems to me that the real and bigger issue is that your CEO wants a system up and running ASAP."

Them: "That's true."

You: "Well, we can pretty much guarantee that we'll have a working prototype up and running in a few months. It's what we do for most of our customers. Our software is designed for rapid prototyping, unlike our competitors. So, let's get the deal done, and concentrate on bringing the system in early and making everyone happy."

Them: "Agreed."

You: "Great! Here's what we do."

Whenever I do something like this, people invariably come up to me afterwards and say, "How did you know where he was headed? He didn't even finish his presentation!" To them, it seems like unknown knowing. And in a way it is. But when you peddle for as long as I have, and you've seen so many people in so many situations, some things are just obvious. You just know where people and situations are headed long before your colleagues, fellow peddlers—even the prospects or customers themselves.

Once you know, then you must act. Jump on the opportunity. Seize the pivotal moment! There are countless ones, and they mean life or death to your deal. Catch the right one, step up to the plate at just the right time, and you have the power to alter the course of events, turn the tide in your favor, change your fate. Pretty heady stuff.

To do this, however, you have to be present in the moment. You can't be wrapped up in the past or dreaming about the future. The here and now is where you have to be. Jacked in, engines humming, gears engaged. Then, just before you peel out, take a nanosecond to put the proverbial finger under your chin and consider how to best use the moment to push your deal forward or get it back on track. Ask yourself, What if . . . ? Then, channel the cosmic energy around you and usher everyone down the better path.

The Art of Dot Connecting

I like to think of myself as a peddler who has a specialty in dot connecting—that is, I can see a scenario or result given only a few pieces of information. All great peddlers are phenomenal dot connectors. They connect the dots faster and better than anyone else—fellow peddlers included. And they do it with such skill and grace that they transform it into an art.

The term dot connecting comes from the game, Connect the Dots, which we all played as kids. If you remember, you are given a piece of paper with a bunch of dots, and next to each one is a number. You draw a line from dot 1 to dot 2, dot 2 to dot 3, and so on. As you do, a picture begins to emerge. If you correctly guess what the picture is with the fewest connected dots, you win.

To be a great peddler—heck, even to be a good peddler—you must connect the dots. Beginning with my first call on a company, I start collecting information and seeing it as dots on a page. I immediately try connecting them in various ways. (The difference between the game and life is that in life the dots aren't numbered.) If a picture doesn't emerge, I proceed to gather more information, more dots. Usually, it isn't too long before I know whether or not there's a fit. If there is, I proceed to collect more dots, such as who I need to pitch and who I need to sell. Soon the image of the deal starts to emerge.

Listen up! Before you can connect some dots, you have to find some dots. The easiest way to do this is to ask questions. It is truly amazing how much you can learn by asking simple, open questions. Questions such as: So, tell me, what do you do? How long have you worked here? Then look the prospect or customer in the eye, put on your most sincere, engaging smile, and silently start to count. Smiling one, smiling two, smiling with bright eyes three, smiling with curiosity four . . . until they start talking. When you hear the words start to flow, move to nodding and active listening. If the person has an ounce of showmanship, they will be off and running. After all, most of us love to talk about who we are and what we do.

Another simple question is: So what do you think? I like to ask this right after I finish a presentation or demonstration. I also often ask, So, how am I doing? Do you think we are competitive? These questions never fail to get the prospect or customer talking, which gives you more dots.

Remember, selling isn't a chess match or a 12-step program. It's a ongoing dialogue. There are times when you have to discuss difficult matters, but great peddlers make every interaction an easy conversation!

PEDDLER'S PREROGATIVE #24

It is your prerogative to remind yourself and your management that selling isn't a chess match or a 12-step program. It's an ongoing dialogue, an easy straightforward conversation.

You are trying to solve a problem for your prospect or customer. You need to understand all the issues as well as how to sell to them. Ask simple, open questions and you'll be astounded at the answers you receive.

Peddler: "Mr. Jones, what is the best way to sell to you and your company?"

Prospect: "You don't have to sell me, you have to sell Bill!"

Peddler: "Thank you very much! Where can I find Bill?"

Back to dot connecting. So you talk to a prospect or customer, get a few dots, begin to see a fit. Talk to some other folks in the company, get some more dots. Find the person who can map how to sell into the company, lots more dots. A rough outline of how the deal gets done begins to surface. Any guesses yet? If so, it's time to round up support by showing it to everyone else involved.

This is crucial to winning the deal. Many times, I have seen peddlers get run over by their manager or some other corporate tyrant who also has connected the dots but sees a different deal image. After you earn your stripes this happens less, as folks are more willing to follow your lead or, if they see it differently, give you the benefit of the doubt. But before then, take time to convince everyone that what you see is true, or watch out!

Once you build a consensus around your image, the deal sprouts some legs and starts hobbling around. Then it starts to morph. It can morph and disappear. It can morph and turn into a three-headed monster. It can morph and turn into the deal of a lifetime. You never know. So watch it closely, see how it moves and where it turns. Keep connecting the dots. If all of a sudden a different picture begins to emerge, go back and build a consensus for the new image.

The thing is, you probably already are a dot connector—but only in your assigned universe. If you want to be a great peddler, you have to think outside the box. Think big. Create a vision!

Vision It!

Great peddlers are not afraid to dream. They open their minds, let the forces guide them, and, SHAZAM!, they have an image in their mind's eye of a smashing, off-the-charts, runaway success. Highly-tuned to people and situations, and lightning fast at connecting the dots, all it takes is a creative spark to ignite one hell of an idea.

Every peddler can (should!) vision bigger and better deals. Start by looking at your deals in terms of your region. Then, break out. Take them one by one and think, "How can I make this deal bigger? How can I expand it beyond my territory into other areas? Other countries!" Think planet big! At first, it may be hard to do. Keep trying. It gets easier with practice. Once you get the hang of it, you'll be surprised at how your mind naturally flies.

PEDDLER'S PREROGATIVE #25

It is the peddler's prerogative to think big and outside the box. To dream about taking a little local deal with a lot of goodness and turn it into a monster of global business. Think big! Really big! BIG, BIG, BIG!

Visioning is what separates the great peddler from the mediocre peddler. Always ask yourself, What's the next step for this deal? And the next one? And the one after that? Don't stop until it doesn't make sense anymore, which may be five or six iterations past where you began. Many peddlers stop where I start. To be a great peddler, however, you must roll your deal imagination up and down every mountain you can find. The first ninety-nine times may prove fruitless, but the hundredth time may bag you a keeper. Your very own mountain!

STORY TIME

I am consulting for a start-up that has some college professors playing with some very cool technology. My job is to bootstrap sales, as they have zero business.

I start by visiting potential customers who have evaluation units to hear what they think of our product. Amazingly, everyone echoes the same thing: We love it! But it costs too much. Several want it so badly that they've actually thought about how we might tweak the design or adjust the manufacturing to reduce the cost.

Back to home base I saunter with solid, first-hand customer research, and solutions to our problems to boot! "Not bad," I think to myself.

(continued)

At the next executive meeting, I tell the team what I've learned.

"A 100% of the feedback is that our product is great, but the price is too high. The good news is that several top engineers at some very large companies have examined our design and suggested changes that will reduce our costs."

I go on to explain our prospects' suggestions. Raised eyebrows all around. Obviously, they're missing the point. I decide to make it clear.

"In short, our price is three times too much. If we make these changes and reduce the cost, they'll buy our product."

"If we make those changes," pipes up one of our illustrious professors, "we'll be compromising our design."

"If we make those changes," I counter, "we'll have a saleable product!"

And with that, the floodgates open and a raging debate ensues over who knows better—them or prospective customers, and whether they are in business to deliver quality products or to do whatever the customer wants.

As they're arguing, I'm thinking, "You're not in business. You have to have business to be in business. And with your attitudes, you won't get any!" But I bite my tongue.

A few weeks later, out of the blue, a company calls and expresses an interest in putting our technology inside their vending machines. The idea was to enable the machines to send an alert to the home office when there was no more product in the machine. The company could then dispatch someone to refill the machine.

"A one off!" the intrepid entrepreneurs tell me.

"But you have NO business," I argue.

"It's not worth our time."

I decide not to push it right then, but I'm already connecting the dots. This company probably has at least a few hundred vending machines. We could charge them an up-front fee for installing our product in each machine, plus a monthly or annual fee for the messaging service. One deal, immediate cash, plus an ongoing revenue stream.

(continued)

I talk to more people. I discover that the prospect actually has at least a thousand vending machines, and they buy their machines from a company that sells tens of thousands all over the U.S. My mind is flying and a vision is starting to emerge: We get this prospect up and running. Then we bring the vendor and the application to the BIG vending machine company. If that works, then we take it to every vending machine company on the planet!

Now that's how you create a vision! It was too bad those folks were so focused on their design that they completely forgot what business is all about—creating products that prospects and customers want to buy! All they could see was one-time opportunities that required them to alter their design and manufacturing specs, and they weren't about to budge. There's another book to be written about that conundrum!

I had a feeling there were a lot more applications for their technology out there, but there was no sense sticking around to find out. No matter what opportunities I discovered, they wouldn't be able to see them. They had no vision. They couldn't connect the dots! Yikes! Do I sound bitter? OM MANI PADME HUM.

Got to, Got to, Got to Believe!

We all know folks with the odds stacked against them, who don't seem to have a blessed chance in the world, yet they have goals so big that you wonder if they're right in the head. Then they succeed—they fly to the moon, make their millions, win the World Series (case in point: Red Sox 2004)—and everyone is amazed. Is it a fluke? Nope. It's BELIEVING!

Key to your peddler strategy is believing—in you, your skills, your vision and ideas, your ability to affect the course of events, your sixth sense for peddling, and the magic you create.

STORY TIME

It's the mid-1990s and I am pacing around my living room trying to decide where I should land next, now that my services are no longer needed at a company I helped found. Having been in this situation enough times to find it vaguely familiar, I am not having the usual anxiety attacks that come with being unemployed. It's more like, "What the hell. Let's see what we (me and the fates) can conjure up!"

I let my mind start to race: embedded systems . . . streaming video . . . ahh . . . the Internet! Now there's a hot sector. Hmmm . . . what's the biggest Internet company? What's the coolest Internet company in the Boston area? I need to get up to speed on what's happening. There's got to be a top ten list on the Web. No, a top 100

(continued)

list! BLAM! A list of the top 100 companies in the Internet space, all neatly categorized, courtesy of a hot Internet rag. This is like shooting fish in a barrel. I dive into figuring out who's who in the Internet zoo and what's what, and come up with a core group of 25.

The more I read, however, the more I realize that what I don't know about the Internet or Internet applications is more than I know. I decide that my game plan should be to find a young company or division that can use a seasoned peddler who knows the sales and business side. I want to be a revenue-generating executive. I don't want to manage a big division or a gaggle of reps. I want to help reps close big deals, have some fun, make some cash. That's my vision! I can see it. I believe it is the right thing for me and the right thing for the right company. I can make this happen!

I zero in on a huge, super-successful company that's on everyone's radar screens. I mean these folks are happening! They are buying and selling companies left and right, and doing IPOs at a rate never seen before. Cool.

One of the companies they own catches my eye. I go through its Web site, map the executives, and figure out a pitch for the CEO: Do you need a black belt in sales who will bring in millions, and who you don't have to manage? Easy enough. I call him and reach his admin, who screens me thoroughly and tells me I have no chance of talking with the CEO.

"Since I don't have a chance," I tell her, "you have to make one for me."

She laughs. "Sure, I'll drop everything right now just for you, Mr. Dennis! Sorry, gotta fly."

"What's your name again?" I ask as she's about to hang up.

"Joanne. Take care, Mr. Dennis!"

I decide to learn more about this high-flying company. After several days of searching the Web and the company's site, I still have no idea what it does or how it adds value. All I have is a name and a number and a goal: to get to the CEO. Dial for some dollars.

"What didn't you get the first time?" Joanne asks me.

I laugh. "Joanne, you gotta help me out! I just need a few minutes of your CEO's time. I think he needs my help!"

(continued)

"Not this week," she says. "He's in California. Call me back next week." Click.

Yee haw! A dialogue is starting. Next week, I give her a call, and in the minute or so she gives me I ask some questions: What's it like at your company? How do you like it there? What's the CEO like?

She gives me some tidbits and says, "Got to go, Mr. Dennis. Talk next week."

On and on we go. Me popping in on her line, trying to establish a good relationship. She being friendly and funny, but still skeptical. Then, one day SHE calls ME!

"I have the CEO on the line. I'm connecting you now." Blam!

I decide to go for it: "I know you have no time, Mr. CEO, so here's my pitch. I don't want anyone's job. I want to come in and help develop and close business. I am sure you folks are wrestling with some big deals. I am a very experienced sales guy who can help you bring them in. I don't want to own or manage anything. Look at me as a revenue generating executive who can add to the bottom line and help you grow."

"Well, you got through Joanne. That's impressive. I've been thinking that I really do need an elephant hunter. We are seeing some huge opportunities go by and need a seasoned peddler to get these deals done. I have to run, but I will have Joanne set up a 15-minute chat for next Wednesday."

"Great! Thanks Mr. Big Time Internet CEO."

An hour later, Joanne calls. I ply a bit more information from her before she interrupts: "OK, Mr. Dennis, the CEO will call you Wednesday at 1:00."

During our next call, the CEO asks me about my previous jobs and I tell about my sales experience. Then I steer him back to his need for an elephant hunter. After a half-hour, he suggests a meeting to be set up by MY FRIEND, Joanne, who by this time is thoroughly amused with my shenanigans.

Again, Joanne promptly calls and in a couple days I'm face-to-face with Mr. Big. We have a nice chat and he asks more questions about my experience. He then tells me he needs a week to see if he can find a fit.

(continued)

A week goes by and we are sitting in a restaurant having lunch. After discussing the details of the position he's creating, he asks me if I am naturally this high energy and flamboyant, or am I now or have I ever been on some kind of prescription medicine.

I laugh. "I take nothing but Budweiser," I tell him. "However, I have noticed that the folks who deal with me often wind up taking meds!" That elicits a nervous laugh as if he half believes me!

As we leave the restaurant, he looks me in the eye, and I get the feeling that I have the job. He shakes hands and says he'll call me, which he does. He offers me a job as V.P. of Business Development for their fledgling software division. He also asks me to teach a few of his folks the fine art of selling.

The moral of this story is, you have to believe in you. That is step one. Never for a minute did I doubt my ability to learn their technology and find a way to bring in business. Never did I doubt my vision. I believed in me and landed a great opportunity. I had a great run and made a pretty penny. Talk about a wild ride, that would be the dotcom days!

Also key to your peddling strategy is believing in your company and your product. I'm not talking about blind faith or arrogant confidence. I'm talking about true, honest-to-goodness believing. Believing because you know what your company and your product can do for prospects and customers, and that it is genuinely useful to them.

I've had a lot of peddling gigs over the years, and I'm proud to say that I believed in 95% of the products and companies. And when I didn't, I hit the road. Now that I think about it, that's quite astonishing, considering that I always have been out there on technology's edge. But it was absolutely necessary. Working for start-ups or no-name companies (as far as the established corporate world was concerned anyways), pitching new concepts to Fortune 1000 companies, and competing against huge companies that have been around for years—well, if you're looking for validation, it's a rare find along this road. When you're peddling leading-edge products, you have to have a lot of faith in you, your product, and your company BEFORE you head out the door.

That's why the first thing I do when I join a company is get the organization and product inside my head (more on this later in the chapters on finding, selling, and closing). The marketing folks usually make themselves (and their "message") known pretty quickly, as they are always anxious to tell peddlers where to go, who to talk to, and what to say (just like preschoolers). But marketing in most companies is a hit or miss proposition, as so many of these experts don blinders, preferring to crunch numbers rather than talk to customers. As a result, they are clueless when it comes to the realities of their market.

So after listening politely to their spiel, I'm off, finding the folks who have a soft spot for the poor peddler; seeking the well-concealed, truly in-the-know corporate folks who can help my army of one; and figuring out how I should really sell the product. I do the latter mainly by asking questions of anyone and everyone. What do the engineers say? How about the customers? What does the support staff think?

All good peddlers are naturally curious; we want to know what everyone thinks about our product. It also ticks me off when the marketeers hold a perfectly good product hostage. My 360 degree polling methodology never fails to dig up the dirt, and give me a complete and true perspective. By the end, I'm either a true believer or the next one out the door.

PEDDLER'S PREROGATIVE #26

Marketing in most companies is a hit or miss proposition. It is your prerogative to listen politely to their spin and then figure out for yourself how to sell your product. There's no earthly reason for letting a bunch of marketeers hold a perfectly good product HOSTAGE!

There's no middle ground here. At the end of this process, you have to either believe or ditch, because believing is a powerful force. It's what puts you on the doorstep of the mystical realm, where planets align, things click, and great deals are done.

PEDDLER'S PREROGATIVE #27

It is your peddler's prerogative to believe or ditch. Believing in you, your product, and your company is square one if you want to experience the magic of being a great peddler.

Once you believe that you are representing great things, you don't worry about what prospects and customers might ask, how you'll answer, or what if they want this or that. You are peddling a terrific product for a terrific company. Things will work out. No need to give it another thought. Believing opens your head, frees your mind. It lets you devote your attention to your prospects and customers, and understanding their issues and solving their problems. It helps you find more fits.

Fits are wonderful things. Not only do they lead to deals, but the realization that you discovered one is a major rush. It's a great high having enough knowledge of your company and product, and a prospect's or customer's issues, that you can recommend your product with complete confidence, describe how it will work in their environment, and how it solves their problem. I live for that connection. And when I make it, I know the sale is mine. It's not IF I'll get the deal, but WHEN. Now that's believing!

PEDDLER'S PREROGATIVE #28

It's your peddler's prerogative to believe that it's not IF you'll get the deal, but WHEN.

Believing in you, your company, and your product—that's the ante into the game right after hard work, a good attitude, and dedication to the details. Now, see if you can take it to a whole other level. If you can believe so strongly that you make things happen. If you can tap into unknown, unseen energy forces and get back unique insights. This notion isn't for everyone. Sticking a butter knife in an electrical outlet isn't for the faint of heart! But if you are of a mind, believe! Channel the metaphysical forces. Generate profound energy around a vision plucked (or given as a gift) from the cosmos. Bring it to life!

When You're Hot, You're Hot

Just as there are bad cycles in sales, there are also good cycles. Times when you are in the zone, in your groove, doing all the things you should be, and suddenly things start going your way—BIG time. You are closing one deal after another. The sky has opened up and good fortune is raining down all over you.

There are also good cycles when, let's face it, you are just plain lucky. Like when you have no pipeline, yet deals roll in. You get a call from a company that has end-of-year money. If you can get them an estimate by noon, they'll get you a P.O. by 5. Or, a company calls that you pitched three years ago. They're ready to buy—today! It's against all odds, but it happens. And when it does, it is a beauteous thing.

The funny thing about a roll is that once it starts, it can keep going. So don't screw up! Stay on the lookout; tune yourself to watch for it. As soon as you see it, hop on and enjoy the magical ride!

Patience Is Suffering

To have unknown knowing, a talent for connecting the dots, vision, belief and, to top it off, moments when the fates smile down at you and set you on a roll—ya, there are a lot of great things about being a great peddler.

But it's not all a walk in the park. Great peddlers are also patient folks. Not by their nature, of course; patience is not in the DNA of any true peddler. And not because they work for patient folks. Sales and corporate managers are known for making unrealistic projections, then trying to figure out how to push our deals along, how to close them this quarter—maybe even this week—to meet their forecasts. Rather than focusing on building pipelines and putting more irons in the fire, managers are all over our prospects and customers trying nine ways from Sunday to get them to sign today.

No, great peddlers are patient because they know impatience is the first bane of all peddlers. It fouls up deals. It introduces unnecessary pressure into the sales dynamic, stressing them, their company, and their prospect or customer. It takes its toll on the good relationships they work hard to establish and the goodwill they build. It sucks the value right out of a deal. (How often have you seen someone give away the store to do a deal? Enough said.)

PEDDLER'S PREROGATIVE #29

When it's the end of the quarter and your peddler reality starts to twirl and whir, it is your prerogative to cease and desist, and be patient. It is better to be patient than to tick off a prospect or customer, or have the value sucked right out of your deal.

I'm not going to kid you. Patience isn't easy for any peddler. In fact, it's torture! But great peddlers learn to suffer through it—gladly suffer—because they know they will be rewarded. They will not only get this deal, but they will have a good customer for years to come. They also will become a better peddler. What doesn't kill us, makes us stronger, and brings us into peddlery's true light.

So, don't get ants in your pants. Don't let yourself be bullied into bothering your prospects or customers. Deals take time, need time. Wait. Be patient! Suffer gladly!

PEDDLER'S PREROGATIVE #30

It is your peddler's prerogative to learn to be patient and suffer gladly for your deals.

The Edge

Being a peddler is like walking a tightrope ten thousand feet in the air and without a net. Day after day, you're out in the world trying to maintain your balance, your composure, your sense of humor, and your integrity as you push your deals along a treacherous path. One misstep and it's a long way down. Tick off a customer, foul up a deal, and it's not only your month or quarter that goes down the tubes, but maybe your region's and your company's as well. Now that's being on the edge! You need another edge to keep from taking the plunge.

Every peddler has some innate ability that sets them apart. Finding it and honing it is imperative, because it's what gives you an edge, a leg up. There are peddlers who are technical. That gives them awesome credibility with prospects and customers, and helps them sell complex products. Other peddlers excel at solution selling. They have a knack for devising compelling solutions, such as for increasing productivity and streamlining processes. These folks crunch numbers for

fun and deliver incredible returns on investment. Still others have an uncanny ability to become part of the fabric of a company, developing close relationships that make them part of the in-house team.

If you are a typical, run-of-the mill sales rep plodding along with a standard product brief and canned marketing presentation, get out there and develop an edge—before the edge gets you!

This is not what your company wants to hear. The corporate sales world spends all its time trying to make everyone's skill sets the same. It wants you to use the same productivity software, the same sales strategy, the same sales materials—even give the same sales presentations. It wants a homogeneous sales force, where all its peddlers walk, talk, and sell the same. Puhleeze!

As any great peddler will tell you, you have an edge when your innate abilities are working with that mystical connection. You have a REALLY big edge when you begin to feel and trust in the magic!

Mystical Communion with the Sacred

There are plenty of rewarding jobs, but if you are a certain type of individual, you enjoy a great feeling of satisfaction from being an adroit peddler.

However, it won't compare to the joy you'll feel when you open your mind to the forces of the metaphysical world; when you open a channel to that world we can't see and can't touch but that helps define us; when you partake of the secrets; when you find solutions coming out of nowhere; when you find yourself making things happen naturally, effortlessly!

But in case you haven't been paying attention, you can't commune with the cosmos if you are not together. You have to be right with who you are and what you do. You have to be dedicated. You must be a caring, considerate, and sincere individual who treats people with respect and creates great and meaningful relationships. You must deliver on your promises and seek truth. Above all, you must do the right thing. Then, no longer will you be simply an adroit peddler. You will find you have magical powers. You will experience long stretches when all is right in your world, which makes for some pretty blissful moments.

The world of you and the world outside of you—your company and your customers—make up this incredible universe. Being truly aware within this dynamic universe is what it is all about. Lots of folks go through the motions and never see the possibilities. Become aware and you will lead a mystical and magical life!

I read somewhere that mysticism in different religions has many things in common: dance, chant, song, the sacred pipe, purifying sweats, fasts, dreams, visions, quests, and the occasional use of psychotropic drugs. Well, I'll be damned if that doesn't describe most of the sales offices I've worked in! (Just kidding!)

PART TWO

YOUR COMPANY

CHAPTER 7

YOUR COMPANY

We must, indeed, all hang together or, most assuredly, we shall all hang separately.

—Benjamin Franklin

When I start a dialogue with a company that may enlist my peddler services, one of my first questions is, "So, who's the founder and what was the genesis that got this joint jumpin'?" Then I train my hawk-like eyes on the interviewer's face for that all-telling reaction to my wired question. Ya, I'm bad.

But the fact is, to be successful, us peddlers need to meld with our companies from the get-go. This requires understanding a company's core origins, and you can't get more core than a company's founder—the dude or dudette with the creative spark that launched the company you see before you.

Founders are folks who see something atop that wondrous idea mountain, grab it, and come down with a strange glow. Then, they jack in, fasten their seatbelts, and go for one of life's wildest rides.

Sometimes these folks are eccentric, maniacal, geniuses, holy fools, sharks, or dolphins. Sometimes they're normal, like us. OK, perhaps not just like us. But the net-net is that they did it. They started a company. And years later they still have that funny look in their eye—one of magical inspiration. Bravo! Thank you for your symphonies.

You are probably wondering why I'm going on about the origins of the enterprise. It's simple. You have a distinct personality, and that personality works with some folks and it doesn't with others. Every company also has a personality (a.k.a. the corporate culture) usually stemming from its very beginnings and the founder. If your personality is not compatible with a company's, you'll be one unhappy camper. So save yourself the aggravation and get a clue *before* you sign on to sell its wares.

I'll let you in on a little secret that will help you: Companies are not really inscrutable entities, companies are people. OK, one more time. Companies are not really inscrutable entities, companies are people.

Here is my definition of a company:

> A group of people threaded together by a spark of creativity channeled through its founder or leader, and which reflects its collective consciousness through its business dealings.

Nope, I am not smoking weed this Saturday morning. In other words, there are hundreds of telltale signs coming straight at you from the moment you make contact with a company. Take heed!

One big tip off for me is how a place sounds. If I walk into a company and I feel as if I'm walking into a monastery, I get a cold chill down my spine. I've worked for companies whose philosophy is, "No laughing, no fun. If you show your teeth or tongue you will pay a forfeit." It really sucks. If a company lacks excitement and noise, I watch out.

STORY TIME

Once during an interview with a CEO, I mentioned that the office was so quiet it was like a library. It was freaky. The CEO nodded and said that the corporate culture was one of the things he was looking to change. He asked me to help, which I gladly did. Thirty months later, the place was hopin', the folks were excited, and I was on to my next gig. Apparently, it was a little too dynamic for him. Such is life. The gig was worth it just to see him curl up in the fetal position every time I went into his office.

Once on board with a company, you need to learn how things *really* work inside and who controls what. Remember, selling to the customer is the easy part. Selling within your company is the hard part. It's one of those freaky truths about peddlery. Believe it! So, getting the "who's who in the zoo" down pat is critical. Read on pilgrim . . .

Who's Who in the Zoo

Inside any company there's the inner circle, brain trust, wired ones, chosen few, whatever you want to call them. They are the team that really runs the place. You need to find out who they are—and fast.

You can start with the company's organizational chart, but remember that org charts can be like Alice in Wonderland adventures: never what they seem. Too often org charts are just generic guides to a company and don't accurately reflect the power structure within.

Rather, look at your company from a peddler's perspective. You'll see it has all the same people you deal with inside your customer accounts: the gatekeepers, evaluators, recommenders, and decisions makers. Create your own org chart and then use it to navigate through your company to get things done.

At a Fortune 500 company many moons ago, I figured out that I could get anything done, and I mean *anything*, through the CEO's administrator. I know this revelation isn't news to anyone. My point is simply that all good peddlers need to find out who can get things done, who can't, who won't, and who always says nope.

PEDDLER'S PREROGATIVE #31

It is the peddler's prerogative to map his or her company, and figure out who can get things done, who can't, who won't, and who always says nope.

Then you need to map and assemble your very own team of trusted folks who want you to sell, and are willing to help you deal with the intricacies of your company so you'll be successful. These are the Go-To folks. You'll find them at every rung on the corporate ladder.

The Go Tos

These truly good souls are the patron saints of the peddler. They are always rooting for you. And they care and are always there to lend a hand.

They are not made up of the peddler cloth, but they have empathy for the peddler's task and fully understand that the company needs sales to succeed. The Go Tos perform miracles and accomplish the impossible. And do so happily! These are the folks that every good peddler needs and takes care of.

STORY TIME

I have been with a company only a short time when I try to get a friend hired. He is the number one technical support person at my previous company and was instrumental in making me a ton of cash.

I set up the required meetings, which turn out to be a four-day interview marathon. At the end of every day, my friend gets a thumbs down. And every day I pick him up and say, "Brother, you are great. You just have to sell yourself. Don't be a dry engineer. Show them some pizzazz!" The next day he tries but fails again.

Finally he says, "Look, I can't sell myself. I'm not made that way."

(continued)

I know what a great contributor this guy is, so I go to see the CEO and put it on the line.

"Have I driven a lot of business to your company and made a big difference since I've joined?"

"Yes," said the CEO.

"If I tell you we need something and that I am 100% serious would you listen?"

"Sure," he said.

"OK," I said. "I know a great tech support guy and we need to hire him. He can make us a ton of cash, because he really knows his stuff and customers love him."

"So bring him in and get him interviewed," the CEO replies.

"I already did and no one sees his terrific qualities because he isn't Mr. Sales guy."

I tell him the team doesn't know what I know and doesn't know me well enough to take my word. I should have stopped right there, but I am on a roll.

"If we hire this guy, I guarantee I'll make my numbers."

A big smile comes across the CEO's face. "Will this guy help you beat your numbers?"

He has me. "OK boss, what's the deal?"

"I get him hired and you give me 25% more on your number for the quarter."

"Deal."

We shake hands and a few days later my buddy gets a call from HR offering him the job. This was much to everyone's chagrin and amazement.

Fast-forward four weeks to the end of the quarter. I have a big deal on the ropes that will save my numbers, the region's, and the company's. Enter my buddy who is brand new to the company and hardly knows the product. I send him out to the customer.

After a few days on site he tells me that the customer doesn't have what it needs to make the product work. He also tells me he thinks he can write a workaround if he can get a product engineer

(continued)

to help him understand how the APIs (application programming interface) work.

I get him an engineer and my friend pulls it off, saving my butt along with everyone else's that didn't want to hire him. We close a huge deal, sign a great customer, and all make our numbers for the quarter. From that day forward, the CEO and everyone else in the company loves him. That's a Go-To guy.

If you're lucky enough to find one, keep him!

As important as it is for a peddler to have a solid team of Go Tos, it's just as important (perhaps even more so) for him or her to avoid the control freaks of every strain and in every unhelpful incarnation.

The Just Say Nos

These are the folks that feel compelled to lecture you about corporate policy, tell you why you *can't* do what you're proposing, and remind you that, hey, this is how *we* do it here. Make an off-handed comment and 30 seconds later all the hall monitors are posted outside your door.

Every company has these self-appointed few. They have nothing better to do then look for ways to say, "Nope, can't do that." You must be on the look out for these folks and spot them before they spot you. Once you are made, the vigils start. Your only hope after that is to devise ways to send them after your enemies or create elaborate scenarios so they lose your scent. Faking your death works well.

The Avoids

Once these characters get a hold of you, there's no escaping. They are masters at consuming your time. The Avoids often show up under-cover. They might come over to upgrade your computer or fix the lights in your office, but before you know it, they're in the middle of a long story about their son, daughter, parents, job, or whatever. You don't want to be rude, but you can't help thinking, "Time's a wastin'! Why are they telling me this? How on Earth could they possibly think this interests me? If I cut them off, will they do as good a job?"

Then there are those who inspire less tolerance and deliberation as they rant and rave about some inane topic, or dig inside your knickers for some information that's none of their business, or weasel a favor out of you—such as selling raffle tickets for their son or daughter. You quickly concoct an excuse for moving on, then wait and wait and wait for them to pause, which they never do.

The solution is simply to avoid these folks from the start. It's tough enough being a peddler. Don't let them waste your time, sap your energy, and lose your focus.

PEDDLER'S PREROGATIVE #32

It is the peddler's prerogative to enthusiastically embrace anyone or anything that moves him or her closer to a sale, and to wholeheartedly ignore anyone or anything that doesn't.

The I'm in Control Heres

These are the head cases of the corporation, as I like to call them. The I'm in Control Heres are a gnarly bunch. They're also just plain delusional. They need to feel they have power over peddlers, children, animals, and the elderly. They weasel their way into nice jobs and turn them into full-scale freak shows. They're different than their cousins, the Just Say Nos and the Avoids, because you have to deal with them and can't easily go around them.

You're sure to find the I'm in Control Heres somewhere in a process chain. They are a string of managers and their administrators who have

collective authority over an in-house process and, therefore, over something you want or need.

They like to be in an environs where there is a before them, a them, and an after them. So you find these folks pretty much anywhere there is a process or procedure looming: resource allocation, expense reports, evaluation forms, loaner agreements, licenses—the list goes on ad infinitum.

The I'm in Control Heres are typically in some sort of sign-off capacity or, even worse, working for someone who has sign-off authority. A nightmare is sprinkled upon you head when you have two or more feeding off of one and other, such as an executive and his administrator.

If all this isn't bad enough, the I'm in Control Heres actually think that they matter, and that the importance of their job supercedes you, your manager, your V.P., your CEO, and God.

I do not begin to understand the dynamics among the I'm in Control Heres, nor do I particularly want to. But I would bet it has something to do with low self-esteem and a general fear of the unknown (which includes you).

The only way to deal with these folks is to get on their good side. Make them laugh, bring them cookies, commiserate with their plight, do whatever it takes. It is very hard to penetrate their barriers, but once they let you in, you are in. It takes time and it is not easy, but hey, what is?

The Measurers and Analytics

Many corporations operate on the premise that they can control reality. Inevitably, of course, this leads to chaos and confusion, as well
as questions such as "Why can't we control reality?"

You might think at this point companies would stop and reflect, and
realize what all good peddlers already know: It's impossible to control
reality. But no. Adding insult to cosmic injury, they try to solve the conundrum by hiring the Measurers and Analytics. They probably would
be better off calling a witch doctor.

As a sales professional, you've undoubtedly been tortured by this
crowd (read: marketers, product managers, business analysts, administrators, and bean counters, just to name a few). They are intimately connected to your daily sales reality (usually trying to measure and
analyze it) even though they don't carry a bag.

Some of these folks may have carried a bag at one time or another, but you'd never know it because they seem to have no recollection
of how hard it was to be peddler. Whatever possessed them to give up
peddlery and join the Measurers and Analytics is beyond me. But now
their job in life is one of terrorizing your sales domain. I have a special place in my heart for the Measurers and Analytics. I can see my
epitaph now:

Here lies Dennis Ford, a peddler who was measured to death.

The In the Ways

This may be getting hard to follow, so let's review and make sure we
know who's who in the zoo. So far, we have:

- The Go Tos—The blessed ones
- The Just Say Nos—Who just say no, no matter what!
- The Avoids—Who drain your life blood and distract you from
  your mission
- The I'm In Control Heres—Who are power tripping and, I'm
  sorry to say, you just have to find a way to cope with them
- The Measurers and Analytics—Who's job in life is to terrorize
  your sales domain

This brings me to the In the Ways. Here's a group that creates as much irony and desperation as comic relief, mainly because they are in the way of the peddler's deals and don't even know it.

The peddler's reality is simple: We sell stuff. This brings in money to produce more stuff. Because we keep the company afloat, *for the love of God,* could you help out just a little bit?

The In the Ways always take exception to such pleas, and want to debate you. A good debate makes them feisty, and when they get feisty they knock over applecarts.

"We work very hard. We're here 'til all hours!"

Can't argue with that. Unfortunately, all their work doesn't make it easy for peddlers to sell and customers to buy.

STORY TIME

I'm working at a startup. They have cool technology, it's ready to sell, but as with most new products it hasn't been proven outside of the lab and a few beta customers.

I'm thinking to myself, been here, done that. All I have to do to sell this puppy is give product evaluations to qualified prospects so they can see what the product really does. After I get a dozen or so evals out there, I can turn a few into sales for this quarter, and another half dozen or so into sales for future quarters. I always had a high percentage of deal closures doing evals before (more than 75%). The strategy works, because it makes sense for the customer, the company, and the product.

I gear up. I'm identifying and qualifying customers (well-qualified prospects are key to this strategy) when I start running into the In the Ways at every turn.

First there's the product manager: "My mandate is to show quick market acceptance. We don't have time to let people evaluate the product before buying!" Eh?

Then I meet with the head of system engineering: "If customers spend a lot of time evaluating the product, they could find problems or want changes. I need to move those engineers onto other projects. I can't spend time on products that are done!" Come again?

(continued)

Even my sales manager turns out to be one of them. "We need to get some skin in the game. Let's charge customers for product evaluations." Ya, right!

Welcome to The Corporate Mindset 101!

Too many people view the world from only their perspective. And here's the scary part: It happens even at the top. I know CEOs who were engineers and it's all about product speeds and feeds, or those who were accountants and it's all about measuring and analyzing. To the CEOs who were consultants it's all about strategy and positioning.

All these things are important, but without sales you're dead in the water. How simple can I make it? If your company has incredible products and no sales, you're sunk. If your company has made a science of measuring productivity and has no sales, you're sunk. If your company has the best three-, five-, and ten-year strategies and no sales, you're sunk.

If sales is the goal, then a company should make it easy for peddlers to sell and customers to buy. All processes that impede sales should be streamlined. All people that get in the way of sales should be removed. Sales must be number one on everyone's hit parade.

PEDDLER'S PREROGATIVE #33

It is the peddler's prerogative to demand that the company makes it easy for peddlers to sell and easy for customers to buy.

The Sales Prevention Team

Just when you think it couldn't get any worse, I'm pleased to introduce the Sales Prevention Team (SPT). The Sales Prevention Team is like a mythical, otherworldly monster that conjures itself up seemingly out of nowhere. It's an evil creature that has only one goal: to eat all good peddlers and their deals alive. GULP!

The fact that the Sales Prevention Team exists is one of the great mysteries of the corporate realm. It starts out as ad hoc groups (usually some perverse configuration of the previously mentioned groups), which band together "for the good of the company" and to "make sure things don't get out of hand."

They believe themselves to be the intelligent and privileged few who understand the whole company, who can see "The Big Picture." So, they make it their business to ensure that your little deal fits in.

In reality, they're just another band of control freaks who have the audacity to cloak their self-serving interests in a moral tone and purpose.

The members of the SPT typically know nothing about selling or closing deals. The major sin that they commit is thinking that they are so smart and such enlightened business minds that they know *all* there is to know about sales. Privately they think that sales isn't a real profession; it's not like their real corporate jobs. Sales to them is just where the pretty boys and girls hang out who get overcompensated for being able to bullshit well. They feel everybody knows it's the SPT that asks the tough questions and does all the hard, meaningful work. The peddlers are just peddlers.

Any deal you try to work through the system can create a conduit for the SPT to manifest. But a surefire way to coalesce this group is to make a request, such as please send customer product ASAP; please provide customer with one product and two licenses; please send cus-

tomer only four of five modules; or customer to buy now and receive free upgrade when it ships in a week. Heaven forbid you want to tweak the product to accommodate the customer.

But nothing gets them together faster than when they realize your little deal isn't so little. In fact, it just might be the biggest deal they've ever laid eyes on. If you're a seasoned peddler, you know what's coming next and prepare for battle. But for the young peddler, it can blow their mind.

Picture this: You've been on the job for 6 months. You've been diligently following up with a prospect, patiently meeting with everyone at his organization and explaining the benefits, and ferreting out more information than they need to make a decision. Slowly but surely you've been reeling in the prospect. And now, just as you're about to bring him up over the side for the big catch, unbeknownst to you, you're about to meet with the Sales Prevention Team.

Your thinking they're just department managers and what not. You walk in confident. You're expecting warm handshakes, the proverbial slap on the back, perhaps some offers to help in the last stretch, when the head honcho clears his throat and asks, "Why are we doing this deal?" So stunned is the rookie peddler that he doesn't even know where to begin and winds up being steamrolled by the SPT.

Why? Why? *Why?* Why would anyone in their right mind allow themselves to be part of sales prevention? Your question is valid and the answer is obvious: They are not in their right minds. Otherwise they would surely realize how demoralizing and frustrating this is—not to mention a waste of time—for even the most experienced peddlers.

Members of the Sales Prevention Team are easy to spot. First they are in a group that is somehow connected to sales and, therefore, kept apprised of the deals in the pipeline and in the field. Usually there are folks from groups such as engineering, marketing, support, legal, finance, manufacturing, and the like.

Second, they typically don't have a grasp of the deals, but take dribs and drabs of information, and create mountains of fear and anxiety over small bumps in the road. Engineers who wouldn't tolerate a peddler questioning their code think nothing of asking a peddler about his customer strategy. Corporate accountants who would be dumbfounded if a peddler asked why it takes so long to process commissions has no trouble asking why a peddler can't close a sale in 4 weeks rather than 12. Customer support managers who would freak out if a peddler suggested that resource scheduling was inefficient thinks nothing of asking a peddler if a prospect is a qualified lead. 'Tis simply amazing. 'Tis a crying shame.

The crime is that many a great peddler has to waste important time going over, under, around and through the SPT. After 25 years, I can't even pretend to be interested in any encounter I have with the misguided lot. The Sales Prevention team exists in every company, however, some companies control it better than others. These companies usually have a CEO who was a peddler.

Frustration Is the Enemy of the Peddler

As you can see, there are many groups that are sources of endless frustration for the peddler. To keep pitching your deals and ideas and know nothing's going to work because they can't or won't listen—well, it can drive even a sane peddler to thoughts of nuking them all. But, in reality, that just gets everyone upset and makes you look like a psycho even if they were the ones that drove you to pushing the button.

Trust me on this one: Frustration is the enemy of the peddler. So guard against it. Acquire extraordinary communication skills, and then try and break through and find some common ground. When that proves impossible, I just try to ignore them as politely as possible and go around them. I also spend as little time in their presence as possible. Any more interaction than is essential with this crowd can whack your reality.

PEDDLER'S PREROGATIVE #34

If folks frustrate you it is your prerogative to ignore them. If you can't ignore them, then it is your prerogative to hide your dismay and limit your exposure. If that doesn't work, it's your prerogative to get someone else to deal with them on your behalf. Forget about explaining or trying to make them see your point. That never works! It is your prerogative to stay away from the last resort, which is blowing up their universe. Stay away from this alternative at all cost. That is unless of course, you are really ready to take that long walk or are really in the mood.

Ladies and gentlemen please stand back . . .

CHAPTER 8

THE EXECUTIVES AND THEIR ADMINISTRATORS

Civilization is unbearable, but it is less unbearable at the top.

—Timothy Leary

Here's something I bet no one ever told you: If you want to make lots of money, you should get to know every corporate executive in your company. In fact, I'll bet your manager, his manager, and everyone else up the food chain tell you just the opposite. Don't listen to them. This was one of the most important (and most profitable) lessons I ever learned, albeit quite by chance.

STORY TIME

It's the early '80s, and I'm now an ex-social worker, having talked my way into an interview and then a job with the Testing Equipment Design Department of a high-tech, Fortune 500 company. My official title is Engineering Change Order Coordinator. It's an entry-level, administrative position, but as you may remember from the Introduction, after trying to transition from social work

(continued)

to sales and landing not a single interview, I decide a better strategy is to get in the door, then work my way up to peddling. So here I am, foot in door!

For the first several months, I focus on learning the ropes, getting the lay of the land, and doing the best job I can. My pay is twice what it was as a social worker, but with a house, a wife, and a daughter, I'm still far from easy street. So it's hard not to notice guys my age pulling up in front of corporate headquarters every day in their Mercedes, Porsches, and Jaguars.

"Who are those dudes?" I finally ask.

"Oh, them. They're the hotshot sales guys."

That gets me back to thinking about Part B of my plan: working my way into selling.

I begin asking around about becoming a peddler, only to find out that the company has no formal path into sales. They have product training for the sales folks, but there's no training for wannabe peddlers like me. Plus, the standard background for a sales position is a degree in engineering or computer science.

Figuring there must be some way, I keep probing and finally an in-the-know HR person tells me about the Executive Briefing Center or E.B.C. This is the place where bigwigs meet bigwigs, where the top sales guys bring top execs to meet our company's top execs. It's also where a guy or gal with no technical background but a hankering for sales can see if he or she stands a blessed chance at wiggling through the sales door.

Off I go to introduce myself to Tom, the manager of the E.B.C. He tells me that there is an opening for a meeting coordinator and explains the job: organizing and scheduling meetings for the sales folk, and their customers and prospects, with the execs; greeting the guests and giving them tours; and serving as all around gofer (as in go for coffee, go for another projector, go for Mr. Smith). In short, the meeting coordinator's job is to make sure all goes well and everyone is happy. I can do that.

"After a year," he continues, "a coordinator usually knows enough about the products and processes, and has enough con-

(continued)

nections, to get an entry-level sales position in the field. However, given that you have no technical background . . ."

"This is my ticket!" I think to myself, and launch into a litany of reasons why I'm the best candidate for this job. After a lot of convincing, Tom finally hires me. Two weeks later, I'm one step closer to being a peddler.

The deal is this: Before executives agree to meet with sales folks and their customers or prospects, they want to know who is coming, why, and the scope of the deal. Only potentially big deals get to this level—deals with Fortune 500 companies. Most of the execs in the company are glad to put on their sales hat as long as there's a good reason. They don't want to waste their time glad-handing though.

My most important task, therefore, is to meet with the sales folks, get the details of their deals, and find out the reason for the meeting and their plan to close some business. Then I write up an executive summary and create a meeting agenda, which I pass along to the administrators of the executives. In the process, I'm getting to know many of the top peddlers and their managers and becoming fast friends with all the admins (whom call to request more information, ask questions, and agree or decline to meet on behalf of the execs). I'm even on a first-name basis with a lot of the execs.

When my one-year anniversary rolls around, I start looking for an entry-level position in sales. This time it's a whole lot easier. I know a lot of peddlers and sales managers, and they know me. The fact that I don't have an engineering or computer science degree no longer matters. Within a month I'm on a sales team.

Fast-forward another four months and I have what I think is a good prospect, but there's a question about our technical direction. I decide to call one of my old admin buddies who works for a product executive.

"Julie! How ya doin'? It's Dennis. I'm good. The new gig is great! Hey, listen, can I talk to Jim? Yeah, I know he's busy, but it'll only take a second. I just want to ask him one question." She puts me through.

(continued)

"Dennis, where are you?"

"Hey, Jim, I'm at a prospect's and they're interested in doing some business, but they need to know our technical direction and when we'll be shipping the next generation of our CPU."

"Yeah, sure. We're just about to announce it, so put the customer on and I'll let him in on some of the details."

"Excellent! Thanks, Jim! Hold on and I'll connect you. Mr. Customer, I have the product V.P. on the other line. He'll fill you in."

That was the first of many calls I made to an executive, and I closed that deal and many others because of it. Ya, sometimes it's like using a bazooka to kill a mosquito, but it always gets the job done and never fails to impress the hell out of the prospect!

PEDDLER'S PREROGATIVE #35

It is your prerogative to truly understand the paradox of using a bazooka to kill a mosquito. It's not the best use of a resource, but it sure as hell gets the job done. It is also your prerogative to share your high-impact weapons with your fellow peddlers.

Listen up! Corporate folks have the power to make things happen. Executives that own the product, pricing, marketing, business model, or some other critical business unit, can make exceptions, provide information, extend offers—in short, grease the selling wheels like no one else. That's why good peddlers cultivate relationships with them. They know that one call and, Wham!, it's done.

Of course, it would wreak havoc to have hundreds of field reps calling a handful of executives with special requests, which is one rea-

THE EXECUTIVES AND THEIR ADMINISTRATORS

son why companies have policies and procedures to keep salespeople away from corporate executives.

Smart companies, however, know that peddlers can sell only about 60–70% of their customers and prospects using their product briefs with the standard marketing pitch, FAQ, competitive analysis, pricing, and field resources. To sign the rest, peddlers have to go beyond the standard offering, which requires enlisting the help of corporate.

That's why good companies create a system for requesting exceptions to the standard policies and practices. It usually involves filling out a form and passing it up the chain of command for approval. Generally, these forms are processed pretty quickly. But as with any corporate process, there are times when the forms accumulate faster than an executive can process them and the system slows to a crawl. When this happens, you're supposed to wait until your branch manager calls the regional manager, who calls the area manager, who calls the National Sales Director, who (finally!) calls the corporate V.P. of Sales and gets the Veep's admin to help out! But again, if you know folks in corporate, you can shortcut the system when time is precious.

> "Hey, Megan, it's Dennis. What's happenin'? Did Bill get a chance to look at my request form? Tomorrow? Does he have a lot of them to go through? Hmmm . . . Can you do me a favor? I'm in a major time crunch with a prospect and need a decision ASAP. Do you think you could put mine on top? Thanks, Megan! YOU'RE THE BEST!"

What can I say? I'm always looking for that edge, as all good peddlers do.

A lot of people thought I was crazy to take the job as meeting coordinator. What could be gained from being a glorified gofer? But as it turned out, the answer was plenty. Getting to know all those execs—that alone was worth it. They not only helped me close deals for years to come but saved my butt on a number of occasions. In addition, I learned how to net out deals, organize the details, and present them to executives. I learned the products, presentations, and the sales process. I learned that it often took a team effort to get a deal done, and the team was interested in forging relationships and partnerships, not just selling product. All good things all new peddlers should know.

Of course, there were the requisite eyepoppers as well, such as the realization that executives fall into one of three categories: the good, the bad, and the ugly, and that the best peddlers are always buddies with the best executives. Coincidence? NOT! Good peddlers make it their business to know all the execs and which group they are in. Then they stick with the good ones.

PEDDLER'S PREROGATIVE #36

It is your prerogative to classify your executive group into the good, the bad, and the ugly, and to facilitate a good and meaningful relationship with the good executives. The relationships you create will spawn an awesome selling team when you need it.

The Good Executives

I can't say enough about the good executives. Let's face it, these folks make the business world go 'round. I have three tests that tell me if I've encountered a good executive. My first one is (drum roll, please), how do they treat others? Do they care about them? Are they HUMAN?

This is not hard to surmise. When you're talking with them, do they criticize, belittle or make fun of employees, colleagues, or the peddler who preceded you? If you walk around the office with them, do they exchange pleasantries with folks or ignore them? If they are interrupted, are they respectful or brusque? Do they exhibit an understanding and knowledge of other people's needs and problems, or is it all about them?

I could go on and on, but I think you get my point. Good executives, it turns out, are good people! They care about their employees, colleagues, customers, suppliers—everyone they have contact with. They also have a healthy perspective on who they are and what they do. They care as much about their family and friends as they do about their jobs.

The second test is, do they have a value system that they live by in life and in business, and do they readily talk about it? The good executives do, and when they see things heading in the wrong direction they don't hesitate to say, "That's not how I do business," or "That's not how we want to act." When they see folks dealing with problems by analyzing all the options and outcomes, gauging reactions, and trying to decide what tact to take, they tell them, "It's simple. We should do the right thing."

Good execs know that actions speak louder than words and they lead by example. Their value system isn't something they drag out for special occasions and corporate ceremonies. It's something they live, day in and day out, and share readily with others. When good executives are in charge, you know it, because their values permeate entire divisions and companies.

My third test is, are they competent? Good execs know their jobs, are technically proficient, are good managers, and take pride in doing all three well. Usually these folks have climbed the corporate ladder the good old-fashioned way—they've earned it. They've worked hard, advanced their knowledge and skills, met their goals, and were rewarded with promotions and new challenges. They are fair and firm; maintain an ongoing dialogue with their colleagues, employees, and customers; communicate in a straightforward manner; encourage exploration within boundaries; are open and honest; ask the tough questions; and go the distance to get the hard answers.

The business world would be a great place if it was full of good executives. But since we know that's not the case, onward!

The Bad Executives

"How did this jolly joker get to where he is?" That's what we all want to know when we meet a bad executive. Here's a hint: the Peter Principle. It states that within a hierarchically-structured administration, people tend to be promoted up to their level of incompetence. So when a person demonstrates his or her competency at one job, they are promoted to another one. If they continue to show their competency, they continue to be promoted to still higher positions. This cycle continues until they are in a position where they are no longer competent, which can be at the HIGHEST CORPORATE LEVELS. That's one way they get to where they are.

Another way is the corporate whammy. A company or division is bought, sold, spun off, or merged, an executive leaves, revenue drops precipitously, or some other momentous change occurs, and Blam!, someone who knows nothing about a division or company is suddenly in charge.

There are a myriad of other ways this particular variety of corporate executives get their front row seats. (Let's not forget nepotism, that wellspring of incompetence, or that these folks are experts at wheeling and dealing.) But the bottom line is they're there and they're inept. Such is life.

Some executives realize their predicament, become paralyzed, and decide on a strategy of avoidance. They lay low, hoping no one will find them and dodging any interaction that could reveal their inadequacies. If they have to attend meetings, they look attentive, nod and grunt, but say nothing. (If you listen closely, you can sometimes hear the wind whistling through their heads.) If someone does confront them, they defer anything and everything that involves a commitment or a decision. "I'll get back to you" and "Let me think about it" are their favorite responses. They hole up in their offices Googling for what they don't know. Oy!

Then there are those executives who are incompetent but have such huge egos that they actually believe that because they have the job, they must know what they're doing or they can bluff it (think dot-com executives). They are quick to take action and make decisions, wreaking all sorts of havoc in the process because they haven't the foggiest notion how things work, who's involved, or the repercussions of their decisions. Bad executives are the reason for low morale and a host of other problems, but my main issue with them is that they screw up good deals and go after bad ones.

As a peddler, you have to map all the executives and know who's who in the zoo. Be ever vigilant. Don't bring a bad executive to a meeting with a perfectly good customer or prospect. No good will come of it!

The Ugly Executives

So far we have some good executives and some bad ones. Then there are those who are crazy, off-the-wall S.O.B.'s. When I first bumped into these execs during my early days at the E.B.C., I thought, "These

guys seem vaguely familiar. Where have I seen these kind of folks be-fore?" Then it hit me: in prison!

I kid you not. So striking were the similarities that I had flashbacks to being a social worker in the maximum security cottage. These execs had sociopathic personalities just like some of the incarcerated folks I knew. I was astonished when I connected those dots! It looked like my experience would be good training for dealing with some of the elite, white-collar business executive after all. Who knew?

Think I exaggerate? Think about some of the characteristics that are often associated with a sociopath. They are smooth talkers and capti-vating storytellers who exude self-confidence. They seem to be charm-ing, but they are secretly antagonistic and overbearing. They crave at-tention and have an overblown sense of entitlement. They have a misguided belief about their own powers and abilities. They never feel shame, remorse, or guilt for their actions. They are outraged by matters most of us would consider insignificant yet unmoved by matters we would find upsetting. They have no ability to empathize with others and have no concern about the impact their behavior might have on others.

Does this sound like someone you know? Some companies actually have a few and they are the folks I think of as the ugly executives. Their follies create layoffs, shutdown plants, rip apart divisions, and plunder companies without shame or guilt. They recklessly manipulate budgets and salaries, yet are first in line with their hand out for the highest bonus. They think nothing of playing with financial results for personal gain. They believe they are the smart ones and everyone else is just a lowly worker. They take everything personally and turn everyday business situations into Machiavellian battles. They don't trust a soul, and will never reveal their true agenda. They know nothing of loyalty. They are incapable of comprehending how their words, actions, and attitudes wreak havoc inside their companies.

The sad part is that these folks usually are brilliant with incredible talents and gifts. They could easily succeed by doing what's right and caring about others. But since they don't, you must recognize them for what they are: a danger to business. They make decisions for the wrong reasons and put their companies or divisions into unsavory situations. Steer clear of them at all costs!

PEDDLER'S PREROGATIVE #37

It is your prerogative to remember that in the world of the corporate executive, there are good execs who can keep companies alive and well, bad execs who can put companies on respirators, and ugly execs who can kill them!

The Administrators

The executives are the main show in corporate, but have no doubt about it, the admins run the joint. They are the reason the plane stays aloft and the train stays on the tracks. They are typically super smart and highly competent. If you explain your situation and what you're trying to accomplish, they usually get it and figure out a solution quicker than, dare I say it?, the executives they work for.

Admins are adept at all things corporate and have mastered the fine art of juggling. They are part manager, expediter, social worker, mother, marketer, and peacekeeper. They are also judge, jury, and executioner of the peddler's reality. You had better be wired into the world of the administrator or you'll perish on the periphery.

I love administrators and they usually take pity on me after seeing how my reality is barely held together with bubble gum and safety pins. That I can be amusing to observe on a semiregular basis helps them to like me. If they like you, they will take you in (like a wet, stray dog) and take care of you. If they don't like you, well, you're dead. I wish I had a nickel for every time a compassionate administrator has saved this Boston-Irish arse from the frying pan.

Woe to the peddler, however, who doesn't understand the admin hierarchy and the awesome power that goes along with it, and makes the mistake of looking at an admin as a worker bee, someone they can order about. Many a bulldog peddler has walked around like a chihuahua after getting his clock cleaned by an executive admin.

Executives often are aloof, autonomous, and up to their eyeballs in alligators. When they're not on the road, they are moving targets, whirring about corporate. The administrators, on the other hand, are always at home base, holding down the fort with all the other executive admins. This group forms a formidable network that communicates fast and has incredible de facto power. When executives are out or not available, it's their administrators who field requests for the executives. They can parse these requests any way they wish, thus putting you on the list or taking you off.

Think about it. Let's say an admin's boss is an Executive V.P. with ten direct reports who have bunches of folks working for them. With one call, the admin of the Executive V.P. can get the immediate attention of those direct reports and anyone under them. One two-second

phone call from the top executive's admin and thousands of people jump off their seats.

Are you following me here, my fine peddler? Are you connecting the cosmic dots? Are you getting an inkling of whom you should pay VERY close attention to?

Play the game correctly, and the admins will teach you the way of the corporate world. Too many peddlers don't have the maturity to navigate the complex waters of these corporate power brokers and wind up taking the longest of walks off the shortest of piers. Take heed: Respect and honor the admins in your life.

PEDDLER'S PREROGATIVE #38

It is your prerogative to realize that you must verily, and I DO MEAN VERILY, respect and honor the administrators in your life. If you do, you have a shot at success. If you don't, you will take the longest of walks off the shortest of piers.

OK, time for another story.

STORY TIME

I'm peddling system software, working for a guy who pushes the limits when it comes to making a sale. It's always amusing to see just how far he goes—unless you are the poor peddler doing his bidding, which in this case is me.

I'm nearing the end of a deal and decide it's time to fly to the west coast and close it down. No sooner than I arrive and the deal begins to unravel. I immediately call my boss to tell him.

"Hey, I'm in a pickle here. The deal's going south, and the executive that must approve it is splitting for vacation in two days and doesn't have time to see me."

"I want that freakin' order," he yells. "I don't care if you have to sit in the damn lobby until hell freezes over. Find a way to see the executive and get the order. Don't come home without it!" CLICK.

(continued)

So I sit in the company lobby; I have no idea what else to do. Unbeknownst to me, however, as I sit twiddling my thumbs, the admin network inside the company starts to whirl and twirl and, one by one, the admins start coming out.

"Can I help you?" each one asks.

"No, not really," I say. "I just have to wait here until I can get a few minutes with Mr. Big. I'm not sure if he has time to see me, but I have to wait anyway."

On and on I sit. I sit until the last person leaves around 9 P.M. Then I shut off the lights and go back to my hotel. First thing in the morning, I'm there in the lobby watching everybody coming in to start their day. A few from the day before notice me, smile, and say hello. At noon, I'm still in the lobby when the admins are on their way to lunch.

"Mr. Big isn't going to have any time to see you," they tell me. "You should go home."

"Yes, I understand," I answer, "but my boss said not to come home until I get this deal done with Mr. Big."

They leave and I continue to sit. An hour later, the admins come back from lunch.

"Aren't you getting lunch?" the admin for Mr. Big asks.

"I'd like to, but I don't want to miss him if he comes out."

They go back to their desks wondering if they have a lunatic in the lobby or a just frightened sales guy with a very mean boss.

On and on the hours go and pretty soon I am the talk of the place. People are bringing me food and candy. Transplants from the east coast are stopping to talk about the Pats, the Celts, and the Sox. By the end of the second day I am an office fixture. Again, I wait until the last one comes out, shut off the lights and go back to my hotel.

The next day is Friday, and I'm back bright and early, sitting in the lobby, and it's like Old Home Week. Everyone asks me how I'm doing, if I've called my wife, and if she's upset.

"Well, we're both bummed," I say, "because my kids have a soccer game this weekend and I don't know if I'm going to make it."

(continued)

Unbelievably, my star seems to be rising and I find myself becoming a cause célèbre.

Around 3:00 in the afternoon, Mr. Big's admin comes running out, grabs me by the hand and says, "Dennis, I got you fifteen minutes. Hurry!" I grab my stuff and follow her. As we approach Mr. Big's office, I ask her if she can give my boss a call and then conference us in. She nods and I give her the number.

Introductions and pleasantries are barely exchanged when the admin announces she has my boss on the line. Mr. Big picks up the phone.

"Why are you being such a mean S.O.B. to this great kid?" he asks my boss.

"Because we have such a great deal for you and I don't want you to miss the opportunity. It's really *that* good!"

"It better be," says Mr. Big. "What do you have?"

Two hours later, I am running to the airport. Everyone's in agreement on the deal and I'm promised a P.O. in five days.

First thing Monday morning, the P.O. starts flying through their corporate headquarters like a hot knife through butter. It flies through the P.O. generation process, flies through the sign-off process, and flies off my fax in two days instead of five. I march into my boss with the P.O.

"Here ya go."

He looks at the P.O. and then at me, smiles, and says, "So, where are we going next week?"

"That is never happening to me again," I say, and he knows I mean it.

Fast-forward eight years, I'm CEO of a start-up company, and we need to get a particular P.O. to make payroll. You'll never guess what I do. Yup. I go and sit in the company's lobby. "I can't go back to Boston without the P.O.," I tell them. "I promised everyone in my company I would stay here until I got it. So I'm here for the duration."

That one took me two days.

The point here is if the admins didn't take pity on me I would have rotted in that lobby. If they didn't decide I was all right, they would have had me tossed out. If they didn't decide they wanted to help me, I never would have gotten the deal done or the P.O. through in record time (a clear demonstration of admin power if there ever was one). They thought I was amusing and they enjoyed the entertainment. I've learned a lot about how to get things done in corporate over the years—and most of it from my admin friends. When you really think about it we all work for them in the long run anyway!

Orchestrating the Executive Choir

You're approaching the end of a quarter and you got a deal on the ropes. Who ya gonna call? You've cultivated inside relationships with some good executives and their administrators, so you have a few well-placed connections you can tap when you're in a pinch. But just as important is knowing who to call when.

Here's a tip: When you're down to the wire on a deal, you want to enlist the help of the good execs whose products you sell.

The upside for folks at the executive level usually is a bonus, which is contingent on them meeting the goals outlined in their Management by Objectives (MBO) plan. Many companies want to encourage a team effort, so they tie individuals' MBO plans to the overall goals of their division or company. So one or more goals of a product, marketing, or customer service executive could be to help their company make its sales goals, get products into new markets, expand the customer base, or improve customer satisfaction.

If you are an adroit peddler, you know where I'm heading. Couple your need to make your numbers with executives' needs to meet their objectives (to get their bonus!), and you can bring some pretty powerful players into your deals that will help

you close business. When those kind of stars align, the joint can really start to rock.

Lots of companies motivate their middle managers using an MBO plan as well. It's worth finding out, because you don't want to be knocking on the doors of the big guys any more than you have to. If a middle manager can achieve his or her goals by helping you achieve yours, he or she will gladly take your case to the higher-ups. Funny how that works.

No matter what type of fix you're in, however, take the time to figure out who you should enlist to help your army of one and what you need them to do. Then create a plan for bringing them together. Orchestrating the executive choir is a something you must do carefully and skillfully.

And in the End . . .

Now you have some insight into how to parse, engage, and navigate the executive web. Don't get stuck in it. Don't get eaten alive by it. Be observant, be astute, and choose your friends wisely. If you want to be good, you have to be good in corporate. Look at the best peddlers and you'll see that they've figured out how to use the executive resources for the good of their prospects and customers. You need to figure out how to do that, too!

CHAPTER 9

SALES AND SALES MANAGEMENT

He who fights with monsters might take care lest he thereby become a monster.

—Friedrich Nietzsche

Everyone who is really serious about being in business should get some hard-core sales experience. Whether their aspirations are in accounting, marketing, product management, whatever, the fact is, everyone needs to know how to sell.

Unfortunately, few corporate folks know this, mainly because few colleges and universities offer courses on sales despite charging big bucks for their business programs. (There's plenty on marketing, though—AS IF THEY WERE THE SAME THING.) It floors me that the philosophy, principles, and ethics of selling are frequently not even on their radar screens when they should be part of the core curriculum! You can major in business as an undergrad, get an MBA—even a doctorate—without having to attend a lecture or be part of a discussion on sales.

What a crock! Shame on you academics! How can you overlook selling, one of the basics of business? If you break it down, ya build something, ya sell it, and then ya account for it. Of this three-legged stool, why do only two count?

I'll hazard a guess. Could it be because you consider sales a job and not a PROFESSION? Or is it that you believe that selling is easy and any schmuck can do it? Or maybe you think selling is what folks do when they can't find anything else? It's the job of last resort, home to the disenfranchised of the planet. Am I warm?

For enlightened folks who pride yourselves on instilling the latest management theories, the hottest marketing techniques, and the best financial practices all using the latest technology and teaching methods, you sure are ignorant when it comes to sales. Could that be because you've never tried selling?

Ya, how did I guess? Because I've worked with some of the brains you've churned out who have this same perception and attitude. And because if you did, you would know that it's a grave oversight not requiring business students to take a course in sales. You would know that there are a thousand things to learn about selling, and without them a business foundation is not complete. You would know it is a real profession.

Here's an idea. If your school offers few if any sales courses, why don't you make *The Peddler's Prerogative* required reading? Hey, at least it's a start! Then recommend that your students spend some time in the field. Theory is nice, but applying it—now that's where the rubber meets the road. Have them dial for dollars for a charity. They would experience first hand what it's like to cold call a target and make a pitch. And let's make it realistic by adding a little pressure— like 40% of their grade depends on closing 1% of the folks they contact.

That goes for you, too, my fellow peddlers. Maybe you've read a few books, taken a couple of seminars, studied your products, and nailed down your tactical approach. Good for you! Now you have to practice, practice, practice. If you can keep smilin' as you're dialing for dollars and banging on doors, you'll figure out whether you are a hunter or a farmer. Hunters and farmers are both admirable tribes in the sales world. Don't let anyone tell you differently. But you have to determine which tribe suits you—which you belong to. It is very important to know where you fit (there's that word again).

Hunters

Hunters are your smart, aggressive, risk-taking mavericks. They are fiercely independent and like living on the edge. Many are also scrappy folks who come from blue-collar and middle-class backgrounds. They work hard and play hard; they're instinctively competitive. Chances are they were making a good buck by the time they were 12, and always angling to get a "friendly" game of ball going before that. Not being born into status or privilege, these peddlers typically have something to prove and, therefore, enjoy doing the seemingly impossible, which is finding and closing new business consistently.

Hunters love sauntering about carrying the big closer reputation (we defrock that myth in Chapter 15, "Closing"). In fact, there's nothing they like better than being called in the clutch—the last week of the quarter when the company numbers are on the line. That's when they can put on the get-me-the-ball bravado, and everyone in the company is cheering them on, hoping that they'll perform their magic, bring in a deal, and make the quarterly goal.

Some companies, such as Oracle and EMC, have cultivated successful sales machines comprised of hunters. Most companies, however, haven't figured out how to use their talents. One week out of twelve, sales managers and corporate executives love these guys and gals. But after the quarter closes and the crisis is passed, they are relegated back to pain-in-the-arse status because they are difficult to manage. They don't check in and say where they'll be when. They won't give the time of day to the measurers and analytics who want to quantify what they do six ways from Sunday. They run over folks who are "just trying to do their jobs" but are standing in their way. There's no doubt about it, hunters can be threatening to mere mortals, which creates problems for management.

But they are the lifeblood of companies for the simple reason that they equate money to success, and they have the ambition, vision, creativity, and leadership skills to make it happen. Make no mistake about it, these peddlers are in it for the cash; they go where the money is. Treat these guys right and they will take a bullet for you (not to mention make you a hell of a lot of money). Treat them wrong and they will vote with their feet.

Most companies never figure out how to fit hunters into their organization. As a result, hunters tend to jump from company to company, always looking for a place that appreciates their nature and lets them use their sales talents to earn themselves a six-figure income. If they get lucky and find such a company, they thrive; if not, they mosey on down the road until they find a decent refuge.

Hunters often wind up selling big-ticket products (the bigger the item, the bigger the commission), or following their entrepreneurial bent by joining a start-up or striking out on their own. What others find intimidating (no immediate source of income) doesn't bother hunters. They know that no matter what, they can take care of themselves. To be a revenue generating machine, all they need is a phone, a desk, and a 'puter.

PEDDLER'S PREROGATIVE #39

If you are a hunter, it is your prerogative to make a mint and be the best individual contributor you can be. If a company can't handle that, it is your prerogative to mosey on down the road, find a better position, or start your own business and buy them!

Farmers

Just as much the lifeblood of companies are the farmers. Farmers tend to be more . . . um . . . hmmm . . . well, OK, more balanced. These peddlers don't have the damn-the-torpedoes attitude of the hunters, but they do have a strong desire to succeed, and they like to show the world that they are good and talented.

Just like hunters, farmers are smart. But unlike their counterparts, they are well-organized, possess an immense capacity for detail, and are wonderful at follow-up. They are really nice folks who can develop and maintain a great rapport with customers. They are great company ambassadors.

Farmers are entrusted with managing large, high-profile, important accounts. The really good farmers make really good money and often get promoted to management, where they can showcase their sociable demeanor and their account management skills. Lots of Fortune 500 companies, such as IBM and HP, have a farmer sales force and it works great. Farmers are underappreciated and don't get the respect they deserve.

By and large, farmers are more centered, more stable, than hunters. Of course, stable is a relative term here. We are, after all, talking about peddlers who are by nature an independent, high-strung, willful bunch. In comparison to hunters, however, farmers are your steady Eddies. They ride out the storms and hold the chaos at bay (rather than create it). They deliver quarter after quarter without much fanfare.

Farmers are a better fit for the corporate structure and understand how to leverage it on their behalf. The key to being a successful farmer

is managing the customer relationship and gradually growing the account; it's not being a hard-core closer. Now, that's not to say farmers can't close. Every peddler must close or you won't be long for the sales world. Rather, farmers close differently. They are facilitators, consensus builders. They are strategic yet adroit. When it comes to getting more and more business from customers, they are the masters, growing accounts beyond expectations. It's beautiful to watch farmers in action. Brings a tear to me eye.

The experienced farmers get the most-prized customers to manage and have high visibility within the executive ranks for their customers. Some folks see farmers as the glad-handers or schmoozers and couldn't be more wrong, although I will grant you it doesn't hurt a farmer to have a low handicap.

PEDDLER'S PREROGATIVE #40

If you are a farmer, it is your prerogative to go as far as you wish up the corporate ladder. If you like, you can work your way right up to chairman and CEO.

You Gotta Be You

Some peddlers are genetically programmed to hunt, others are meant to farm. Really good peddlers understand both but know that most peddlers lean one way or the other.

Figuring out which one you are usually comes with experience—somewhere between one and three years as a sales rep. That may seem like a long stretch, but to figure out who you are and get good at what you do really takes a lot of practice, and that takes time. Deal with it or risk being outed. I like nothing better than interviewing junior sales puppies who finagled their way to the head of the line, got promoted, and think they are big-dog peddlers. I usually begin with, "So, tell me, what's the biggest deal you've ever done?" Here's a hint: $150,000 is NOT a big deal.

Get some solid experience under your belt, find out if you are a hunter or a farmer, and then scout out your next career move. Your choices are roughly as follows:

Experience	Hunter	Farmer
3–5 years	New Business Account Executive	Account Manager
5–10 years	Senior Account Executive	Sales Management
10–25 years	V.P. Business Development, or President or CEO of a small- to medium-sized company	V.P. Sales and/or Marketing, or President or CEO of a medium to large company
25+ years	Write a book, seek professional help, or buy a bar in Thailand, Vietnam, or Costa Rica!	Sell your stock and retire, then golf, golf, and golf some more

OK, I threw in that last one just to see if you were paying attention.

Listen up! Be honest with yourself. Whether you're a hunter or a farmer, it's OK. Don't take a job that goes against your nature. If you're a hunter and take a job as an account manager, you will be bored silly and screw up royally. If you are a farmer and take a job as a high-commissioned, new-business-only peddler, you will get fired.

Both hunters and farmers are overly optimistic (after all, they are peddlers). They think they can do anything, that everything will work out. What the hay! They wake up every morning, put on their happy ears and their dancing feet, and shuffle off in search of today's rainbow and pot of gold. But going against nature causes anxiety and stress, and let's be honest, peddlers don't need to add anymore of that to our reality.

Of course, it's possible that you are a hybrid, in which case you can go wherever the pay is best at the moment. It is very rare, however, to have the instincts of a hunter and the patience of a farmer, so don't pretend you're something you're not. Leave that up to your sales manager! (Just kidding!)

Committed Soldier or Hired Gun?

Being peddlers, hunters, farmers, and hybrids have many things in common, one of which is being committed to their customers and their companies.

After many years on the job, however, some peddlers (particularly hunters) can get a mercenary bent. Knowing they can sell anything to anyone, they decide to be in it just for the money. They cherry pick markets, companies, and products, exploit opportunities, and make some fast money. When mercenaries jump into the middle of a hot market, they bring a level of professionalism and business acumen to the team. However, when it starts to slow down or look played out, these folks take off like a turkey through the corn.

It's too bad. These folks are good, professional peddlers. Ya have to wonder how they would do if they could commit themselves 100% to a gig. Probably unbelievably well, not to mention their customers and companies!

Sales Management (Everybody's Got One)

There are two kinds of peddlers: those who can sell and those who can't, and they manage!

What's the difference between a lawyer and a sales manager? The lawyer pretends he cares!

A motivational moment with a sales manager can sound like the narrator's advice to Alice in Lewis Carroll's *Through the Looking Glass*: "Now here, you see, it takes all the running you can do to keep in the same place. If you want to get somewhere else, you must run at least twice as fast as that." Thank you very much!

I do love them. It's just that sometimes they can be such dolts, clowns, jolly jokers, and imposters that, well, it's hard NOT to make fun of them. I can't help myself. Sometimes I'm so juvenile about it that, yup, it's a problem.

Let's get oriented in the world of sales management. The global view is V.P. of Worldwide Sales. Reporting to him or her are various Sales V.P.'s or Directors who manage big countries or groups of countries. Following them are Area and Regional Managers who are responsible for smaller geographic regions and cities and oversee the Branch Managers. Depending upon the size and stage of your company, you may have some or all of these. For sure, there's always a lot of sales management.

That said, the person that most affects your reality is your sales manager. I've had a few really great managers and we've always wound up being friends for life. Good sales managers keep their egos in check, understand what makes peddlers tick, and are fair but firm. They help guide the farmers and leave the hunters to do their own thing (within reason). They know when to stay out of a peddler's way and when to get involved. Good sales managers act as if their only job is making you and your customers happy, not vice versa. To top it off, they are genuinely good people. I'm always happy when good sales managers get promoted. The higher up they go, the more people will benefit from their great attitudes, and the better the company will be. It's also nice to see good, competent folks be rewarded.

It doesn't seem like it should be too hard to find good sales managers, but considering how many horrid ones there are, apparently it is! Why? What does it take to see that peddlers are a diverse group, all of whom have different ways of thinking and different ways of approaching problems? How hard is it to figure out that a seasoned, competent team does not need an overly inspired, know-it-all leader to make them do their jobs better. Why is it so hard to grasp that what your peddlers need is a complimentary resource, a sounding board for tactics and strategy, and a Go-To guy or gal for those things they can't pull off? Above all, how hard is it to see that peddlers have their own problems and don't need someone else's? That they are quite capable of making mountains out of molehills, of making things more complex then they need to be. They don't need sales managers taking seemingly simple problems and turning them into intergalactic holocausts in a nanosecond just for something to do! Geesh!

But I digress. Sales managers come in different flavors. They are younger (the hot shot), older (the war-torn soldier), or your peer (your brother or sister who just sold out to management); they are coming and staying forever, or going as soon as they have a chance to evacuate the premises. This creates a rather interesting dynamic depending on how you match the variables up.

Peddlers become sales managers because they are looking for more responsibility, stability, and a shot at a corporate career path; it's not for the money. When it comes to compensation, top peddlers make really good money. Top managers make good money, but never as much as the top-gun sales guys in their groups. If they do, there's something wrong with the program.

Some sales managers subscribe to the Bill Parcells' philosophy: The more you beat 'em, the better they do. Others take Dr. Phil's approach: The more you love 'em, the better they do. It's the yin and yang of sales management.

News Flash: The best sales managers use a combination of both! Let's face it, managing peddlers is kind of like managing a bunch of teenagers. You really can't tell us much, we won't really listen, we do want to please you, we do want you to be proud. But the problem is that we just get caught up in our daily lives and you just rarely enter our heads unless we need money or are desperate for help!

It's in the teenage years that parents asks themselves why they ever wanted to be parents in the first place and that's why I always laugh when a peddler asks me whether they should go into management. I usually try and talk them out of it except on those rare occasions when I see that it really makes sense. But even then I recommend with great trepidation that a peddler actually jump into that frying pan. Being a sales manager is no walk in the park, and being a good one is even harder.

Oh Goody! Let's Have a Sales Meeting

As peddlers we all have to suffer through daily or weekly sales meetings, which run the gamut from being very helpful to utterly ridiculous. I've been a sales manager for many years and run my fair share of good and bad meetings. I prefer the rough and tumble, Bill Parcell's school of management to Dr. Phil's. If you play the odds, it's likely you're going to pay. In other words, I don't take kindly to peddlers who try to fake or dodge their way through a meeting. As a result, I have had some pretty wild and tumultuous sales meetings. Think really good opera!

I learned this approach from a few good managers I had over the years. They knew all the right questions to ask to get a REAL status on an opportunity. They were big fans of the binary approach to sales management and didn't suffer fools gladly. What all that means for the peddler is, honesty is the best policy. The following story is from one of their meetings. The names have been changed for no apparent reason.

STORY TIME

Sales Manager: Greetings . . . Let's get rockin'. Here are our ten biggest deals. Let's take it from the top. Deal number one. We said we were going to get our techie to do some work for the prospect. Is that done?

Peddler #1: Um . . . no . . . we didn't have the time.

Sales Manager: EXCUSE ME? Who is "we"?

Peddler #1: I mean me. I got busy with other things and didn't get a chance to arrange it. I had to help marketing with some trade show stuff and some new leads surfaced.

Sales Manager: So the top deal on the list for the region—and maybe for the company—is sitting in nowheresville because you decided other stuff was more important? We brainstormed on your deal, we freed up resources to help your deal, we made ourselves available to close YOUR deal, and then you blew it off BECAUSE YOU'RE TOO FREAKING BUSY? Why did we waste our time?!

Peddler #1: I will get right on it. Sorry, you are right.

Sales Manager: OK, make sure I am the first one to know TODAY when it's arranged. All we really need to do is concentrate, ladies and gentlemen. Set 'em up and knock 'em down. Please, for the love of Pete, try and focus on what we say we are going to do.

(continued)

It's why we have these inspiring meetings. On to deal two. We were going to set up a call with the decision maker. What happened?

Peddler #2: I called and he said he didn't have the time.

Sales Manager: Last week you said getting the decision maker to talk about a deal was no problem. Now, here we are a week later, talking about the number two deal in the region and—DARE I say it—maybe the second biggest deal in the company, and we learn that the decision maker doesn't have the time. That does not give me a warm and fuzzy feeling. Have we successfully passed the technical review?

Peddler #2: Well, we don't think the reviewer gets it. He may not be technical enough.

Sales Manager: So we gave a technical presentation to the wrong person. Hmmm . . . what's wrong with THIS FREAKING PICTURE?! Is it any wonder why the decision maker won't talk to us?! Oh sweet Jesus! Call the decision maker, ask him who the REAL techie is, get him on the phone, and set up another presentation.

Peddler #2: Will do, boss.

Sales Manager: OK, let's go to the third deal on the list. Let's see . . . We were going to demo our product. How did that go?

Peddler #3: It went great!

Sales Manager: Really? Who did you demo to?

Peddler #3: Bob Brown. He's a product manager.

Sales Manager: Product managers don't evaluate our products. Engineering Directors and V.P.'s buy from us; it's never the product side of house. SOOOOO . . . Why are we talking to this guy?

Peddler #3: I told him that would be a concern, as he didn't meet our typical profile and it wasn't the typical process. He said he understood, but that the folks in engineering are too busy, and that unless they get a nod from him, they won't take the time to look at it.

Sales Manager: Got it. So when do we demo for engineering?

Peddler #3: I'm scheduling it today.

Sales Manager: Good! Deal number four . . .

Peddler #4: Well, um, er, they are not returning my calls.

(continued)

Sales Manager: Not returning your calls? That's just great! Sounds like we have a real wonderful relationship going here! What do you think happened?

Peddler #4: Search me. The guy fell off the planet.

Sales Manager: Searching the account would be better. Who's the highest contact we have?

Peddler #4: I met the COO once for about 15 minutes.

Sales Manager: Good. Send him an e-mail and say we are not sure if we are in the right place or talking with the right folks, as we don't seem to be getting anywhere. Make sure you state the value proposition, give him a quick status, and then ask him if, in his opinion, we should continue or not bother. Tell him we don't want to waste anyone's time.

Round and round it goes until we get through the ten top deals.

Sales Manager: OK. Enough torture for the day. Now onto the counseling and shock treatment sessions.

That manager's basic theory was to get all peddlers in a room once a week, have the top ten deals on a board with the status and action items, and start at the top and dissect each deal. More often than not, he'd get all the peddlers involved in brainstorming problems and kicking them around, playing out what-if and what-then scenarios—whatever it took to solve our dilemmas.

Sales meetings such as these focus everyone and get the group in synch, in the same headspace. Eventually, they become perfunctory regarding customer profile, sales process, and closing tactics, which let's everyone focus on the deals. Ideally, they don't waste a lot of time debating and bullshitting about other deals in the pipe. Good peddlers are able to watch the comings and goings of the really big deals, grasp how typical deals fly, and apply that to the rest of the deals in their personal pipelines.

Here's a tip: When times are getting tough and your sales manager is getting tense and willful, invite him or her to listen in on your conversations or go with you on your sales calls. Give him or her the chance to see what you are doing, what you are up against. Ya, it's not always the most pleasant way to spend the day, but trust me. It's better than letting them sit in their offices guessing about what you are or are not doing. That only drives you—and them—crazy.

Who's in Charge Here?

One of the ways that peddlers fall into a rut is by letting themselves be controlled by the routines and processes created by their productivity applications. It is the most bizarre thing. They get drawn into these symbiotic man–machine relationships that stall their thinking and creativity. For instance, you probably have sales-tracking software that essentially organizes your daily sales-call activity. Go to work, fire up the 'puter, read your e-mail, check if your team won, boot up your sales software and BLAM!, you have the list of folks you have to ping, and your notes from your last attempts to reach the prospects: Not in, left message. Sound familiar?

Grunt work is a big part of being a peddler. All the tedious cold calling and follow-up is dreadful. You will lose your mind, not to mention prospects, unless you push yourself to make your pitch compelling. Good peddlers spend a lot of time learning the ins and outs of their markets, products, and companies so they can make a persuasive pitch and meet a prospect's objections or concerns with creative solutions. Good peddlers also find creative ways to move their deals along (if the routine processes are not working, that is).

Implementing productivity software is often management's idea. They like nothing better than to see a bunch of peddler drones dialing for dollars, working the system. But the notion that scorekeeping software makes peddlers sell more is a fallacy. Selling is not about being a nonthinking slave to a piece of anal-retentive software. But it's up to you to steer clear of its clutches, fight the temptation and follow your sales instincts. The more you learn what works for you the more you will sell. Selling is not just a system and you are not just a parrot.

On to THE NUMBER, the holy grail of sales!

The Number

Inside every company is the number—the yearly sales goal. As a fiscal year winds down, the powers that be come up with this number for the next year. Then they divide it by four to get the quarterly numbers, which are further divvied up among the various regions and branches, and finally reps.

There are two ways companies figure out the number. The first one starts with the peddlers. Each peddler predicts what he or she can sell for the upcoming year and gives that number to his or her manager. The manager reviews each peddler's number, tweaking it based on what he or she knows about market conditions, the peddler's customers, and the peddler's ability to forecast accurately, among other things. Finally, the manager comes up with a number for the group, which he or she passes along to his or her manager, and on up the chain it rolls.

The second way also starts with the peddlers but quickly takes on a life of its own, as folks from all corners of corporate decide they should have a say in determining the number. The first ones to butt in are usually the marketers. No matter what sales predicts, the marketers determine that the peddlers can sell more. How they come up with their number they never say; it's a process shrouded in mystery. Pure hocus pocus in my humble opinion.

The corporate executives are the next group to get in the game. They take marketing's inflated number and huddle behind closed doors. Remember, these are the guys and gals who want to look good to the board and Wall Street, and who own a lot of corporate stock. Is it any surprise when they goose the number even higher? Nope. No conflict of interest here!

Then the bean counters and business analytics jump in. They've been diligently measuring the number of calls, evals, proposals, and

P.O.'s, and turning the art of selling into a mathematical equation. If anyone should be able to predict the number, it should be them, right? Not a chance. Year after year they're off the mark. Gee, I wonder why? It all seems so easy and logical!

Sometimes the number makes its way to the Board of Directors. Of course, by then the number has been through so many departments and people that the board doesn't really know what it's looking at. But that doesn't seem to matter much if they have an agenda. They have no problem adjusting the number some more.

The amount of jostling for input and tweaking usually is directly proportional to the amount of pressure to improve revenue, beat last year's sales, best the competition, gain market share, and the like—despite the fact that forecasts really have no affect on how much a rep can sell. If you have some fine folks, a decent number can emerge. But more likely than not, black holes and chicanery abound, and the number is far afield of practical, which produces sales' biggest past time: bickering about the number.

From reps to management, no one ever likes the number he or she is handed. But there's a difference between a number everyone grudgingly acknowledges is in the ballpark, and a number that is so inflated it is ludicrous. The latter is bad for morale, a real confidence buster, and mayhem is sure to follow.

The Good Fight

There is a saying that goes something like this: If you ever see a good fight, get in it! The fight over the number is a good fight and probably the greatest testament to whether you have a good sales manager or not. A good sales manager doesn't overcommit but fights tooth and nail to get a number that is doable. It is so easy to commit to an unrealistic number at the beginning of a year and so impossible to get out of it once things start going south.

The net-net on a sales manager, from the field's perspective, is always going to be whose side is he or she on? Is he or she with us or against us? There are three sides, for any sales managers who are reading along. First, there are the peddlers and the customers, and good sales managers fight the good fight for and with them. Second, there is the sales managers' side, in which the managers fight only if they benefit. This attitude is predatory. The third side is the corporate side, where sales managers blindly follow whatever garbage the execs are throwing their way—real yes men and women.

Should I tone this down a tad, Mr. or Ms. Sales Manager? Can you handle my straight peddler speak? Which one are you? If your answer is anything other then the first, I strongly suggest giving the devil a ring and trying to get your soul back. Remember, you can bargain and trade your next in command.

Pays Me, Don't Praise Me

There are many types of companies, but for a peddler there are really only two. The first has a leader that understands that the person with the biggest W-2 at the end of the year should be his best peddler. The second type has a leader who does not think peddlers should make the most cash.

I always choose companies that give me a tremendous upside—the chance to make more money than anyone else in the house. When the compensation plan rocks, I know I'm with folks that recognize the importance of sales, which is truly delightful.

I have a wall full of plaques from various companies for my peddler achievements. Most of the plaques went hand in hand with a great financial result. Thus, I got praised and paid. Unfortunately, that hasn't always happened. I have also worked for companies that believed public and peer recognition was a fine substitute for stock options and dollars. To them I said, "Pays me, don't praise me." It is up to all peddlers to remind management that we want to be paid well.

PEDDLER'S PREROGATIVE #41

It is the peddler's prerogative to make sure management understands that he or she prefers to be paid rather than praised. It is your prerogative to suggest they save the money spent on recognition meetings and sign some checks for the best peddlers.

Your Fellow Peddlers

Every day you are under one form of pressure or another: tracking leads, getting appointments, making presentations, following procedures, and meeting quotas, just to name a few. So it's no surprise that we often don't take the time to get to know our fellow peddlers, our band of brothers and sisters. But we should!

We lead a unique life, and no one understands that better than other peddlers. Forge relationships with these folks and they will help you, commiserate with you, make you laugh, and get you back on track. You'll find that ya, you compete, but you're all part of the big peddler clan. You're all in the same boat, fighting the good fight, trying to keep body and soul together, paddling against the tide, quarter after quarter. It's an experience that bonds you together for the rest of your life. Most of my best friends today are peddlers I met during my selling career.

Move Along, Now

Before we move on, I have a Public Service Announcement to make. The next chapter is about marketing. As a peddler, your inclination is probably to skip it. DO NOT SKIP THIS CHAPTER. In some companies marketing is a helpful entity; in others it can drive a peddler to drink. Are the marketing folks in tune with sales or are they as mad as hatters? It is your business to find out. Read the next chapter.

CHAPTER 10

THE MARKETING DEPARTMENT

No one wants advice—only corroboration.
—John Steinbeck

Can't live with 'em, can't live without 'em. That's pretty much how I feel about most marketers (or marketeers as they're sometimes called). I've been told that's pretty much how they feel about us peddlers, too. It's a love-hate relationship. Both sides love to hate each other.

At best, we tolerate each other. At worst, well, no need to get into that. We've all been there. But here's the really scary thing: *Customers* have an equally ambivalent and contentious relationship with marketers. It's not just us peddlers!

If you're a peddler, you know I speak the truth. Customers take time out of their busy days to tell you their ideas, suggestions, complaints, and requests. You spend precious face time listening and making careful notes. Then you dutifully report back to marketing, only to have the feedback fall on deaf ears. 'Tis a sad fact. Most marketers aren't listening to customers and customers are getting pissed off.

It wasn't so long ago that we seemed on the cusp of a major marketing breakthrough. Some cool heads surfaced and had some pretty compelling ideas about the company-customer dynamic. Pundits such as Peppers and Rogers introduced the concept of one-to-one marketing, and told us that companies will succeed or fail depending upon their ability to cultivate individual relationships with their customers.

Then along came Seth Godin with *Permission Marketing*, in which he argued that businesses can no longer rely on traditional forms of advertising. There's so much of it that customers no longer notice it. To capture customers' attention, Godin told businesses that they should discover customers' problems and ask their permission to pitch a solution. Pitches that are relevant and expected will be welcomed and, therefore, work.

When it still didn't seem as if anyone was listening, the *Cluetrain Manifesto* gang chimed in and took aim at corporate marketing. In eyebrow-raising commentary they observed that "markets are conversations," that "markets consist of human beings and not demographic sectors." The *Cluetrain* authors warned companies that "their markets are often laughing—at them," and that "markets do not want to talk to flacks and hucksters."

Could the message have been more clear? Marketers must talk with customers. Engage them! Have a dialogue! They should ask customers how they can help them, what they need. They should deal with customers fairly and honestly. Marketing isn't rocket science, as most marketers would love to have you believe. It's common sense and common decency!

A few marketers got the message and for a moment, change was on the horizon. But ultimately, the marketing majority chose to ignore it despite the promise of higher revenues (if they took heed) or the threat of irrelevance and extinction (if they didn't).

Then there were those marketers who managed to twist these simple, straightforward concepts beyond all recognition and take them to the bizarre extreme. They thought, why go to all the trouble of caring about customers when we can use technology to create the illusion of caring? Why spend a lot of time and money actually getting to know our customers when we can use technology to appear to know them?

Single-handedly, these marketers turned what was supposed to be the age of personalization into the era of impersonal personalization. Not sure what I mean? Let me ask you a few questions.

How often do you get calls, IMs, and e-mails from 'bots rather than people?

How often do you hear "Your call is important to us," only to be left hanging on hold?

How often do Web sites offer you "personalized recommendations" when you haven't spent even a minute talking with anyone at that company?

How often do you get a phone matrix instead of customer service or a knowledge base instead of technical support?

When was the last time you received a letter from your credit card company that someone actually signed?

Let's face it, most marketers think personalization means having a computer insert your name on a form letter or etch your initials on a mass-produced tchotchke! Unfortunately, this is indicative of the broader corporate marketing mindset.

The Truth about Marketers

There's no doubt about it. Most marketers are measurers and analytics at heart. They like nothing better than to gather lots of information, crunch the data, and spew out reports. And they've made enormous investments of time and money in the infrastructure and technology to do just that.

One of their favorite things is collecting hundreds of data points and creating detailed customer profiles that read something like this: Our typical customer is a 40-year-old, white-collar, male professional who lives in the suburbs, commutes less than 1.5 hours to work, is married, and has 2.3 kids who attend public school. His wife is between 38 and 42, and a working white-collar professional who commutes .5 hours or less to work. They have owned their home for 5.8 years, have 2.2 cars, and travel for vacation 9.3 days per year. They have 2.5 computers and 3.1 TVs. They eat out 2.2 times per week and order in 1.4 times per week. Yada, yada, yada.

To any peddler, compiling such statistics sounds like pure drudgery. So you're probably thinking, if that's what floats their boat, let them knock themselves out. Normally, I'd agree with you. But their obsession with collecting and processing massive amounts of data is harming relationships with customers.

The Smartest Guys in the Room

Those would be the marketers—or so they think. They have gathered so much data that they believe they know all there is to know. Are you wondering why customers buy (or don't buy) a product? The marketers will run the numbers and get you the answer. They don't need to talk to customers. What do they know?

STORY TIME

A friend of mine is hired by a venture-capital group to be the CEO of a start-up. His assignment is to reposition and relaunch the company. He writes up a new business plan and interviews some big-league talent to get the place hoppin'.

One of the folks he interviews is a well-known marketer with tons of experience, a successful track record, and a list of marquee names on her resume. She says all the right things during their meetings and her references rave about her skills. Suitably impressed, my friend hires her and she puts together a great plan with a new message.

Fast-forward several months to a meeting of the executive staff. After a few people update the group it's her turn. "All is going great," she reports. "I've presented the new positioning to sales, engineering, support, and all the product folks. I've had it critiqued by a well-know consultant, and I've briefed several leading analysts. Everyone loves the new positioning and has given it a thumbs up. It should fly."

"Great!" says the CEO. "What do the customers think?"

The marketer looks befuddled.

"You have talked the customers, haven't you?" asks the CEO.

"What for?" asks the veteran, world-class marketer.

True story. I couldn't have made it up if I wanted to.

The Target Audience

That would be our prospects and customers. If I haven't convinced you before now that corporate executives see themselves at war that should do it. But it's also indicative of marketers' focus on data. Prospects and customers are analyzed and categorized and stripped of everything that makes them human, that makes them individuals. Then they're lumped together into segments, clusters, heads, eyeballs, and seats. Where peddlers see folks to get to know, marketers see targets to be managed and manipulated. Unfortunately, this is what happens when you spend too much time with data and not enough time with customers.

Here's a tip for all you brilliant marketeers: Customers don't like being targets!

Measurement for Measurement's Sake

If some is good, more is better. That's corporate marketing's thinking when it comes to data. They spend millions of dollars measuring everything and everyone under the sun despite the fact that most marketing can be done with three or four basic data points. Most consumer marketing, for example, can be done knowing a person's age and sex, and where they live. Marketers relentless pursuit of measurement is one of the biggest (and most expensive) hoaxes foisted upon corporate America. But more importantly, it's turning off customers. They are tired of forking over more and more information in the hope of getting products that suit their wants and needs—products that never materialize.

The New Corporate Weapon

Make no mistake. Data is the new corporate weapon, and marketers wield it better than anyone. They use it against competitors. They use it against executives and colleagues. And they use it against customers.

Ya, CUSTOMERS! Have a personal item shipped to your office and soon you are receiving two catalogs, one at home and one at the office. Provide an e-mail address for order confirmation, and soon your in-box is clogged with solicitations from that company and others you have never heard of. Pay your credit card bill on time, and soon you are bombarded by telemarketers with "special offers" because "you have been such a good customer." Sheesh! Is it any wonder why their relationships with customers are increasingly adversarial?

Listen up, you know-it-all marketers! We are just simple human beings. We love to talk. We love to listen. We love to be heard. We need things. We want things. Ask us who we are and what we want. Be kind and understanding. Engage us. Create real and meaningful conversations. Respect us. Love us. Treat us as you would want to be treated. Oh, one more thing. STOP INSULTING AND ASSAILING US BECAUSE YOU'RE REALLY PISSING US OFF!

There's a Priest, a Rabbi, and a Shaman . . .

The mistake of the enlightened pundits was making their cases to the marketers. Strategically it made sense, but not tactically. It was like trying to convince the fox to come out of the hen house. Most marketers nodded politely and went back to slicing and dicing their data. They didn't believe the pundits—or didn't want to believe them.

Or, they really didn't want to talk to customers. That's my opinion (even though they swear up and down that they REALLY do). After all, developing one-to-one relationships takes time. It means going out into the field, listening to customers' stories and problems, understanding how they work, and asking questions. It takes thinking about one customer's problem and finding a solution—a solution that you may never use again, that may not be applicable to tens, hundreds, or thousands of other customers, that at best may only make one sale.

That's not marketing's bag. They prefer to sit in their offices crunching numbers and spotting trends. Predicting the next big thing. Hatching strategies in a vacuum. Dictating to peddlers and customers: One way, baby. Our way or the highway. Do it or lose it! Dealing with the everyday problems of single customer? Where's the fun in that? But rolling out a national media extravaganza of opulence and cluelessness, now that's fun!

Some pundits also pitched their theories to the CEOs, but that's proved equally as hopeless. If it doesn't affect this quarter's earnings, CEOs don't want to hear it.

Surprisingly, the gurus overlooked the peddlers who are in the best position to bridge the divide between marketers and customers. The best peddlers are honest, caring folks who cultivate great, meaningful relationships. As the purveyors of business relationships, we are the ambassadors of our companies and, conversely, we are the customer evangelists and liaisons to our companies. We can be the priests, rabbis, and shamans of our companies and bring together the marketers and customers. We can show marketers the rewards and satisfaction that comes from putting customers and their problems first.

It won't be easy. The disdain most marketers have for peddlers and customers is so great that you may just have to grab them by their polo shirts and haul them out to the field. But I promise, you will be rewarded for your efforts.

PEDDLER'S PREROGATIVE #42

It is the peddler's prerogative to advise the marketer he deems relevant (the higher the better) that he will be taking him or her out to the field. It is also the peddler's prerogative to tell said marketer that resistance will be futile, as he will take him or her kicking and screaming out of the building by any means necessary. It is the peddler's prerogative to delight muchly as the customer reads the marketer the riot act.

Hey! What's That Noise?

Marketers have felt the rumblings of the new customer-company dynamic for some time, but for some reason a good majority still resist. They tend to be the super control freaks who believe peddlers are merely mouthpieces to deliver their messages, and customers are just vehicles to gain market share. They believe that, any day now, they will achieve two long-held objectives: to completely control the peddler and the customer. Ya, that's how bad it is.

You're mission (should you choose to accept it) is to show these marketeers that peddlers and customers are real people, not robots and data segments. Shazam! You're a person, Pinocchio.

It may very well happen that the first few times you put such a marketer in front of a customer, they simply repeat their scripted messages over and over and over again. They're doing as they've always done, what they expect peddlers to do: look for validation of what they have created. When this happens, gently intercede and begin a dialogue with the customer. Show the marketer how it's done, how the customer opens up when you skip the script and ask him or her questions. Peddlers know how to do this better than anyone, because we already do it!

Back at the office you may notice your marketer planning more silly ads, more annoying e-mails, more fake white papers, more phony infomercials—more of anything but honest to goodness, face-to-face communication. Take them aside and explain that it's not more, more, more, it's real, real, real. Then make a mental note to take them back out to the field ASAP. Keep in mind that you're dealing with control freaks. They have a fear of letting go. They may even try to make you think they've changed horses when, in fact, they haven't moved an inch. Be on your guard. Be patient. It usually takes about six months or more in the field before a transformation can take place.

PEDDLER'S PREROGATIVE #43

It is the peddler's prerogative to think of the corporate marketers as spoiled brats when they refuse to listen and think they know it all. It is the peddler's prerogative to readjust that view when the marketers start acting like responsible corporate citizens.

CHAPTER 11

SOMEBODY'S WATCHING YOU

No man is good enough to govern another man without that other's consent.

—Abraham Lincoln

In the previous chapter, I said that one of marketing's objectives was to control the peddler and the customer. Take heed: they are not the only ones who have a fascination with control.

In every company there lurk a few individuals who for one reason or another coalesce as the monitors of the company. They usually surface simultaneously with the availability of some new and nifty corporate tool. In the sales realm, it was sales tracking software (also known as customer relationship management or sales automation software). When this was first introduced, some corporate types, like thugs in an alley, saw their chance to pounce: We can't control everything our peddlers do, but now we can monitor it!

On one level these types of productivity tools are useful. They help peddlers keep track of their prospects and customers, and their interactions with them. Peddlers can enter notes from calls and meetings, action items, and their schedule for follow-up calls and visits.

On another level, these benign applications are being exploited to monitor you. Yup, MONITOR. Telemarketers have it the worst.

Management can push a button and get real-time statistics that tell them who you call, how many calls you make an hour, the length of each call, if you follow the script, your success rate in delivering the message or securing information, and on and on.

Road warriors used to have it a little better, but the monitoring folks have even figured out how to reign in the field under their watchful eyes. Whether in the office or out, these programs monitor your e-mails, analyze your sales reports, track the length of time it takes you to do a deal, and more. If you turn in your cell phone bill for reimbursement, the date, time, and length of your calls from the road can be added to the mix.

As usual the data is never the problem. It's how it's used. The best managers use it to help their folks become better peddlers and to build a stronger sales team. Other managers use it to get rid of employees. They scour reports to find reasons for dismissal. If they can't find anything, they might manipulate the data. Or they might start scanning through the records of one of the many other surveillance devices they have.

Recently, a friend of mine popped up on my buddy list. We hadn't spoken in a while, so I sent her a message. Immediately I received this automated reply from the IM admin at her company (I'll call it XYZ to protect its privacy): "This Instant Message conversation is monitored to ensure adherence to our compliance guidelines. XYZ Company retains copies of all messages sent in this conversation and from time to time that content may be reviewed."

Think about it. Most companies monitor e-mail and Internet access. Some tape your phone calls. Video cameras in the hallways record your comings and goings. If you have an ID badge, your company has a record of every door you go through and the time. Put all these things together and management can tell how much time you spend away from your desk, how much time you spend at lunch, who you call or visit when you're in the office, even how often you hit the restroom. Your digital footprints are easier to follow than you think.

Yeah, but who has the time to piece it all together, you might ask. A lot of people. Many companies have a full-time staff that does nothing but monitor their employees. They're just the folks who can put the pieces together and paint an unflattering picture of your corporate life for a devious manager.

Monitoring is very blatant in sales departments in particular. The monitoring droids have convinced the powers that be that this is necessary in order to deliver a consistent message and meet sales goals. The monitors also have persuaded the higher-ups that they should play a big part in selecting the sales tracking software that you use. And they've colluded with HR and IT to make it all happen. Here's a group that has no problem acting like Big Brother.

If you find this creepy or appalling, you're not alone. On a lark, I went to Wikipedia, the free Internet encyclopedia, to look up the word fascist. I discovered that Mussolini encapsulated his philosophy in the following maxim: "Tutto nello Stato, niente al di fuori dello Stato, nulla contro lo Stato," which translates to, "Everything in the State, nothing outside the State, nothing against the State." Mussolini then reasoned that "all individuals' business is the state's business, and the state's existence is the sole duty of the individual." Substitute the word "corporation" for "state" and you might just have the same epiphany that I'm having. That sounds a lot like business today!

If you find yourself in a company that acts like a dictatorship and forgets that we live in a free society, you have the right to call a spade a spade and let them know—in the nicest way, of course. Explain that the present level of scrutiny does not create an open, productive, and enjoyable work environment. Rather, it creates an environment of hostility and mistrust that is stressful and inefficient. It sends out the message, loud and clear, that it's US versus THEM. Explain that the result of their actions is a company that is at war with itself. Explain that it doesn't have to be this way.

STORY TIME

It's the early '90s and I'm CEO of a high-tech start-up. We have a great product, but as is typical of new companies, we're strapped for cash. To keep costs down, I decide not to allocate any money for traditional marketing. After years of being a peddler, eliminating the traditional marketing overhead seems like a no-brainer.

Instead, we hire lots of smart engineers and aggressive peddlers. Aside from a few finance and admin folks, we decide that everyone will either write code or sell product. (They will also ski, but that's another story.)

Right from the get-go, we anoint Friday as meeting day. Everyone (and I do mean everyone) meets in the conference room at noon for pizza, after which we review the top 10 deals and brainstorm on how to move them forward. I'm intent on having everyone in sync and avoiding departmental fiefdoms.

The first meeting proves to be a real eye-opener. Peddlers throw out ideas—each one wilder than the previous one—as possible next steps. The engineers, getting their first glimpse of how peddlers think, are dumbfounded. To their credit, however, they take a deep breath and patiently explain the technical issues involved and how the peddlers' ideas might affect other projects and ship dates. The peddlers toss out more ideas. The engineers analyze them. Finally, finance weighs in, explaining how various ideas might affect our pricing, revenue, or profitability. Round and round we go until we all agree that the path to take is the one that puts the customer first.

It takes several more months of weekly meetings to get everyone in sync, but eventually we are and the joint is rockin'. The direct connect from sales to engineering, engineering to the customer, and the customer to sales is helping us close deals left and right. Sometimes it's like using an elephant gun to shoot a mouse, but the good news is nary a mouse escapes!

The moral of this story is, it's not necessary to control and monitor peddlers or other employees when everyone is working together, heading in the same direction, and aware of what others are trying to accomplish. Our first year in business, we received the Product of the Year award from a prestigious industry magazine. No one was more surprised than us, because there were some big players—Fortune 1000 companies—in our space. Nevertheless, a band of peddlers and hotshot engineers beat them to the punch. We did it because we really listened to our customers, facilitated real two-way dialogues, and all worked together. The result was a top-notch product.

Granted, the ideas that work on a small scale don't always work on a large scale. Company-wide meetings quickly become impractical and unproductive when a business grows beyond 50 people. However, they can be adapted, and should be, because the lessons are clear. When there's an environment of trust and support, mutual respect for skills and intellect, an understanding of the business, and a customer-first mindset, a company starts to click. People work together. They produce good products. And peddlers make hay while the sun shines.

It is the epitome of stupidity to coerce and force sales folk into the latest and greatest automation and organizational schemes in the hopes of improved productivity. For the love of Pete, sales folk are not an assembly line of automatons that can be run by machines. Ya, it's good for peddlers to use some basic tracking and scheduling software, but RUDIMENTARY is all they need. It's a waste of time and money to make everyone conform to the latest hot sales system and its processes.

Here's an idea for all you corporate folks: Boost sales by making your products more compelling! Pump your dollars into research and development. Stop blowing your cash on monitoring and policing. One more time: STOP BLOWING YOUR CASH ON MONITORING AND POLICING.

CHAPTER 12

SALES SUPPORT, ENGINEERING, AND PRODUCT MANAGEMENT

It is not the employer who pays wages. He only handles the money. It is the product that pays the wages.

—Henry Ford

Support for the peddler is key. Good support wins you business, bad support blows your deals. Yet, the very folks who are there to help you can, in fact, hinder you. It's a paradox. You line up a prospect for a demo, call up the support manager to schedule your favorite techie and, Blam!, everything comes to a screeching halt.

"Tell me about this sales call and *I'll* decide if you need to take Bill."

This is part of the "peddlers must justify themselves to everyone" corporate mentality. Woe be it to the peddler who has a comment or question about someone else's job. But when it comes to peddlers, evidently everyone has carte blanche to judge our strategies and tactics. The upshot is that peddlers often don't receive support—from the SUPPORT group! The reason? Some corporate lackey decides you don't need his resources. Oy!

Several constituencies is another reason. Support groups are often autonomous or part of another department or division, such as product management, in which case they have many (and more important) folks to please other than you. One group of techies may support both sales and customers, for example. In small companies, the engineers often do double duty as sales support. This leaves peddlers competing for techies' time, which is the kiss of death if you are looking to move fast and furiously.

There's a lot less negotiating if the support group is part of the sales organization. In this case, the support group also is more in tune with the needs of the sales folks and the objectives of sales management. However, even sales support groups can be part of the problem rather than the solution if they are not involved in the sales process.

Ready, Set, Engage!

The best salesperson in any company is always your best support person. Ya, you read right. Best as in even better than the top-dog peddler. This is because prospects and customers trust them. Peddlers are thought to be interested in only one thing: making a sale. As soon as we walk into a room, prospects and customers have their guard up. But bring in a support techie who knows the product really well, answers all their technical questions, shows them how they can use the product to solve their problems, tells them how other customers use it, and he or she quickly wins them over.

Now, here's the cool part: the trust and confidence the prospect or customer has in the techie reflects on you. The fact that you brought in this smart, credible, earnest person to speak with them wins you points.

That's why my M.O. is always to hook up with the best support person, pronto. There's another reason as well. I know that what product knowledge does for a techie it also can do for me in spades—mainly, help me gain the trust and confidence of my prospects and customers. Listening to a knowledgeable support person meeting after meeting helps me to really grasp the product. Even dense technical details begin to sink in. And the more I know the more I sell.

PEDDLER'S PREROGATIVE #44

It is every peddler's prerogative to discover who knows the most about the product he or she is selling. It is also your prerogative to engage those folks in your deals, overtly or covertly.

Once you've identified the best and brightest support folks, then you need to get them on your team and into your head space. Make sure they know that they are part of your sales process and your Go-To guys for tactical questions.

I usually start off by saying I'll make a trade with them. If they teach me what they know about a product, I will teach them what I know about peddlery. Usually their first thought is, "Oh, boy. What a deal." But after a few calls, they start to come around. I show them a different way of looking at things, and dealing with people and problems. I teach them how I spot opportunities and avoid bad deals. And, of course, they get to see my philosophy up close and in action.

It takes some time, but usually I win them over. I explain that they are analytics who see a complex world and try to ignore problems, hoping they go away. I, on the other hand, am an emotional person who sees the world as black and white, and likes to run headlong into problems, engaging them, and figuring them out. After a few days in the field with me, they tend to agree.

Hey! Make the time in the field with your support folks quality time. This also helps get them on your team. This is no different than forming a relationship with anyone else. You're together in planes, trains, and automobiles. You're eating three meals a day with each other. You're preparing proposals and squeaking by deadlines. Get to know your partners. Do they like baseball? Fishing? Are they married? Do they have kids? What kind of music do they listen to?

Then, take care of them. Treat them right. Let them know you REALLY appreciate them. Over the years, I've treated support folks to drinks, dinner, weekends, ball games. They helped me close some pretty big deals and make a ton of cash, and I wanted to show my appreciation. You should, too. Let's face it. We put our support folks through hell. The least we can do is make it as comfortable as possible.

Comrades in Arms

Once you have the support folks on your team, things start to cook. The first few times out with a techie, you plan your approach, script your parts, and rehearse your presentations. But after a while, you know each other so well that calling on a prospect or customer becomes second nature.

STORY TIME

I'm in Florida making a call on a well-known retailer. The company asked me in to explain how they can use the Web to extend their business. There are a bunch of Webophiles in the room and the presentation is going great until the V.P. walks in. He's your classic "I'm ME and you're not" kind of executive, always pulling his trump cards. The type that demands clarification on trivial points and misses the big picture in the process.

After everyone's been introduced, he sits down and I begin bringing him up to speed on what has been a really good meeting. I've hardly begun when he interrupts with one of those "I have the power, so you listen to me" rants. As his staff sit back and then slide down in their chairs, I realize that this is your classic power play. He needs to be in control and he isn't going to put up with anyone who won't play his game by his rules. As he's correctly surmised, that would be me.

Now, I can be patient and accommodating with some folks, yet easily irritated by others. I stopped trying to figure it out long ago. What I do know is that I can quickly determine who's in which camp. On this day, it's clear Mr. V.P. is in the latter. If I keep talking, we are going to bang heads and the deal is going to go south, because the cold fact is, he has the power. So I close my mouth.

Along with me on this call is Tim, a great engineer. He is oblivious to what my years of experience have told me. Because we've worked together so long, however, Tim picks up the ball and runs with it without batting an eye. He presents the product and fields questions, unaware of the potentially hazardous dynamic between the V.P. and me.

Luckily, the V.P. takes a liking to Tim and confides in him about his objectives. I watch as the relationship starts to develop; the deal is getting some legs.

Back in the car, I explain to Tim what I had seen. He shakes his head and laughs. "What different worlds we live in," he says.

Tim and I have been on a lot of calls together. We're different, but we make a good team because we enjoy working together and have great respect for each other's smarts and talents. That's the way it's gotta be.

Listen up! Peddlers fly in and out of accounts and typically don't get the face time with prospects and customers that the techies do. The support folks not only give product demos and answer technical questions, but interview the staff to understand their technical needs and problems, and create and implement prototypes — and that's just a few of their jobs. By the time the deal is ready to close, they usually know the prospect or customer better than you.

That's why you need to forge deep partnerships with the support staff. They are your ears and eyes on a prospect or customer. They are the Trojan horses who can bring you inside the gates. They are the ones who can deliver the all-important G2 that helps you win business, because prospects and customers ask support hundreds of questions. Discount their influence and importance at your own peril.

The other reason to build alliances with the techies is because, sooner or later, you'll need their help. You'll need someone to go on a call at the last minute. Someone to explain, once again, how a feature works. Someone to calm a hysterical customer and assure him that this really is the solution to his problem despite what his golf buddy says. Someone to come to your rescue and not insist you go through the chain of command first.

STORY TIME

I'm courting a prospect and slowly wending my way through the corporate maze. Finally, I'm in front of the decision maker.

"I understand the vision. I understand the product. And I believe it will help us expand our market. So, set up a meeting with Joe and go over the numbers with him," he tells me.

One week later, I walk into Joe's office. He has spreadsheets and financial models spread out all over, and I realize I'm in this deal with a numbers freak.

"Let me explain this to you," he says. As he begins reviewing the spreadsheets and his analysis, I realize that I'm a dead man. I have no idea what he's talking about. I'm a big picture guy. I connect dots, not numbers in tiny boxes.

Not knowing what else to do, I confess.

"Joe, I'm sorry, but I can't help you. This is not my area. But I know someone who can. Let me make a call."

The next day, I'm back with a techie who is a gem at this kind of modeling. As they begin reviewing Joe's spreadsheets, I can see that they are perfectly in sync, like two peas in a pod.

The moral of this story is, you better know your strengths and weaknesses, and get cozy with folks who have the talents you lack. This is an obvious statement, but in peddlery it's an important point we tend to forget. That deal would have been a goner if I hadn't been able to call for backup. Don't think you can do it alone.

Who's Driving This Train Anyways?

The architects or engineers of a product are always my favorite to haul out into the field and the hardest to spring. Being the folks who design or create the product, they can educate and impress prospects and customers like no one else. On the other hand, the demands on their time are great. If they are helping you sell, they are not working on their products, which can play havoc with deadlines. So before you request the assistance of an architect or engineer, you better make sure you're not making a frivolous call.

PEDDLER'S PREROGATIVE #45

It is your prerogative to figure out how to bust out the cavalry from corporate. If you're going to be good at anything, be good at that! Be adroit, but never cavalier or wasteful. You'll screw it up for the rest of us.

Here are my rules for tapping these precious in-house resources:

- I need to penetrate a big-name company and all avenues are jammed; the only way in is through the prospect's engineering division.
- I've been to several meetings, it's a highly-technical company, and I need firepower to go head-to-head with the prospect's evaluation team.
- I have a meeting with a top executive who is bringing the V.P. of Engineering or the CTO, and they have requested that I bring my company's gurus.
- An important prospect has the product in house, doesn't "get it," and I need some technical intuition to tell me what the problem really is.
- I keep hearing the same objections customer after customer, and I need to get the message, loud and clear, into corporate engineering.
- A prospect wants to use the product in a way that is beyond support's technical understanding and abilities.
- A prospect needs to understand the product's architecture.
- I have one last shot at a really big account.

If the call meets any one of these criteria, I usually have a shot at getting it through the powers that be. If they turn me down, then it's time to cash in on my relationships, which are usually pretty good.

Like peddlers, engineers know they are cut from a different cloth. Maybe that's why we get along so well. Neither of us fits into the corporate world in which we find ourselves.

There the similarities end, however. Engineers typically like to build things whereas peddlers like to build relationships. Engineers are cerebral and independent types who marvel at peddlers' back-slapping, give-me-five nature. And whereas peddlers have the attention span of a gnat, engineers can spend days, weeks, or months taking things apart, seeing how they work, figuring out how to make them better, and then rebuilding them.

STORY TIME

I'm president of a startup and trying to drum up interest in a product that's still in development. After writing code for months, the founder has several modules ready for debugging, and a prospect tells me he'll buy the product if we can deliver the first three modules in 90 days.

We need some help fast, so I start dialing. I find three hot-shot engineers, all gurus in their respective areas, and invite them in.

"Here's the deal," I tell them. "A company will buy our product if we deliver the first three modules in 90 days. The modules have to be debugged and the customer wants these additional features. Here's the code. Can you do it?"

Each of them takes the code home, studies it, and comes back with the same answer, "Sure. No problem."

"Great!" I hire them and let them go to work while I go back on the road to drum up more business.

Three weeks later we meet. "How's it going?" I ask.

"Great," says the first engineer. "I've rewritten about a third of the module. I'll be ready to debug it in another 6 weeks."

"Same here," the second and third engineers chime in.

(continued)

"But we didn't want you to rewrite it," I say. "We wanted you to debug it and add these features."

"But this is *sooo* much better," says the first engineer, who proceeds to explain why by drawing arcane diagrams on the white board.

"How much more time will this take?" I ask.

"Oh, a few weeks at most."

One hundred and eighty days later we delivered the first three modules. The lesson I learned was to automatically doubled any estimate from engineering.

I also learned to carefully script any customer meeting with an engineer or architect, because in addition to deadlines, they often are oblivious to the social norms we take for granted. It's not unusual for them to show up for a meeting in shorts, t-shirt, and sandals, and that's on a good day. Or for them to go off on a tangent that has everyone either tapping their fingers or nodding off.

In short, these folks often don't have a lot of experience dealing with prospects and customers, and it can show very quickly. So before you take these folks on the road, detail everything they should do from start to finish: What they should wear, the goals for the call, who is attending the meeting and their roles, the questions the customer may ask, the answers they'll give, and so on. Then practice, practice, practice. Review the script with them over and over again.

Ya, it's a lot of work, but it's worth the effort. It avoids any embarrassing moments for you and them. It helps you make the sale, and the architects and engineers learn about the needs of prospects and customers. It's a two-way street.

Architects and engineers are used to making decisions in a vacuum. That's how corporate has laid out the process and they do their best. Unfortunately, because of this, they don't really know what customers want or need, the environment in which their products will be implemented, or hundreds of other factors that could influence their design or implementation decisions. So when they're finally dragged down from their ivory towers and forced to converse with real people, it can be a real eye-opener.

Architect:	One of the newest and coolest features is that our device wiggles!
Customer:	Wiggles?
Architect:	Operating with lasers, temperature sensors, and a custom chip, our device begins to wiggle when it detects the slightest change in the environment.
Customer:	But we don't need it to wiggle.
Architect:	Its wiggling capability doesn't affect the battery life at all!
Customer:	But we don't need it to wiggle. However, if it could roll . . .
Architect:	Roll?

Some architects and engineers are devastated when a prospect or customer doesn't take to their product. Others are so arrogant that they see prospects or customers as being too ignorant to appreciate the brilliance of their creation. They may justify continuing by pointing out that it's just one person's opinion, or use their high rank to continue creating a product that no one wants.

Then there are those who act reasonably and ask to visit other prospects and customers: "We are spending a lot of time and money making this wiggle. If we're going down the wrong road, we better find out quick!"

These are the folks you want along on calls. They are also the ones who can make good peddlers. Their product knowledge and pragmatism make them good candidates—once they're rid of their bizarre notions of what peddling and peddlers are all about. One of the most prevalent views is that peddlers are the gentleman's gentleman, the butlers of the company. Another, at the opposite end of the spectrum, is that peddlers are hired fiends who pillage and plunder customers.

Bring them into your world. Show them what good peddling is all about. When you're in lockstep with a really good architect or engineer, you can start the joint jumpin'! But let me reiterate, haul an engineer or architect out on a frivolous call and you will be a marked man or woman.

Onto product management . . .

The Keepers of the Flame

The product managers essentially own the products from an organizational perspective. They are the keepers of the product flame, responsible for the care and feeding of the product. They are notoriously hard to reach, usually because there are only a few of them and lots of others banging down their doors.

Product managers come in three flavors: good, bad, and indifferent. The good ones are, well, good. They tell peddlers the unvarnished truth: Here's where we're competitive and here's where we're not. Here's what you'll see in the next product update. They're on the level.

The bad ones, on the other hand, suck. And the indifferent ones really suck. They think nothing of manipulating the facts to serve their own purposes. They insist that a product is competitive even when you cite several others that are faster, better, and cheaper. They refuse to acknowledge any problems with the product despite a chorus of customer complaints to the contrary. They refuse to discuss the features and fixes in the next version, insisting that you sell what you have.

Do these folks really think that if they admit that a product is at the beginning of its life cycle and has fewer features than its competitors, or at the end of its life cycle and slower than the competition, that we'll stop selling it?

Grok this, all you product mavens! The reason we're peddlers is to make money. The way we make money is by selling products. So we're not about to stop selling yours even if they aren't the latest and greatest. In fact, what we may be able to do for you—if you're HONEST with us—is find you a market: prospects and customers who want and need your product, warts and all. So for the love of Pete, stop with the spin.

PEDDLER'S PREROGATIVE #46

It is your prerogative to remember that every product has a product manager and you have a one in three chance of it being an enlightened and engaging one. It is also your prerogative to find out fast if you are blessed with a good one or in need of an alternate strategy.

Pardon Me, Is This a Real Product?

The fact is, my fellow peddlers, good product managers are few and far between, and even they can be blinded by the radiance of their wonderful product plans and strategies from time to time. So to get the real skinny on a product, you have to do your own due diligence. I usually start with the product folk, then move along to the support staff, engineers, and anyone else whose path I cross.

One of my favorite questions for the product manager is: Do you have a product? That always gets the meeting off to a lively start. I tend toward technology's outer edges, however, so that question is crucial. I've talked with numerous companies that were supposedly up and running, only to be shown a demo or prototype rather than a real product. Software companies are so notorious for selling products that don't exist a word was coined to describe it: vaporware.

If a product exists, then I continue down my list.

- Is it shipping?
- Is it at the beginning, middle, or end of its life cycle?
- Who is the competition?
- Why is it competitive?
- How does it fare in objective competitive analyses?
- How many customers are using it?
- If it's being phased out, why?

On and on I go, asking as many questions as I can before the product manager kicks me out.

My next stop is usually the support staff or engineers to verify the information, and get answers to any remaining questions. This is a lot easier than talking to the product manager. Sneak them out for a few drinks at a local pub and it's amazing what you learn: "We stopped working on that product over a year ago. Are you still selling that? Oh my God! This next one's a killer! It's half the size and twice as fast. You should bring that to the customer. Stop by tomorrow and I'll give you a copy."

Getting the real answers may be like slogging your way through a maze, but it's essential. A brand new product with technology and features that leapfrog the competition is exciting and generates a lot of buzz. On the other hand, it has no customers or historical performance data, so gaining market share is an uphill battle. You need to press whatever corporate button it takes to get the REAL FACTS.

Once a product is accepted, it gets a life of its own and you just have to keep up. As soon as it proves itself, however, up your tailpipe come the wannabes. They start to encroach on your territory and the market becomes crowded and cloudy. As the product's life cycle winds down, things are pretty gnarly as you hang on, trying to sell something that has pretty much played itself out. Identifying the sweet spot in the product cycle and capitalizing on it is something all good peddlers must do.

Not of This World

Keep this uppermost in your brain: Some product managers are oblivious to how peddling works and how damaging wrong or insufficient information can be to your relationships. They are in slow mo, driven by processes and measurements. It's a different world than you and I live in. That's why they call it the corporate world and not the real world.

STORY TIME

It's 1980 and I'm getting my feet wet selling for a large high-tech company. It's the end of a quarter and a bunch of us peddlers are trying to earn some incentive dollars with a new product. The product is so new, however, that not even the in-house support team has been trained on it. Undaunted, we dial for dollars. If we schedule some calls, our plan is to have the corporate product manager sit in and help us out.

(continued)

Within a week, I have several prospects lined up. I call up the product manager's assistant and work out a schedule.

The calls happen over the next several days, but with no help from the product manager. He misses the first two calls, is testy and rude on the third one, and acts like a jerk on the fourth. At first I'm in shock, but then I start a slow burn.

There's one more call scheduled with a marquee account and I don't want a repeat of the first four calls. Being one of the leading mini-computer vendors of office automation systems, we have company-wide e-mail, so I whip out a blazing message to the product manager. Steam is still coming out of my ears when my good buddy John strolls in. He manages the support group. Fuming, I show him a copy of my e-mail.

His eyes widen. "Dennis, we need to drive down to corporate right now."

"Why?" I ask.

"The product manager should not read this. Let's hope and pray we can get into his cube and delete it before he does."

"Huh?"

"What you wrote will get you in BIG trouble, probably a trip to HR, and maybe canned!"

"Oh."

Into the car we fly and make the 12-mile drive in record time. We jump out of the car and race through corporate to the product manager's cube. It's empty.

"Go in, find the e-mail, and delete it," John says. "I'll keep watch."

I dart into the product manager's cube and see a maze on his screen that goes beyond my modest comprehension of computers. I run back out to my buddy.

"No clue," I gasp.

"Geesh. OK, keep watch. I'm going in."

In a minute, he's back. "Done," he says, white as a sheet. Just then the product manager walks around the corner.

"What are you two doing here?" he asks.

(continued)

"We've come to see you, brotha," I say testily. He really had my Irish up. "We want to confirm that you will be participating in the last call we have scheduled, as you are currently batting zero for four and this one is a big account."

"Yes," he says warily eyeing the two of us. "I think I can make it."

I'm on the verge of taking him by the collar and telling him that he damn well better make it, when my friend speaks up. Calmly, John explains the problems it causes when he commits to a call and then doesn't show or is unhelpful. He explains how we in the field take calls seriously, and how the sales guys have families to support.

The product manager looks stunned but nods his head. "Got it. I'll do better for you today."

We had a good call that day and on many other occasions as well. From that day forward, that product manager came through for us whenever we asked for his help.

The moral to this story is that no matter how clueless or irritating some product managers are, don't do anything that alienates them or, worse, gets you fired. Rather, try to solve problems with product managers as you would with a prospect or customer—by creating a dialogue. Perhaps if I had explained to the product manager ahead of time why I needed his help and what my prospects were looking for, I wouldn't have had four calls go down the tubes.

Selling inside your company is as important as selling outside. Ya, it's hard work and time consuming. It also takes time away from being the field. If all was right in the world, you'd be fighting off engineers, marketers, product and support folks, and executives, all wanting to go along on your calls. But that ain't the way it is. No one is interested in customers, so you gotta work corporate. Work it and work it. Such is the life of the peddler. Deal with it!

PART THREE

YOUR CUSTOMER

CHAPTER 13

FINDING

When you go in search of honey you must expect to be stung by bees.

—Kenneth Kaunda

Finding deals is kind of like fishing. Number one: They are either there or they're not. Number two: If they are there, you need to know how to catch them. To catch fish you have to think like a fish, no matter how weird it gets (my friend Demi buys Storm Lures with that saying on the package). The same concept applies to finding prospects and customers, bucko.

If there aren't any customers around, then there are none to be had. I know that is stating the obvious and probably seems ridiculous to point out, but peddlers spend a lot of time looking for prospects and customers in the wrong places, and are shocked when they come up with nada.

Repeat after me: I won't do that.

So where do you find customers? A lead can surface in any number of ways. You might find a company on the Web, see a name in a database, get a tip from a friend, or perhaps the poor peddler before you left his contact list on the computer or a stack of business cards in the desk. All are fair game.

Before I tell ya how I find accounts, I've got to tell ya that leads are relatively easy to come by. The hardest part for most peddlers is IDENTIFYING them.

Identifying Leads

Your job as a peddler is to identify leads as good or bad, and then move them on or off your plate as fast as is humanly possible.

Most peddlers do just the opposite. They collect leads, horde them even, and keep adding to their stash. They like nothing better than having a lot of leads. Being the optimists that they are, there's something comforting knowing there are all those possibilities in the queue just waiting for them.

If that's you, consider yourself forewarned. When peddlers let themselves be seduced by stacks of leads, they have slipped into what I call the *Peddler's Magical Reality*. They believe everything will be all right as long as they have leads; leads will somehow, some way, turn into accounts. Their natural optimism is running wild, leading them into the fantastic, and heading straight toward the magical.

PEDDLER'S PREROGATIVE #47

It is the peddler's prerogative to avoid getting stuck in *magical reality* and not to be led astray by unreasonable hope, quiet desperation, or fanciful, wishful thinking, as it is the quickest way to get your ass in a sling!

Listen up! You don't just want leads, you want GOOD leads. A few good leads are better than a full pipeline of poor ones. In fact, I firmly believe that it's as worthwhile spending time getting bad leads off your plate as it is getting good ones on your plate.

Let's face it. In our fast-paced peddler world we don't have a lot of time every day to pick among our leads and decide which we're going to follow. We can't be indecisive or confused as to where to focus our efforts. We have to be able to grab a few and start dialing. You can do this only if you've got all good leads.

Another reason is that the bad leads on your plate can obscure the good ones. Ya, you know what I mean.

So, when you get a lead, the first thing you must do is IDENTIFY it. This takes practice and discipline, but it's what successful peddlers do.

It also takes a certain amount of vigilance. Too often good leads get snatched away and bad ones are slipped on your plate. Your manager thinks a company is a better fit for someone else. (Not so fast, pal!) A marketing 'bot gives you a lead. (Hmm . . .) The big, big boss asks you to do a favor and call on his friend. (What can I say?) Greet all with healthy skepticism. Be a good detective. Then make your own decision.

But again, you don't have all day, which brings us to the concept of right accounts and wrong accounts, and account profiles.

Right accounts are really what it's all about. If you know what a right account is, you'll be able to separate the good leads from the bad ones.

PEDDLER'S PREROGATIVE #48

There are two kinds of accounts: right accounts and wrong accounts. It is your prerogative to pursue right accounts until the cows come home. It is your unequivocal duty not to kid yourself and waste time on wrong accounts. Every peddler knows up from down and right from wrong. Stick with right accounts and ditch wrong accounts.

Some companies develop right account profiles. They analyze their product, market, customers, and so on, and create a description of their ideal customer. If your company doesn't have one, you must create one. And if it does, you must verify it.

First, look at industry segments, such as education, finance, manufacturing, retail, and so on, and select those that have a lot of right accounts—in short, vertical markets for which your stuff makes sense.

Then, within each vertical, construct an account profile of the type of company you should go after. An account profile typically specifies some broad, minimum requirements, such as company size or annual revenue, number of employees, location, or number of years in business.

It also includes the folks whom you have to get to and blow by to move down the line and make a sale. This cast of characters includes the gatekeepers, the information gatherers, evaluators, and the recommenders.

Keep account profiles simple and logical. That way, you'll be able to keep them in the front of your brain and quickly zero in on the good targets in your turf.

Peddler's Prerogative #49

When you find a right account, then it's just a question of strategy and timing before you hook them. If you pursue a wrong account, you will never get them. So stop. Don't go after wrong accounts. Peddlers have an incredible capacity to try and make wrong accounts right accounts. This is a frivolous act.

The Measurers and Analytics

If you started reading this book at the beginning, you know by now that I have a healthy disregard for the corporate types who think that the solution to any dilemma is more tracking, processing, and measuring. They firmly believe that they'll be able to divine an answer if only they have more data to analyze. Peddlers are one of their favorite subjects, if only because the age-old question from corporate is, "How can we sell more?"

Having said that, I have to agree that there are good reasons to keep score. First and foremost: We get paid by how much we sell, so they had better keep track. Second, to run a business, you need to have some idea how much money will be coming in the door and when.

The key to keeping the measurers and analytics off your back and out of your face is to agree on how to categorize prospective accounts so, ultimately, it's a binary conversation: "Mr. Measurer, it is exceedingly difficult to appease your desire to count that prospect in this month's forecast as I spoke with him for the first time only three hours ago. However, for your purposes, I can say that I've identified him as a lead."

You can see where I'm heading here. You don't want to classify any old lead as identified, only a good lead. Because you can be sure that next week, or next month—at some point—Mr. Measurer will be angling to move your identified leads onto the qualified list, and then, BLAM!, there they are on the forecast. If you try to pass off bad leads as good leads, you'll be doing a lot of backpedaling down the pike. (I'll go into the other categories for leads and prospects in the next chapter, "Selling.")

So treat every lead as suspect. Focus on who really buys your products and for what reasons. Does a lead fit the bill? You should prove to yourself that a lead is worth your time. This will also help you avoid getting stuck in the *Peddler's Magical Reality*. Be ruthless. There are no maybes here. It's either yes or no. Here's a tip: If it isn't a good lead, it's a bad one.

Generating Leads

While leads may never be in short supply, good ones always are. I often prefer to generate my own rather than slog through someone else's list. (There's probably a reason why those business cards were left behind.) Here's how I do it.

Grokking Your Company

After I join a company, the first thing I do is find out what the heck I'm selling and to whom. I start walking around with my eyes and mouth wide open in earnest curiosity asking tons of questions of anyone who will listen. Depending on their answers, I usually go pretty quickly or stay until I am thrown out. What usually happens for me is that I find one or two folks whom I like, are smart, and I can hammer constantly. I make them my friends and then bother them all the time. What are friends for?

I ask questions and I listen and I ask more questions and I listen some more. I figure that in my first couple of fly-bys I hit most of the obvious questions, which are in no particular order:

- Who are the biggest customers we have?
- Why do they buy our products?
- Who else is similar that we have not sold to yet?
- Who is the customer we can't sell no matter how hard we try?
- Who is the best peddler selling the stuff? (My new best friend.)
- Who really knows the product the best? (My second new best friend.)
- Who is the best support person? (My new bestest best friend.)
- What do customers like most about our products?
- What do customers like least?
- Who is the best executive in front of customers?
- Who likes to help?
- Who doesn't like to help, but when made to, is very good?
- Who sucks?

And the last question I always put to whomever I am chatting with is this: "So, if you were me, how would you sell the product and whom would you go after?"

I get some of my best targets from asking this *simple* question constantly. On and on I go, circling my wagon around the products and the in-house players. Because remember, boys and girls, the first thing you have to do is map your company and product.

In the finding phase, the inside folks are your best resource. They can help you find leads and grok the product. Then when you have one of those targets on the line and need help reeling them in, guess who you're going to call and who's going to be more than glad to help? The hardest sell is always going to be the inside sell—unless, of course, the prospect you're bringing in is one they recommended. Remember, we are dealing with corporate here, so if it was their idea it had to be a good one because, let's face it, they are corporate and they are truly wonderful.

I also want to find out the history of the company and the product. For these questions, I typically hit the executives first—the CEO and the V.P.'s of Sales, Marketing, and Business Development. Then I go after the product and engineering folks. Finally, I track down the founding players. These folks have been around for a while and know where all the bodies are buried. Having been there from the beginning, the founders have chronicled the entire goings on of the company in their heads and have been eyewitnesses to most of the pivotal moments.

PEDDLER'S PREROGATIVE #50

It is your prerogative as a peddler to understand the entire history of the company, its products, and services. It's your prerogative to know why and how they were created. It is important to understand the historical perspective so that you become an authority and can chronicle the product inside your head. It is your absolute prerogative to get this information from the people in the know. It is not their prerogative to put you off, ever.

Back to Ground Zero

After I learn the history of my company and the product, how the product works, and who's who in the zoo, I typically try to validate my obvious hunches about how I would sell the product. To do this, you have to find the person or persons in house who understand the product technically and are savvy about the market.

It may sound brash, but I go right back to ground zero and start validating all the assumptions and big decisions that have been made to date with regard to the product, as well as the positioning, marketing, and selling methodologies. I do this to make the product and the company mine.

If you are going to be a good peddler, you have to go through the magic act of taking ownership in your brain of the company and the product. Once it becomes yours in your mind, then you innately do the right things for the care and feeding of these great possessions. It's the Zen of peddlery: You need to get the product inside your head and you have to get inside the product's head.

It usually takes me anywhere from three to six months to really learn and validate a product. My goal is to know as much about the product as anyone else. Sometimes, because I am fresh I know it better than some of the in-house folks who are stale. It is so funny when in a relatively new position and armed with enough product knowledge to be dangerous, I go into a meeting and start spouting off. Looks of horror and surprise, mental notes all around: Watch out for this guy. Who me?

Don't let the three to six months fool you into thinking that in the meantime I am doing nothing, because that is far from the truth. If I don't know the product yet, I have no problem dragging the folks in the know along with me on calls.

When you think about it, if you have to be productive from the get-go and you don't have the knowledge, it only makes sense to find someone that does. Then, while you're preparing for a sales call and traveling together, you have an expert with you for hours on end. I take full advantage of this time to get fantastic, one-on-one training. It's a fact of life: The more you know about your product, the more you will sell.

I also grok the product by living with the techies and the in-the-know product folks. In the beginning, I may have no idea what they're all talking about. But I hang around them so much and listen to the ongoing dialogue that I begin to learn the product literally through osmosis. Eventually, I'm at the point where I have a pretty thorough understanding of the product.

I also sit through bunches of presentations. In particular, I listen to the CTO's pitch until I have it memorized, along with his answers to the 25 or 30 most-commonly-asked questions. Pretty soon I can parrot his pitch. Having repeated this process so many times over the years, I am a pretty quick study. But please make no mistake: This is a quick and dirty solution only; you need to really learn your product!

The Rub

Let's see, where are we? OK, we start learning the product, which can take as long as six months. The rub is that we never have that luxury. While we're learning the product, we also have to find some leads, map the company, line up some meetings, make presentations, and get some deals cooking at the same time. This is the peddling life. You're never allowed to really figure out what the heck you're selling before you sell it. Deal with it.

Another funny thing about being a peddler is that the conditions under which you are selling your product are never good. You have a proven product, but it lacks new features. You have a new product, but no installed base. You're an established company, but in a mature (read: saturated) market. You're a new company trying to figure out where the market is. And on and on it goes.

In peddlery everything is in more or less of a whacked-out state constantly. Your job is to keep your head screwed on straight enough to find deals despite it all.

Here's a tip that can make your job easier: Peddle quality products that are genuinely useful. Peddling useless stuff to folks who don't really need it is ridiculous.

Your Competitors' Customers

This is a no-brainer: An account that is using a competitor's product is a prequalified lead. The good news is that all it takes is a little investigating to map out how that particular deal got done. With a few calls, you can find out who evaluated the product, who signed off on the purchase, who bought it, who administers it, and who actually uses it. You can get to see the whole process laid out.

STORY TIME

I am working for a content management company, helping them ramp up sales. We have a great little product, but sales are at an all time low (tough economy). We need to get something cooking fast, so we go to one of our competitors' Web sites, right to the customers/partners section and, BLAM!, there's a list. One particular customer is a big financial player in our geographic area, so we make a few calls.

Because we know this company bought our competitor's product, we know who to call—the V.P. of Content. When we get him on the phone, we tell him the reason we are calling is to see how he likes our competitor's product and how our product might augment or complement the current solution.

Being an astute executive, he agrees to see us. It doesn't take him long to figure out that although he isn't going to change vendors, he does see a use for our product. The competitor's product is complex and unwieldy, and difficult to use for the company's ad hoc, one-off, content needs. On the other hand, our product is simple and straightforward, and would be a good fit for that purpose.

As we chat, we discover how much the client spent on the competitor's solution, and how long it took to implement it. We also learn the duration of the sales cycle and who was the champion that ran the deal through.

We had a choice. We could have ruled out the competitor's customers, believing that the sales had already been made, or, as we did, we could call them up, get a meeting, and learn why they bought the competitor's products and what they had that was so compelling. We didn't let the obvious fact that we had already missed the boat stop us. As it turned out, we found a fit and got a deal done. We were happy to be sharing the account with our competitor instead of being on the outside looking in.

After you map out the process for one of your competitor's customers, call the next customer and see if the process was the same or different. Then the next one. And so it goes. After you've validated the process several times, you have a selling map—the in-house purchasing process, and the players. Now you know where to go, what to do, and who to talk to.

This is also a way of validating your company's selling map. If your company's marketing department is suggesting another approach, you can say, "Hey! This is how it is bought in our market! CHECK YOUR DATA, CHUMPS!"

The Look Alikes

If you know who your competitors' customers are, you can target companies that look just like them. You can also use that selling map to assess leads and find prospects. Let's face it: Whether you got a new job, a new product, or a new territory, you don't have a lot of time to show some results. So, you have to be adroit and find the obvious leads first. Pick the low hanging fruit and get some deals cooking. Then figure out a way to get on up the tree.

Front and Center

I keep track of my leads on a whiteboard. It's not high-tech, but it works for me. I hang it on my wall so I have all my leads in front of me at all times. I can always see what I have and, more importantly, what I don't have in the pipeline.

I divvy up the board into four or more columns and write my leads in the appropriate one:

- Targets that fit a unique profile
- Competitors' Customers/Look Alikes
- Industry Vertical #1
- Industry Vertical #2

Seeing where particular leads fall can help you decide where to spend your time. If you need to get some deals in the works fast, you might focus on a Look Alike. However, if one of your verticals is government and it's budget season, then maybe that's where you should spend your time.

Desperation

Finding leads can drive peddlers to distraction. Perhaps you are a new peddler or new at a company and your pipeline is drained, your goal has been increased (it's never decreased), or you are facing some new-fangled pressure tactic that management has contrived to get you to produce more. In spite of it all, on some predetermined schedule, usually monthly or quarterly, you must show your stuff and bring home the bacon.

At times like these, it is very easy to fall down the desperation rat hole. You are constantly being monitored and measured. You're stressed. You allow demons inside your head. Then nothing is the same. I've seen desperate peddlers walking around with a glazed look in their eyes, chanting, "Must find deal. Must find deal." I've seen the nicest peddlers become bullies, and salt-of-the-earth peddlers become delusional and psychotic. When a peddler gets into this state, it is not a good thing for anyone in his or her orbit.

So, let's get down to the real issues that surface when a peddler is desperate. First, you lose your sense of right and wrong, and your reality gets pretty fuzzy. When you are not thinking straight, you are not acting straight either. Desperate peddlers do desperate things.

Second, because you have a distorted view of reality, you may lose the clarity you need to keep all your sales stuff simple and straightforward. Third, how can you accomplish anything when you are losing it? In short, when you let yourself become desperate, you've just given the proverbial snowball a big push down the "I'm going to run myself over" mountain.

The peddler's world is stressful and can seem desperate especially in the finding stage, because guess what? You always start with nada. A peddler literally has to create something from nothing all the time. This is not for the weak of heart. It all boils down to the fact that finding opportunities is really hard, tedious work.

Keep in mind that the better you are at finding, the better you will be at selling and closing. You have to learn how to find good prospects. Don't think that once you get past the finding stage, you'll be fine. Not so. Here's the key to being a good finder: knowing your company well, having an intimate understanding of your product, and last but not least, having a clear understanding of the customer that buys your product.

When you feel yourself slipping into the desperate realm, pull yourself back out. Enlist the help of others if necessary. Often, peddlers try to hide—or worse, deny—the problem. Don't!

STORY TIME

A group of venture capitalists invested in an Internet direct-marketing company. They put a lot of money into this company, hired the requisite engineers and sales folks, got the product almost done, but weren't seeing any sales. Sound familiar? Someone recommended that they contact me because of my sales and Internet marketing background, and send me in as a troubleshooter.

They book me on a flight to Boulder, Colorado, where the company is located. When I get to Logan Airport, I meet one of the directors of the company. He's the CTO of a big software company on the west coast as well as an Irish kid from Boston. Hey, just like me!

We board the plane and have a great time on the flight. He's a real hot ticket. When we finally get around to talking about the company, he reiterates his and the VC's concern about the head of sales. He wants me to check him out, peddler to peddler. In short, he wants to know if the guy is for real or slinging B.S. He tells me everyone's frustrated because no one can get a straight answer to

(continued)

a simple question: Are you finding any business? Needless to say I laughed and told him that I would be able to tell fairly quickly. I didn't tell him I could probably tell just by looking at the guy!

So we mosey on into the People's Republic of Boulder and meet the engineers who are trying to launch an Internet marketing company. What's wrong with this picture? But that's another story. The director and I meet with the CEO, CTO, V.P. of Sales, and V.P. of Engineering. The director introduces me and explains that I'm here to help assess how sales are going. I start out by asking them each to tell me something about themselves.

As the introductions roll around to the alleged peddler, I size him up. As he tells me about himself it becomes apparent that he has spent his career in medium to big companies, and has little knowledge of bootstrap startups. So I ask him, how's it going? He gives me an unfriendly look (no points for that, bucko) and says it's going real well.

"What does real well mean?" I ask. The engineers start shifting around in their seats.

"Well, we haven't closed anything yet, but we're close."

"Great! How many deals have you got cooking?"

"About a dozen or so."

"OK, let's go through the top three." I get up and walk to the white board. "What's your biggest deal?"

The peddler becomes enraged, saying he doesn't have to play freakin' sales 101 and doesn't have to explain his deals to some fly-in from Boston.

"Be very careful with the rope you're tugging on," I warn him. "You might not like what you find on the other end." I wasn't about to back down or be intimidated by a temper tantrum from this new-age peddler from Boulder. I also knew it was a sure sign that things were not going well.

In jumps the rest of the team, trying to calm the situation and telling the peddler that we're just trying to get a status on sales. The peddler collects himself, goes to the white board, and starts to talk about his best deal. I listen and then start to ask some questions.

"Have we mapped the account?"

(continued)

"It's not necessary. I've sold to one of the guys before."

"Has your guy explained how you can get the deal done?"

"No, I don't have to worry. He'll come through."

"It's real hard for me to feel all warm and fuzzy about this deal."

The peddler turns red, but stays calm. Onto the next deal . . .

"I feel real good about this one."

"How many meetings have you had?"

"One, but it was very promising."

"Really. How long did you meet with them?"

"About 30 minutes."

"If these are your top two deals, Houston, we got a problem!"

With that, the peddler picked up his things. "I don't have to stand for this," he says, throws me a look, and marches out of the room.

Within hours, the powers that be decided to dismiss the peddler. I met with him later that day to tell him. Surprisingly, he was polite and solicitous during our meeting. It was as if it was a relief. Who knew?

The moral of the story: Be honest with yourself and your manager. This isn't a peddler self-help book, but if any work group needs to be hyperaware of stress and desperation it's the peddler. Don't ignore it. Don't give in to it. Be on the lookout for it. Because it can kill you.

On that cheery note, it's time to take a look at more finding techniques.

Finding 102

After you've ramped up and are feeling more comfortable with your company, the products, and your territory, you should try other techniques for finding leads.

The Perfect Fit—It Just Feels Soooo Right!

Understanding the similarities between your products and your competitors' is essential when looking for leads and prospects. Equally important, however, is how they are different, because you can turn differences into an edge and pull accounts that fit your company's unique target profile.

Here's a tactic that is simple yet works. Always be questioning your company's product positioning. If you do, you may find an edge that's been missed or glossed over. It may be insignificantly small or glaringly large. Ya, glaringly large. But the only way to find it is to constantly rethink the product positioning. You don't need to dwell on it for hours on end, just keep it in the front of your brain and be on the lookout for something that will give you an advantage.

STORY TIME

Once upon a time, there was a high-profile, tech company that was run by a bunch of venture capitalists who hired only seasoned, best-of-breed managers who knew how to make things happen.

One day, one of my buddies gives me a jingle. He tells me he's been hired at this company, and asks me to come on board and help ramp the puppy. Of course, I jump in with both feet. Because it's my buddy, I believe the story he feeds me regarding how sales are doing. My bad. He is not a sales guy. I should have known to do my own due diligence and run the flag up the proverbial pole.

Like a lot of companies, it was a bunch of engineers that started this one. Unlike a lot of companies, however, the engineers decided they would do the initial selling. In true engineering fashion, they went after the folks who they thought would like the new product, who of course were folks just like them—engineers. Then they narrowed their target market to academic science labs. Heaven help me!

It took me all of one week to realize that all the business they allegedly had lined up equaled zero. Oh, the engineers had had lots of meetings and they did lots of presentations, but they hadn't closed a single deal, and they weren't going to. What the engineers-turned-peddlers didn't know is that generally, academic science labs don't have the budgets for such a high-ticket item,

(continued)

and the engineers in the labs have no decision-making responsibility or authority over the lab budget.

To make matters worse, when the company finally hired marketing folks, no one questioned or verified the basic premises. They just took up the cause and charged blindly ahead. I was in an insane asylum of cavalier, wanna-be peddlers and frivolous, would-be marketers.

Needless to say, it was my job to explain to the engineers, who were sure that they'd close a deal any day now, that it wasn't going to happen. It was also my job to break the news to the watchmen and stewards of the company, and explain that engineers can't be peddlers any more than peddlers can be engineers.

I also had to figure out just where sales were going to come from. I eventually found a great vertical for the product where we could demonstrate compelling savings using our product. (But that's another story.)

I don't want to cause a riot in corporations (well, maybe a little one), but I have to tell ya, QUESTION, QUESTION, QUESTION everything coming out of corporate! The most relevant data in the world is what you learn in the field, first hand, from your prospects and customers. The fact that this information is disregarded or misunderstood is the problem of the corporate marketers and the feeble executives who support them.

When you come up with something that might give you an edge, try it! I'm not saying to do this every time with every call. But don't stick to the script if you have something worth trying. Don't tell yourself that it's too far out or it just won't work. You won't know until you try it. OK, now say it: I just won't do that!

The net-net is that differences give you an edge, so find them and make the most of them.

The RFP: Someone Writes It All Down!

Companies and government agencies often announce that they are looking for a product or have an RFP (Request for Proposal) out. After you are in a market a while, there are many ways to monitor and be part of the RFP process. However, getting started can be tough. These are usually very controlled situations, so you must be vigilant and find ways to get yourself in the running.

I like to find the straightest line between two points, so I find the group or person that is tasked with writing RFPs for my product. Then I find a way to work with these folks, be helpful, and wire myself into their RFPs. The best way to get a leg up is to send the RFP writers your responses to other RFPs. They can glean the information that should be in their request from your answers. This makes their jobs easier, as it takes a lot of time and energy to write RFPs, and helps you gain the advantage.

I cannot tell you how many times I have obtained an RFP only to read it and realize that I don't have a shot, because another peddler has wired it for his product and company. Sometimes it is so obvious it's laughable. It's a two-way street, my friends.

The Peddler's Prospect Mall

I like to think of my region or area like a big mall: the peddler's prospect mall. Everything's conveniently in one place and I'm shopping for all kinds of deals. Like at any mall, I'm interested in finding out which companies are the anchors; they are typically the marquee names. I do this for three reasons. First, you always want to know the prize accounts in your turf. Second, often there are secondary accounts that are nearby. Third, in some cases, between two anchor accounts is a corridor of companies. So locate the big names, and you're bound to find some smaller targets nearby.

This strategy pays off when you get on the road. I like to set up as many calls as I can when I am out. If I know where the accounts are, I can line up meetings in geographical order and jam my schedule. This takes some planning, but it's important to spend most

of your time in front of prospects and not driving around. When you're in an area, you might as well do as much shopping as you can, which means if your schedule isn't packed or something falls out, cold call for "that day" visits.

Prospects and Customers

Here's another one of my must-ask questions. Whenever I'm with a prospect or customer, as the meeting ends I always ask, "Now that you know what our products are, who else would you go after in this region?"

Ask this simple question to all the right people. It's amazing how much intelligence you can gather this way. A right person would be someone who is breathing and can speak your language.

Line 'Em Up!

When you get a strategic or important call scheduled—something worthwhile to put on the radar screen—the next step is to line up some of the key characters at your company and enlist their support. Then, plan to use the heck out of them. You pretty much own the day and night of them, so make the most of it.

Figure out who else you could call on in the same vicinity, region, and state. A good peddler works these guys from one high-profile call to a week of meetings. The results are always better when you have the heavy hitters from corporate in tow. Not only does it help you get some deals cooking at the prospect's, but back home, they'll champion your deals when you're doing that all important inside sell.

I ask whomever I am hauling with me if there is anyone in the area with whom they would like to meet. Inevitably there is someone whom, as long as we're going to be in the area, they would like to drop in on. Pretty soon I am working a list of targets with whom my executives would love to connect. I am now calling high with a reason, and my hit rate for closing these meetings is high: "Hello, I am calling for Mr. V.P., and he asked if it would be possible to set up a meeting in two weeks, as we are going to be in town. We are very flexible and can meet any time, including breakfast or dinner."

The last minute, "we just happen to be in town and close by" call works wonders for filling in any scheduling holes. For some reason when you call someone on the spur of the moment, tell them you are here with so and so, explain that you have a call right next door, and say that if they have a minute you would really appreciate being able to stop by, Blam!, they find the time.

Take heed, peddler. This tactic works whether you are cold calling a prospect (first visit), meeting a prospect you've been calling on, or trying to see someone else at a company even though you're already inside. While this technique works amazingly well when you have the extra firepower with you, it also works just fine when you are alone.

When traveling with corporate types, don't hesitate to leverage them in every which way you can. You have all the face time you need and can create. Use it well and you'll look good; screw it up and you'll look real bad. It's a double-edged sword; you need to be hyperaware of this when you are playing host to the most.

I could give you the full list of do's and don'ts, but you can figure that out. Just use your peddler head. Always make sure you know where you're going; never, ever, get lost and wind up being late, or screw up the time and place of a meeting. Always validate the meeting times and places the day before. Always. Prep the corporate folks a few days ahead of time, explaining where you are going and why, and what they need to do and look out for. Don't wing it! Prepare thyself.

When you are planning a trip never block yourself. For that matter never block yourself, period! When you are asking to set an appointment, keep it wide open and don't ever close off your options. Go after accounts with a wide-open schedule, not an hour slot that you have to squeeze someone into.

For example, if you have an afternoon open, say afternoon, dinner, or anytime the next day. That way you have given more than enough leeway to the person you want to see. It is that flexibility that gives them the opening. If they really do want to see you they can find some time. If you give them enough flexibility and they still can't make time then guess what? They don't want to see you or the timing may be wrong. So ask them if this is the case: "Hey, Mr. V.P., is it that you are too busy and don't have the time, or is it you just don't think it's appropriate yet? I figured I would ask, Mr. V.P., so I know whether I should or shouldn't bother you some more." I love when they say, "No, no, it's OK to bother me."

Some peddlers know that they can always get the important folks out on the road if they have secured a meeting with a big name. So they line up key corporate personnel to make calls on certain big accounts or prospects, only to have the meeting be mysteriously canceled (wink wink) as soon as they all get off the plane. No problem, they still have a full schedule—albeit meeting with prospects the big honchos typically wouldn't see. And, after a "we're in town" call, it turns out the BIG prospect suddenly finds time later in the day. You peddlers get my drift, aye?

Be the Best in Your Company

Finding deals for me is easy. I am a very creative thinker, and I have a burning desire to show everyone just how gosh darn smart I am. One way I have found to do this is by finding leads better than most anybody else. I love putting on the show and bragging, give me a phone and a desk and stay out of the way. I like to back myself into a corner and then prove how good I am. I am a confident, cocky, wise-guy peddler when it comes to finding leads. So pay attention and you, too, can impress and amaze your friends and family, not to mention keep your boss out of your pajamas.

STORY TIME

I once was a peddler in a Fortune 500 sales force. Believe it or not, these organizations have the same issues as their small and mid-tier counterparts, which is how to get the sales representatives more focused and more productive. The real question, of course, is how to get the hunters hunting and the farmers farming.

The V.P. of Sales got an idea to have a two-pronged sales strategy, which divided the sales force into existing account managers (farmers) and new account managers (hunters). The existing account mangers did the care and feeding of customers that had already bought. This meant they were to focus on servicing and growing the existing accounts. The new account managers had no accounts and were tasked with going after new business. Any new business they closed they kept for a year before turning over to the other side of the house.

(continued)

This new program generated a ton of discussion in my regional sales office the few weeks before it was implemented. At that point in time, most of us were married with young kids, and making the mortgage and car payments was crucial. The big question buzzing around the office was who was going to have to drum up new accounts, which was dicey by most peoples' observations, and who was going to get the existing sweet accounts, which was just maintaining and milking them for add-ons and upgrades.

The existing account reps would receive a higher salary and a 2.5% commission; the new account reps had a lower salary but got a 4.2% commission. The incentive was that after you made your number your commissioned doubled. I was never really very good at math, but it took me all of a nanosecond to figure out that 8.4% of a million dollars was $84,000.00.

Needless to say, I was the first one at the door to volunteer for the new account program. I have always been a risk taker and that program to me was risky, but the upside was incredible. I had the confidence that I could go out and break the bank. Also, because I was just starting out in sales, I knew there was no way I was getting anything handed to me on a silver platter.

I will end with this: About nine months into the program I received a frantic phone call from my wife. She called and said the bank made some kind of mistake and that there was about $84,000 extra in our bank account. When I got home she showed me the statement and I was in shock. Then I realized, hey, that's our money! The company had paid me my commission through direct deposit and I was in double money. I knew I was on a roll, but I had just kept my head down, sold my butt off, and never even looked at how I was doing or how much I was making.

That night we went to the local Volvo dealer (what can I say, it was the '80s) and paid cash for two spanking-new Volvos. I closed eight new accounts that year from scratch. I wound up getting the "Salesman of the Year" award for my area and region. I went to Hawaii with the "Million Dollar Club" and all was right with the world.

Until I got back and got my new goal.

It is important to remember that your peddler attitude has a lot to do with your success. Before you call on an account, you need to believe there is a fit. Then, you need to visualize yourself selling that account. If you've done your homework—you know your product and your prospect—and you're not skirting the *Peddler's Magical Reality*, then you can go in with confidence.

Also keep in mind that tenacity is key when finding accounts. You may get unequivocal no's the first several times you call into a new account. If you persevere you will get a meeting eventually. I like it when I get no's because I have to figure out how to get a yes. I look at it this way: Any company I think is a right account eventually will be a customer of mine. They just haven't realized it yet!

Let's face it, sometimes everything's right but the timing. If you see a fit but you're too early, be patient, wait for the right moment, and then strike!

PEDDLER'S PREROGATIVE #51

When you find a target or prospect that's "right," it is absolutely your peddler's prerogative to immediately start to see and think of them as a customer, they just haven't realized it yet! So be it.

Keep It Real

If you look at it from the perspective of the people at the other end of the phone or the other side of the desk, they probably get tons of calls every day from bothersome, pushy sales folk. So your first goal is to bring some humanness to the conversation. Of course, I'm presupposing that you are indeed human and not a poser. On guard, poser!

This may seem like I'm emphasizing the obvious, but as I've said, being a good peddler is all about simple concepts and truths. Once you bring another person into your reality then you have a place. Once you become a real live person to another person they hold a place for you inside themselves, and that spot gets reactivated when you call again. Eventually, the person you keep calling will get to know you and when that happens, a relationship begins.

I have this crazy notion that giving people a glimpse of my life at any particular moment is amusing to us both. So I tend to be a color commentator on my life to just about anyone and everyone. If someone does listen then I try to engage them in a conversation, usually something funny, topical, or philosophical. And I use my Boston accent to the maximum when traveling outside New England. The deal is you have to try and find some common ground that takes you from being just a peddler doing your obligatory spiel to somebody that is real. Getting to be "somebody" is probably the single hardest part of the cold-calling process.

The Peddler's Truth

Before I stop yakking about finding accounts, I'll leave you with some truths that I have learned along the way. First and foremost, get yourself into the finding mode. It's hard to go traipsing about, looking under every rock for new accounts to call on. But you have to do it, and it is so much easier when you have your head into it and are fully engaged.

Don't try to go it alone. That's a waste of time. You need to ask everyone and his brother if they were you who would they go after, and then cherry pick the best suggestions. I like to start with the CEO and ask which account in my territory he or she would most love to see as a customer. Then I set up the meeting.

Finding deals is about getting up and away from your desk, and asking anyone and everyone who you should go after. Sure you need to come up with a bunch of targets on your own, but getting as much input is what it's all about. Don't try and be a one man band. Assembling your team and getting many folks engaged on your behalf is a beauteous thing.

Think out of the box. Get way out in the margins and open up your mind. The best way to find deals is to really, really think about who would be a great account to call upon. Thinking is more important then action in peddlery. It is imperative to create activity, but mindless activity is fruitless.

When you are thinking about how to find deals, always go to the blatantly obvious first, then to the polling method, on to the grand castle in the sky scenario, ending with the bold stroke vision. Never say never, and don't presuppose that you know anything about anything until you have picked up the phone and heard a prospect say "no way" or get laughed at in an unfunny manner.

PEDDLER'S PREROGATIVE #52

When prospecting and finding deals it is your prerogative to never say never on any idea or presuppose that this or that will not work until you have actually tried it by picking up the phone or getting in front of and talking to the prospect. If you think you can't then you can't! This kind of predictive attitude is stupid. Says me!

When you get a hot lead, stay cool and keep it under wraps. This is imperative. Peddlers have a penchant for making mountains out of molehills and announcing a prospect as if they just closed a deal. Filter yourself. Don't brag. The longer you can keep it off management's and corporate's radar screens the better. Once you reveal it, it is gobbled up by the "process," and now you and your prospect have to deal with process mojo, which in most companies is a pain in the butt.

The strategies above should serve you quite handily. We will leave the Viking method of pillaging and plundering your fellow peddlers' leads and turf for your illustrious sales manager's pontification. I wouldn't be surprised to learn that the Viking method is how your sales manager got to where he or she currently is! Quick hide your leads! JUST KIDDING!

CHAPTER 14

SELLING

Everyone lives by selling something.
—Robert Louis Stevenson

In the previous chapter we talked about finding deals. The world is full of targets. Your job is to find the leads among them, identify the leads as good or bad, and then get them on or off your plate as fast as possible.

A good lead is a company that is within a vertical market that you've identified as chock full of opportunity, is within your territory, and matches your account profile. A good lead has a good chance of being a fit for your product.

So, what's a fit? This is the obvious question for the peddler. As I mentioned previously, you have a fit when a company has a real need for your product; when the timing is right; and when a company has the money to pay for it. If a lead passes this initial qualification test, SHAZAM!, it becomes a prospect. It becomes a HOT prospect if it wants your product in a time frame that is relevant to your current monthly or quarterly goals.

Sometimes, these three simple things are easy to recognize. More often than not, each becomes a universe unto themselves in the sales process. No matter. Easy or hard, peddlers must train themselves to honestly assess when this metamorphosis occurs, and not mistake leads for prospects or prospects for leads.

The Ten Percenter

The first stage of the sales process is what I call The Ten Percenter. It's the phase when a lead expresses an interest, shows some signs of life, and officially becomes a prospect. Ideally, a lead articulates some need related to a project, a goal, or some kind of defining event with a real deadline. This is when you have a meeting or two and a dialogue starts to happen. When you get a prospect, you are in the game and playing for money, although your chances of turning a prospect into a customer are only 10% at this stage. You are at the beginning of the pipeline, or "the pipe" as I like to call it.

The pipe is a way to measure the progress of a prospect or deal. It's the antidote to fruitless and exasperating forecasting meetings. Ya, the ones where field reps assess their deals, the corporate folks press for more, the field reps reassess, the corporate folks toss out numbers and closing dates, the field reps hesitate, and the corporate folks move in: "We're in control here. Show us everything you got and we'll decide what goes into our forecast." This is not a good thing.

First off, this lets corporate select potential deals that fulfill their projections, rather than forces them to analyze the status of prospects and deals, and make projections. As a result, deals wind up on forecasts before the prospects have even been qualified. If a prospect hasn't been qualified, there's NO WAY a deal will be baked and ready to close any time soon.

And yet, as we all know, once a deal's on the forecast, there's increased pressure to close it. This is the second problem. Whether or not it should be on the forecast to begin with, whether or not the prospect has been qualified, whether or not it's ready to close—that's all besides the point. It's on the forecast and immense pressure is put on the peddler, the prospect, and the corporate folks to get it done, generating bad vibes all around.

The third issue is because the forecast contains unqualified deals, it is unreliable. We have seen this backfire time and time again. Wishful corporate thinking replaces honest numbers, which at the very least wreaks havoc, and at the worst results in fraud.

The root of the problem is really the lack of consensus between peddlers and corporate as to how to classify deals, which usually stems from a lack of dialogue. Tasked with forecasting sales, the corporate folks set out to develop a model to measure peddlers' progress. Corporate, however, is clueless about carrying a bag and gets zero input from the peddlers. Therefore, it creates a model that has no relevance to what's actually happening in the field. The outcome is more useless meetings that would tax the patience of a saint:

Mr. Measurer:	"What I need to know is when you're going to close the deal, how big it is, who's going to sign the contract, and when."
Peddler:	"Before I can help you, Mr. Measurer, I need to get the blessing of the gatekeeper, pass muster with the evaluator, find the navigator, and befriend the recommender."
Mr. Measurer:	"OK, I'll put you down to close by the end of the month. Now, how big is the deal?"
Peddler:	"What I'm trying to say, Mr. Measurer, is that you should take the deal off your forecast."
Mr. Measurer:	"That won't look very good for you."
Peddler:	"But I wasn't the one who put it on the forecast, Mr. Measurer."

If your company doesn't have a way to classify your deals, do WHATEVER IT TAKES to get everyone singing from the same hymnal. Get the peddlers and corporate in the same room. Get a dialogue going. Have the peddlers outline what it takes to do a deal. Have corporate decide how to measure those milestones. Get the peddlers' feedback. Get corporate input. See the pattern?

It's imperative that every peddler understands the dynamic between corporate and the field, and that corporate understands the peddler's wacky world. There will be a lot fewer schisms if everyone can grok what the hey is going on, not to mention a lot less fuzzy math.

PEDDLER'S PREROGATIVE #53

When it comes to deals, pipelines, and forecasts, it is the peddler's prerogative to understand the agreement between corporate and the field. What is a qualified prospect? When does a deal enter the pipeline? And when does a deal go on the forecast? If the answers seem fuzzy or look funny, the adroit peddler should adjust accordingly and vacate the premises.

Typically, I consider deals to be in my pipeline when they meet the criteria of a ten percenter. Before that I call them noise. Deals can fall out of my pipe at any time for any number of reasons, although if they reach 100%, they exit as customers.

By the way, do not confuse your pipe with your manager's. Yours kicks in with a ten percenter. But you shouldn't let a prospect enter your manager's pipe until there's a 50% probability you'll close a deal. (Says me! Your manager and the corporate measurers probably disagree.)

Customers are accounts on the books of your company. Accounts owe your company money, because you sold and they bought. When accounts pay, you get paid. So listen up, students of peddlery. We are going to discuss how to make you cash, which is why we are all here. True dat, Bill!

When you're in the 10% stage, you're likely talking or meeting with the information gatherers or the gatekeepers. These two groups are part of the corporate geography, and you must meet with them to qualify a prospect and figure out if you have the makings of a deal.

The Information Gatherers

Usually, the information gatherers are folks who are good at ferreting out information and understanding technical details. They don't necessarily know all the specifics as to why they have been assigned a task, what the information will be used for, or when it will be used—in short, they can't answer our all-important peddler questions. All they know is they've been asked to collect info on some stuff.

Sometimes peddlers try to make an information gatherer more important or pivotal than he or she is; this is always a waste of time and effort. Recognize it as a simple information transaction. That's what it is! Provide the info in as nice a package as you can, then go on your merry way. It is not an automatic lead, prospect, or deal when you hand out some information. Maybe it's a target. Deal with it!

Having said that, you can't take anything for granted. You must probe to make sure the info gatherer is just a lowly marketing 'bot and not more than that. I remember a conversation I once had with an info gatherer. I asked him what he was looking to do.

"Who me? I'm just getting some data for some stuff we're looking at."

"What stuff?" I ask.

"Oh, I'm trying to understand what companies are doing in this area and the products they have, and then I pass the info along to the folks in our company."

"What for?" I ask.

"We are trying to make some decisions, I guess."

"Well, who are you and what do you do?"

"Who me? Oh! I'm the CTO of IBM's Life Sciences Group."

Bingo!

Keep in mind that the answer could have been that he was a student doing an internship. In fact, most info gathers are interns rather than key players. A CEO asks his S.V.P. to identify the top 10 vendors that sell a specific product. The S.V.P. delegates the task to his V.P., who gives it to a department manager, who assigns it to an associate, who passes it on to an assistant, who gives it to the intern. That's corporate for you.

However, sometimes CEOs and other top-level executives are in a hurry and don't want to wait around for the information. They can do a Google search as quick as the next guy and line up a couple of meetings. So ask who and why. You never know!

Open Sesame—The Gatekeepers

The gatekeepers keep you out or let you in. Most accomplish this by making all roads lead to them. They tell the receptionists, administrators, and everyone that counts, "SEND THEM TO ME."

Other gatekeepers, however, are pulled into the game on an as-needed basis, or as you and your product are qualified by the prospect.

Let's say you are calling or e-mailing high, and you actually get through—you get someone in the C suite on the line. They refer you down the ladder to someone else, or then days later, someone else calls you back. You're thinking, hmmm, maybe I will see some action here. This person is the gatekeeper.

The gatekeepers usually are the in-the-know folks, and part of their job descriptions is to parse good things into the company and turn away nuisances. For the most part, gatekeepers are easy to find, as they tend to be in the product organization or the executive suite. They usually are knowledgeable about their company's markets and products. They are easy to get by if you have something that makes sense, but they do not suffer fools gladly.

The gatekeepers are also busy folks, and besieged by peddlers who are trying to get by them, so it's hard to get their attention. Your best bet is to send them some crisp, timely information that you know they need. Of course, to know what they need, you have to do your homework. These are binary folks. You won't get by them with glad-handing and chicanery, but solid, concise, bottom-line rationale works well. Oops! There's that credibility thing again (although it never hurts to be friendly and personable, too).

The gatekeepers are not going to give you a lot of opportunities to get into their companies. Your first attempt must be well thought out and well planned, and you must be organized. Before you contact them, for example, have an e-mail package ready to send as soon as you get off the phone. Before you meet with them, make sure you know your stuff. If you don't, bring someone with you who does. If you tell a gatekeeper that you want to bring one of your company's great folks to talk to him or her personally, most likely you'll get one of two reactions. They will volunteer to bring some of their folks as well—or not. If they don't, then you know this gatekeeper's got clout.

Either way, get a meeting scheduled. Get in there! Use the gatekeeper to map the company's players and how their process works. Of course, you should do your own map first.

Mapping a Company

There are various ways to map a company. At one extreme are the peddlers who approach it like a reconnaissance mission. They gather all the information they can find and comb through it before the big meeting. They do nothing short of an exhaustive analysis of the prospect, its competition, and the industry.

At the other extreme are peddlers like me who do enough research to have a general idea of the prospect's business, and gather the rest through real-time, toe-to-toe dialogue.

STORY TIME

I have a friend, Dave, who I've worked with at a few companies over the years, sometimes as a peer, and sometimes as a direct report. He is one smart dude. A screaming analytic. A guy's whose motor is always humming.

As a CEO, Dave is famous for his all-hands-on-deck summonses. In anticipation of a first call or an important meeting, he often calls a time out for his executive team and launches a full-court press on a prospect and its industry niche. He's a Web maven, and his capacity and skill for collecting and associating massive amounts of data in a short time is almost frightening. In a 24-hour period, I've seen him go from knowing nothing about a company and its market to having a rollicking, right-on-the-money, straight-to-the-heart-of-the-matter, impressive chat with a prospect.

(continued)

The thing about Dave is he knows that there are other ways that work just as well. He realizes that this methodology is right for him, but he also respects and accepts alternatives. This makes Dave a great leader in my eyes. Flexibility and openness should be the guiding principles of the methodologies used in corporate environments. Too often, however, the way of the guy or gal at the top becomes law. But what works for some peddlers doesn't work for others. Is that so hard to see? THIS IS NOT ROCKET SCIENCE.

Anyway, Dave always leaves me out of his drills, because he knows my attention span is that of a toddler when it comes to dissecting a company's soul via the Web. He also knows that my method is opposite of his, but it works for me.

I pick up the phone or get in front of a prospect having a general idea of their business, but not the nitty gritty details. I then use my people skills to get the prospect to tell me what I need to know. I get the facts straight away and synthesize in real time. I check my interpretations and clear up any misconceptions on the fly. Don't get me wrong. Before I meet with a prospect, I gather as much data as I think I'm going to need. I'm just comfortable with a lot less than Dave.

It's a freaky thing for a guy like Dave to go into a meeting cold (which is his perception of what I do). He wants to assemble all the data beforehand and then confirm it through dialogue with the prospect. He also has the idea in his head that this puts him on a level playing field with the prospect. I, on the other hand, have no problem asking a lot of questions and having the prospect educate me through dialogue. I can read in between the lines of a one-on-one conversation better than Dave, and he can parse Web bullshit better than me.

It gets raucous when Dave and I double-team a prospect. We have them surrounded. We both find it amusing when half-way through the meeting I ask a seemingly dumb, open-ended question such as, "So, what do you think so far?" and, against all rationale odds, the prospect starts spilling the essential information, laying it out on the table. Dave furiously takes notes while I just nod and listen, and watch my deal start to unfold.

There are many pros and cons to these two methods. One advantage to Dave's information-overload approach is that prospects perceive him as well-informed, credible, and perceptive. This evokes respect and trust, which helps him forge solid relationships. On the other hand, I've seen peddlers who spend way too much time researching and not nearly enough on the phone or on the road. And, when they finally do talk with a prospect, they are so focused on verifying their data that they don't really hear what the prospect is saying.

Now, don't get me wrong. You must verify your data. Some peddlers simply assume that the info they gathered up front is correct, don't take the steps to confirm it, and they pay the piper later on. All I'm saying is, don't let the data run the meeting.

A strength of my seemingly cavalier approach is that the prospect talks and I listen. I draw people out, read between the lines, verify what I hear, connect the dots, and ask and answer questions. It's an honest, real-time dialogue, which also garners respect and trust, and lays the foundation of a good relationship. It also maximizes the amount of time I spend in contact with prospects. Unfortunately, many peddlers believe themselves to be faster on their feet than they really are, and they misconstrue less prep for no prep, leading to disastrous results.

It's hard to gauge how much up-front time you should spend, but good peddlers find a happy middle ground between these two extremes. Here's a tip: The amount of time should be determined by the importance of the call.

First Impressions

OK, so you are meeting the information gatherer or gatekeeper and starting a dialogue. This is a critical point. During the first few meetings, prospects form an impression of you and your company that sticks with them and becomes their long-term view. Are you the glad-hander, slick Willy, or carnival

barker that promises the moon to make a sale? Don't try to pull the wool over anyone's eyes. You may win a prospect's business, but your prospect sees you for who you really are. So, don't go putting on airs or silly costumes. Just be you, baby!

Just as self-destructive are the peddlers who think they must sell themselves in order to sell their product—they think they must make prospects like them or they must show prospects how funny and witty they are. Still other peddlers believe the best sales tactic is the all-powerful offense combined with brow-beating and intimidation. Nope, they're not going to buy it!

To lay the foundation for an honest dialogue with your prospects, know your product, listen to their issues, ask them questions, answer their questions, show them how you've solved problems for other customers. They will see you as a credible peddler.

The process of qualifying a prospect is extremely helpful here. During a meeting, you confirm your map of the company, verify that there is a project and the timeline, outline the purchasing process, discover a few pain points, find out if they're talking to your competitors, and zero in on who will be the ultimate navigator of the deal. You draw the prospect out, open up a dialogue, have an honest exchange of information, and everyone gets comfortable.

Hey! Here's a notion for your peddler head. Every time you call on a prospect—whether it's an info gatherer, gatekeeper, or even a decision maker—look at it like you are going to get to know a new person. You ask about this and that, and you tell them what you are up to and what you are trying to do.

I always go into a meeting being the friendly, knowledgeable, prepared, and genuinely-caring peddler that I am. I want the prospect to form the impression that this guy and this company are in the know. I want the prospect to say thanks for a great meeting, we learned a lot, and look forward to working with you. I want to say the same back to the prospect.

One way I do this is by being a color commentator, just like the sports folks on TV. Their value is providing insight into what's happening at any given moment in a game. When you think about it, this is something peddlers can do easily. If you have been in an industry or territory for a while, you know all the key players and who's buying what from whom. You know who's doing well, who isn't, who has the latest and greatest, and who's playing catch up.

Such knowledge is fascinating and interesting to prospects and customers. Synthesize and deliver it in a lucid and cogent way, and you can enhance your credibility, not to mention be someone they like to talk to. Ya, you, too, can be a pundit, a bon vivant raconteur, or an industry analyst, just know your stuff!

It's Only the Beginning

During the 10% stage, a picture begins to emerge, a relationship forms, things are off to a great start, and many a peddler is led astray. He or she sees a deal when there really isn't one or shouldn't be one.

Let's face it. Peddlers feel pressure to put something on their manager's forecast, get overanxious to turn a lead into a prospect, or slip into the *Peddler's Magical Reality* and are off in la la land. They begin to see things that aren't there, they try to force a fit, or they use every peddling skill they have to sell something they shouldn't. Don't do that!

Listen to your gut. Think back to a deal that came together as it should have. Remember the circumstances that gave you confidence in that deal, and the moment you knew you could honestly say to yourself, "They'll be a customer, they just don't know it yet."

Even when you've made a hard, critical assessment of your prospect and you know it's just a matter of time before you reel this one in, for the love of Pete, keep it to yourself. I know it's hard not to get excited about these opportunities. It's also hard to keep a poker face when your tense sales manager surfaces with a tight smile asking you to go over your pipeline. But you know as sure as the sun will come up tomorrow that anything you mention will wind up on his forecast, and anything in this stage isn't far enough along.

Heck, even anything in the next stage, the 25% stage, is not ready to put on someone else's forecast. 25% opportunities come and go. They change, get postponed, stumble and fall off a cliff, lay there, or out and out die. They are very tricky creatures. They prey upon your optimistic nature. They get you in a fix. That is why it's imperative to concentrate real hard on the good ones and 86 the bad ones, pronto!

I have found in my years of experience to only surface a deal when it's truly at the fifty-fifty stage. Those are better odds to play from a peddler's standpoint, if you get my drift.

Movin' Down the Pipe—A Quarter

After initially qualifying a prospect, you must develop the prospect. A good peddler recognizes this and doesn't rush, overwhelm or hassle prospects no matter how much pressure is being exerted by those up the corporate food chain.

One of the hardest things for me to learn as a peddler was patience. But the fact is, deals take time. They can't be rushed. That's why it's important to have many irons in the fire. You get killed if all you do is worry and bother the few deals you have cooking. I have learned to say, let's wait! Let's give it some time! Let's not overwhelm the prospect with our overzealous desire to close him or her. Hold off, take a deep breadth, chill, be calm, relax. The deal isn't going anywhere. Let the damn thing be so it can make its way up the qualification chain.

Don't smother or piss off the prospect because you have ants in your pants. Take the time to develop relationships with the right folks at the account. The right folks at the 25% stage are the evaluators, the navigators, and the recommenders.

The Evaluators

When the evaluators enter the picture, the game is afoot! Here's the skinny: The evaluators are the ones who roll up their sleeves and actually take a look at your product.

It is really easy to do a good job with evaluators and just as easy to foul up your deal. I have seen countless peddlers pass off the technical due diligence to their techie counterparts in the sales group and go about their business thinking all will be fine.

Don't be stupid. Weird things can happen when you put a bunch of engineers or techs together in a room. I have seen what I thought would be slam-dunk evaluations turn into full-blown firestorms over nonissues: the programming language a product is written in, the architecture choices that were made, the way you search through the documentation, and on and on and on.

Techies love to belly bump each other over how smart or knowledgeable they are about esoteric subjects. Technical knowledge and strong opinions go hand-in-hand. When your hot tech sits with their hot tech it can be a melding of the minds or a battle royal. They might get along famously or dig in their heels and get downright stubborn. Good peddlers know to be ever vigilant during this process. They leave nothing, and I mean absolutely nothing, to chance. If the sparks start to fly, they are there to put out the fire and calm the group.

PEDDLER'S PREROGATIVE #54

It is your peddler's prerogative to leave nothing to chance, be ever vigilant, monitor everything, and maintain a meaningful dialogue with all key players—inside your prospect's company and inside your company!

As the arbiter of all good things rationale and sensible, one of the things a peddler should not do is go toe-to-toe with the techies. There's no quicker way to lose credibility with this group than to act like you know more than you do. I'm honest with the techies. I tell them that I understand geek, but I can't write it, read it, or speak it. Then I listen very closely. When I detect they're getting off track or a little hot under the collar, I pipe up: "It sounds to me like you're saying this and you're saying that, but what we really need to discuss is this thing over here." This type of tactic boosts your standing with the techies. A peddler should never, ever argue with them or try to engage them in a technical discussion.

PEDDLER'S PREROGATIVE #55

Never, never, never try and be a techie with a techie. He or she knows you are not and will think you are a dope if you try.

Another thing to avoid at all costs during evaluation meetings: allowing folks to take each other down rat holes. It happens all the time. Two people are off topic and heading straight into never-never land. A good peddler keeps the group focused and doesn't let them get diverted, and never gets involved in the chase.

The best way to start an evaluation meeting is to set the stage or create the context for the evaluation. Keep it simple. First, go over the agenda for the meeting, making sure everyone agrees with it, knows why they're here, and understands what they're trying to accomplish. Then take them through it step-by-step.

Part of your agenda should be to present your product as you would to any other group, set their expectations, and highlight the synergies between your product's features and their company's needs.

Someone may object to a product overview, saying it's unnecessary or a waste of time. No matter what anyone says or demands, simply smile, nod, and start from the beginning. It is imperative that no one gets by without hearing about your product. You can give them the short version, hitting just the high points or touching just on the basics, but you can't skip it. You must present your product, no matter what. Otherwise, they'll soon be asking why it won't fly them to Mars.

Many peddlers skip this step. Some are not in tune with the process or their prospect to recognize the need for this, others simply don't know how important it is to doing the deal. But it's one of those subtle techniques that separates successful peddlers from the rest.

Of course, before the evaluation, you want to get a list of points they want covered. Of course, you want to go into the meeting with a crisp and well-prepared presentation. Of course, you want to make sure that you are getting validation as you move along through your talk.

As you explain what your product does, what you understand the prospect's needs to be, and how your product can solve or fulfill those needs, you should be seeing some sort of positive feedback from your audience. They may be smiling, voicing their agreement, or simply nodding—all good signs. If there's disagreement, smirks or scowls— or worse, no reaction whatsoever—you are in trouble. Step in fast— and I mean freakin' pronto.

Start with some open questions: "Mr. Evaluator, are we showing you what you want to see? Did you expect something else? Did we misunderstand what you are looking for or what your needs are? I'm sensing a disconnect. Are we disconnecting?"

Such direct, open, frank questions should be enough to elicit some feedback. Then you can adjust or regroup. However, never let the evaluation deteriorate without trying to understand why: "Mr. Evaluator, I feel we are heading south here. Please tell me why."

One of the mind-blowing aspects of peddlery and presentations is the shoulda-woulda-coulda phenomenon. You're in the car, restaurant, or back at the office after a presentation. One by one, the team starts to dissect the meeting and participants: Do you think the V.P. understood all our new features? Do you think the CEO bought our delivery date? Do we know how the CIO is planning to deploy the product?

All good questions THAT SHOULD HAVE BEEN ASKED DURING THE MEETING.

I always tell the folks on my team not to waste a meeting with a prospect. If they have thoughts, questions, observations, or insights, speak up! Now's the time, while we're all together. Get it all out on the table. Point out any issues you see or perceive on their side or ours, and let's get them resolved. The alternative is catch up mode: You ask for another meeting so you can address some open issues, or you track down the participants individually to clear things up. It sucks. It's time consuming. Ya, sometimes it's necessary, but often it can be avoided.

Listen up! Evaluations are good. Evaluations are necessary. No company is going to buy a product without evaluating it. From time to time, you'll hear sales managers and corporate measurers encourage peddlers to try to get around the evaluation process. They believe evals slow down the process, that you could close deals much quicker if you didn't have to go through that step.

The fact is, evaluations are probably the most important part of the sales process. It provides the prospect with a hands-on look at your product. Evals can be anything from a sit-down, in-depth demo to an in-house installation and implementation (try before you buy). Yes, it's true that some products don't require an evaluation. For products that are well known, ubiquitous, or widely accepted, the sales process is different. It isn't necessary to go through all the steps I'm describing here, because these types of products don't require a peddler. ALL THEY NEED IS AN ORDER TAKER!

The Navigators

Sometime, somewhere, as a deal progresses through the pipe, the navigator surfaces. He or she usually appears during the evaluation or recommendation stages, and is the person who has the most skin in the game. His or her success is riding on the outcome of the deal— whether it be with you or your competitor.

The navigator is your Go-To guy or gal, your sponsor, your new best friend, and the person you need to sell. Learning to identify the navigator is imperative. It is also tricky, as everyone you meet along the way may tell you that they are the navigator. They don't mean to mislead you, but at some point in the process, they are the one making the call. You have to figure out who's really going to guide you through the deal. This is why I mentioned earlier to always verify who you're talking to. Miss the navigator and you can miss your deal.

The navigator is the person most closely associated with the reason this company needs your product in the first place. He or she may be running the project or responsible for a deliverable. Whatever the reason, this person and that compelling need are locked together, and you need to be the key that delivers success. It is imperative that you build a solid relationship with the navigator.

PEDDLER'S PREROGATIVE #56

As a peddler with a qualified deal, it is your prerogative to first find the navigator and second, determine the reason or compelling scenario that creates a sense of urgency about doing the deal.

The Recommenders

The recommenders are the folks who are pivotal to your deal. It's their opinions and recommendations that really count. These folks surface in every deal, but they generally stay behind the scenes until they need to get involved.

A recommender is usually a techie, middle manger, or maybe even an executive who is tasked with scanning the market for products and companies that fit a need. When you meet with a recommender, you start talking more seriously and more in-depth about implementation, time lines, costs, deliverables, and so on. The recommenders are the folks who get the deal tied up into a neat little package, bow on top.

If you get to the recommender you have a sure shot at winning the deal. The recommender will narrow his choices to a handful; you can bet all your competitors are in the running. It's here that you, your product, and your company all have a major bearing on who gets recommended to the decision maker. (I talk about closing and the decision makers in the next chapter.)

A good peddler gets cozy with all the folks in the selling process: those helping out at his company and those helping out at the prospect's. But he or she gets as tight as possible with the recommender. The better your relationship the easier it is to get the real scoop of what the issues are and how to close the deal.

Let's face a simple fact: A deal will start out with a particular set of requirements and end up with different ones as it comes to fruition. It is the nature of deals; they move and change, they zig and zag. You have to keep your eye on what is happening. The peddler who stays on top of the nuances of a changing deal usually wins, because he is current and in context.

The Importance of Context

One reason why so many opportunities get blown and why so many deals go south is because of lack of context. You know the moment: You're in a meeting, trying to get some commitment that will move your deal forward, when someone pipes up and says, "I thought it leaped tall buildings in a single bound." The tech guy's eyes dart over to you and you say, "Well, not exactly, but it's faster than a speeding bullet."

Before the words are even out of your mouth, you know that was the wrong answer. But what's the right one? Who is that guy? And why do you get the distinct feeling that your deal is suddenly on the ropes?

I'll tell you. During the sales process there are lots of meeting and lots of people moving in and out. It is hard to keep everyone on the same page, and this is the person that you missed. He or she has some wrong information. At this critical juncture, when you're looking to confirm that all's right with the world and your deal, he's raising doubts.

Nothing can derail a deal faster than a prospect with the wrong information. It may be about your products, your company, the deal, their needs, their objectives, the fit, or any number of other things. It doesn't matter. It gets you off track.

This is why at the first sign of a change, rewind and start over. As soon as someone new comes in the room, give them a summary of your presentation so far. As soon as you move up a notch in the selling process, present your product from scratch. As soon as someone makes a statement or asks a question that could foul up the percep-

tion of what the product does, jump in: "OK, Ms. Prospect, let's take it from the top. Here's what the product does. These are the needs you have. Now, is that a fit?"

PEDDLER'S PREROGATIVE #57

It is the peddler's prerogative to summarize the product and opportunity to every new face that appears during a meeting. This revolving door lets you reinforce the fit among the other participants. Turn a negative into a positive whenever you can.

This is not something you do just for the evaluators. It is something you must do for everyone every time they come into a deal's orbit. And in defense of the evaluators, let me say that they are not the only ones to get off track. Everyone you meet during every stage of the sales process tends to do what-if scenarios, start brainstorming, or just go into fantasy overdrive. Don't let them derail your deal. Put everyone in context. THIS MEANS EVERY SINGLE PERSON EVERY SINGLE TIME.

This drudgery can drive a peddler batty. It is tedious, boring, repetitive, time consuming, and hard to do. If you keep every sentient being who is involved in the sales process on the same page, however, your deal will go smoother and you will be in a better position than your competitors who don't worry about context. If you don't, your prospects will miss important points about you, your company, your product, your deal, and so on. This is why, dearest people of the planet Earth, that it takes so freaking long to sell something!

A typical context-setting session might progress like this:

- This is who we are and why we are here.
- This is who you are and why you are here.
- This is our product, what it does, and how we have helped similar companies.
- These are your current needs and why our product is a fit.
- Here is where we are in the sales process.
- This is a summary of our last meeting. Do you agree?
- The goal of today's meeting is to keep moving toward a relationship.
- Here is the agenda for our meeting today. Is this correct?
- Here is what we hope to accomplish.

- If there's a fit, here is how things work in our company.
- If there's a fit, here's how we understand things work in your company.
- Here's where we're heading next.

This is a simple approach to getting everyone on the same page.

Keep in mind that you are selling in a dynamic environment. People, specifications, requirements, the market—any one of a hundred things can change that affect your deal. Despite it all, you must keep everyone aware of and in agreement of the status. Provide the context for participants in meetings and calls. Establish the context for the players running the deal. Follow up with status reports to all. Do it constantly. Or else prepare thyself for the weird and the bizarre.

Time Out

OK, before we go any further, there are a few things I want to say about peddling in general. These things are important, so keep them in mind or you can forget about the fifty-fifty realm.

It's the Product, Stupid

Selling something that is good and useful is a lot easier than selling junk. Trying to sell stuff that isn't useful to folks who don't really need it is ridiculous. There are companies and people out there that sell junk and they should be eradicated. (Says me!)

Sell What You Got

After you find out what the heck you are selling, you have to sell it. It's that simple. Time and time again, I have seen peddlers moaning and groaning about their product—it doesn't have this or that feature, it is priced to high or too low, there are too many or too few models, and on and on.

Stop already. You really need to sell what you have on its own merits, which is another good reason to make sure you're selling something that is good and useful. It's also important that it is ready to be delivered to customers and performs as advertised from the get-go.

That said, customers often want to customize your product. It's what customers do. Corporate types, on the other hand, don't want to change a thing, and fight tooth and nail to keep the product as is. It's what corporate types do. That's life.

As the one who's forever in the middle, it is the peddler who must decide when to stick with what he or she has, and when to explore product enhancements and changes; when to show the customer that the product meets all his or her requirements and is a fit, and when to confront the corporate types and demonstrate the upside of accommodating the customer. It's up to you. Make the right choice.

Get on the Road—or the Phone

If you are a field rep, you must leave the building. Get out of the office. Figure out a way—any way—to get your feet on the road. You will not sell anything, ever, sitting around your office. You need to get in front of leads, prospects, and customers if you are going to sell stuff. If you find yourself stuck in the office you are dead meat. Get up off your chair, walk around outside, even talk to people at random. But get the heck out. Any peddler who is in the office more than he or she is out making calls will fail. If this is you, quit or get your butt out the door. There is not one iota of middle ground here. Once you have deals you have to work, you need in-house time—but not a lot.

For all you peddlers doing over-the-phone sales, you better dial fast and furious, folks! Gabbing with your colleagues and surfing the Internet is not going to bring in the bucks. You must pick up the phone and talk to leads, prospects, and customers to sell your product. If you don't, you will fail. Plain and simple.

I have a theory about peddlery: The peddler who is the first one into work and the last one out sells the most. Here's why: A good peddler is up early planning the day and making sure everything is prepared. Then, it's out to the field or on the phone for a call-filled day, spending time at the end of the day on follow-up. That peddler works late, taking care of all his action items, then repeats the process the next day. This is how you spell success in peddlery, boys and girls.

The Competition

I talked about checking out your competitor's customers in the previous chapter. Suffice it to say that most people in business are afraid of their competition and stay as far away from them as possible. My vote is to always keep them close. The reasons are many, but the best is so you and they can share valuable info and insights about your market. Think about it: You and your competitors are in the same boat. Who better to talk to?

As I'm getting some traction, my favorite thing is to reach out to the competition. Yes, you read right. Somewhere out there is a competitor and it always behooves you to make nice and have a chat. Depending on who you are and your level or position within your company, you can pretty much gauge who you should be talking to. Keep in mind that this is always done on the up and up. And no matter what anyone tells you, it is perfectly—and I mean perfectly—OK to do.

PEDDLER'S PREROGATIVE #58

It is your prerogative to meet with your counterparts at all of your competitors. It's an essential part of understanding and familiarizing yourself with the market. It's extending your web. It shows you are a smart peddler. It's OK to be friends with the peddlers you are competing against. Remember, it's a very small world.

Calling on the competition as well as the competitor's top accounts is always a good thing. First, no one ever thinks of it because they are the competition. Second, it dispels your fear of the competition. Of course, being afraid isn't always a bad thing in business, but dispelling that fear is always a good thing.

Understanding your competition is second only to knowing your products. When you have those two things down you start to develop an expertise that gives you credibility. A peddler who has a grasp of the market and the products in that market earns respect from the customer.

I think it makes sound sense to go to your competition and their major accounts with your top execs and say hello. It accomplishes two things: One, it shows everyone in your company you are aggressive and think strategically. Two, it shows you have a lot of, um . . . gumption! Ya, gumption.

Let's face it. The competition probably has your company on their radar screen as well. Putting together a little gathering of the right leaders at the top can never be a bad thing and might yield some G2. It is only good business sense to talk with the competition no matter whether you are a peddler, company executive, or customer.

These meetings are relatively easy to set up. "Hello, company XYZ, this is Dennis Ford with company ABC. Could I please speak with your CEO's administrator? Great! Hello, I am calling to set up a meeting with the appropriate executives to say hello and make sure we understand where each other is going in the market. We want to determine whether we are friends or foes. Also, we'd like to validate that we are both selling in the same market to the same customers. Last but not least, we'd like to make sure we know where our products overlap, augment, or complement each other."

I have done this kind of meeting countless times and they are always good. Bringing together the product and marketing executives who are competing for the same customers can give you some real insight into the market. It does take a bit of finesse to get over the initial awkwardness, but that's what good peddlers are for: putting it on the table, moving everyone past their paranoia, setting the tone, connecting the dots.

Selling Is Not for Wimps

Even if you do your job right, the sales process is rarely smooth. Be alert, be aware, and don't be afraid to make the tough calls.

Deals can change at any moment. They can grow or shrink and die. Don't freak out when weird things happen. One thing you must never do is get jumpy and start nodding your noggin, saying yes to things you should be saying no to. Always stay straight, honest, and in control.

As you work with a prospect to define a project, rarely is it a perfect fit. You may be able to throw resources at the problem and fix it. But if a deal morphs outside your product's and company's capabilities and it's no longer a fit, say so. If it's not worth your company's extra resources or your prospect's, speak up. Many peddlers think, "Oh my God, this isn't going to work. I hope we close this deal before they find out."

Don't let this be you. Call 'em as you see 'em: "Mr. Prospect, I've realized that my product really isn't a fit for your company. I appreciate the time you've spent with us. Here's the company to call. Ask for Bill. Tell him I suggested you call him. He can help you." Your good karma will be rewarded. Everyone appreciates a no-bullshit peddler who doesn't waste their time. Don't hide and hope, face the facts, Jack.

The kiss of death can come from nice people wanting to be nice. They agree with everything you say just to be nice. You explain your product, you ask the prospect if she gets it, she say yes, and it takes you all of a nanosecond to know she really doesn't. She may know that she needs your product, but not why. Or she may know why, but doesn't understand how it will help her.

You cannot pass Go. The nice folks are easy to blow on by, but getting by someone is not the point of being a good peddler. You want them to buy in, because you know that's the only hope you have of having a happy customer. You also know that eventually, you are going to run into the not-so-nice guy, and when he starts asking all the nice people why they like your product and he doesn't get the right answers, your deal is over.

If you have a prospect who says he understands your product but doesn't, the first thing you should do is verify if he or she is the right person.

Peddler: "Gee, Ms. Prospect, it doesn't sound like you're the person I should be talking to."

Prospect: "I'm not really. I'm just sitting in for Mr. Bill who's on vacation."

Peddler: "Perhaps I should call Mr. Bill when he's back and set up another meeting."

Prospect: "Yes, that would be a good idea."

Now we're getting somewhere.

Just as likely, however, is that this is the prospect and you have to find a way to help her understand the product even as she's saying she does. If you move the process along before a prospect understands your product, it will come back to haunt you. You must make sure that everyone along the way gets it, no matter what. Don't let yourself slip or you could hurt yourself!

Fifty-Fifty

When you enter the fifty-fifty stage you have something that is alive and kicking. Yours to lose is another way of looking at it. At this stage, you are fully engaged and have a 50% chance of turning your prospect into a customer. The evaluations are in full swing. The relationship and dialogue are good. You've teamed up with the person who is going to get you to the end of the deal. When your phone is ringing with questions and your calls are being returned, it is truly a great thing.

The Value Propositions

As a peddler, you are continually conveying the value propositions of your wares. But as you head into the fifty-fifty realm, you need to get the prospect's buy in to your value propositions, or have a clear understanding of what your prospect sees the value propositions to be. When a prospect sees the value, wants the product, and knows why it's a good thing, the game is getting interesting.

It is precisely at this point that you as a good peddler don't fall all over yourself trying to get the deal done. You must make sure that the prospect truly understands the value and that he or she is convinced your product is a fit. Don't assume a prospect truly understands the value simply because he or she says so. Verify. If you try to close a deal when the value propositions are not fully understood, you decrease your chances of closing the business.

"So, dear prospect, it seems that you see the value of my product and a fit. Please take a moment and explain to me what you've learned and why it works for you. It would help me to hear it from your perspective."

Now, it's likely that one of three things will happen. The prospect may echo the value propositions you conveyed. If this happens, bravo! You've done good. The prospect also may cite one or more value propositions that you've never heard before. This is also good. The fact is, IT DOES NOT MATTER WHAT YOU THINK THE VALUE PROPOSITIONS ARE. Your prospect knows what they are for him or her, so listen closely. He or she is giving you a gift: new value props that you can use to pitch other prospects.

However, if the prospect is unable to articulate the value propositions—yours or theirs—either he or she doesn't really understand what they are or you missed something along the way. GO BACK TO SQUARE ONE. It's what you must do. Start the selling process over, right from the get-go. Take the prospect on the sales journey that you thought got you to fifty-fifty. Pull up a chair, cancel all your calls, get some coffee, and repeat after me: "So, we started talking to you folks about three months ago. . . ."

PEDDLER'S PREROGATIVE #59

It is the peddler's prerogative to make sure the prospect understands the value propositions. Anything less than 100% will proportionately decrease your chances of closing the business.

The Long and Winding Road

After the value propositions have been laid out and bought off, and a proposal is submitted, you and your counterpart are winding your way through each other's corporate gotchas. You have bonded and you both want to get the deal done. You keep each other well informed and forewarn each other about any unwritten rules—the ones that explain what truly can and can't work at each other's companies. You've set the tone, choreographed the dance, and the deal is moving in step.

Speaking of dancing, you must do the pricing tango ear to ear. Never negotiate pricing in a room full of people. If you have an audience, only talk about your published pricing. At most say your company tries to be flexible and meet companies' needs. Then stop and say no more. Not a word. Nada.

After you discuss pricing and general contract terms with your counterpart, he or she confirms a date for buying the product and a timeline for implementation. As you head toward the end of this stage, it is appropriate for your inside contact to connect you to the person who can give you the nod.

When the time is right, explain that it would be great if you could get in front of or on the line with the decision maker. When you get that call, you are heading into the final stretch—75% land.

As part of the sales process, most companies require that an executive gets on the phone with one or two of the potential suppliers and says, "Ya, you are in the running." If you take a quick step back and put yourself in the prospect's shoes, they have to have a strategy to get the best deal they can. Anyone worth his or her salt knows that the best way to do that is to play one vendor against another vendor. So, typically, you find that the executive who is the recommender or decision maker is courting a few vendors to keep the one vendor he wants honest.

Please remember that because you have talked to an executive and were told that you have a shot, isn't going to get you to the next level, which is the VERBAL. The verbal is when someone in the know, behind the scenes, or the main guy in the deal says to you verbally, "Dennis, you and your company have the deal." We will talk about the verbal in the next chapter.

The Poetry of a Deal

Reading this aloud before each sales meeting saves everyone a lot of time.

Deals are funny. They come. They go. They're alive. They're dead. They come roaring back to life. They're dead again. They're on fire. They're as cold as ice. They're wiggling. They're moot. They're winking at you. They're closed. They aren't closed. Their owners went on vacation. They got sick. They had an emergency. They forgot about the meeting. They said there are open issues. More and more open issues. They killed the deal. They're back. They want it. They said it costs too much. They want a discount. They want to try before they buy. They think our company is too small. They think our company is too big. They went to our competitors. They came back. They're gone again. They're mad at Jim. They love Jim. They say Bob pissed them off. You apologize. They apologize. They're mad again. They want too meet the CEO. They canceled the meeting. They're back and ready. They want to do a deal. The deal has changed. The new deal has changed. Everyone's confused. Everyone's involved. Nobody's in charge. THE DEAL IS OUT OF CONTROL.

Work the deal. Follow the deal. Be nice to the deal. Don't push it too hard. Just run with it. Treat it good. Stay the heck out of its way. Don't get run over by the deal. Be the deal. Feel the deal. Free the deal. Do the deal. Do the deal. Do the deal. CLOSE THE FREAKING DEAL. Ta Da!

I just had to get that off my chest. Once deals become real they are like living creatures with all the foibles, silliness, and randomness that comes along with life. Someone wrote a book about the art of a deal, maybe someone should write a book about the poetry of a deal. Oh my, could that be me? "No," said the spider to the fly, "You're writing *The Peddler's Prerogative*."

The Battle for Control

During the sales process, someone has to take control. It is part of the archetypal dynamic of every negotiation. Here's a surprise: It doesn't always have to be you! One thing I learned the hard way as I came up through the sales ranks is that it doesn't matter who is in control of the deal or what side of the table he or she is on. What does matter is that the owner of the deal knows what the heck he or she wants and how to get it.

So, my friends, on a deal-by-deal basis, make a rational call as to who is going to be in control. Then, if it's not you, be cool and calm. Surf the deal. Follow the lead of the person in the know. It is more important to have a person who can get the job done than it is for you to be in control of the deal. Most peddlers foul this up.

When you have someone to run the deal, then fill in where you're needed. Sometimes you may be the quarterback, other times you may be in the backfield or on the line. Countless times I have made the choice to follow the prospect's guidance in getting a deal done.

One thing I always keep in mind is that I am in the deal to make a living. If my boss or his boss wants to run with my deal, or if someone at the prospective company wants to move it through, it's not a problem. He or she is my new best friend. I don't have to be the sunshine glory peddler, I just have to be the guy they write the check to.

PEDDLER'S PREROGATIVE #60

It is the peddler's prerogative to avoid fighting for control of a deal, and make a rational call, deal by deal, whether he or she or the prospect is going to run the deal. When the prospect leads the deal, the good peddler remains in the game, participating and influencing accordingly. The smart peddler makes sure he or she is always sitting at the table.

Never Lose Your Sphere of Influence

You may relinquish control of a deal, but you should never ever give up an opportunity to influence it. Exerting influence is one of those subtle techniques successful peddlers use. In fact, confidence in their ability to persuade is one reason why they can let someone else run the deal. (Another is the realization that fighting for control is a loser's game.)

Most peddlers, however, let opportunities to influence the game slip by time after time. Here's a common scenario: A peddler has a meeting with a prospect. At the end, everyone agrees to a follow-on meeting. Someone at the meeting volunteers to organize the next meeting and the peddler lets them. BLAM! The deal just moved out of the peddler's sphere of influence.

A smart peddler doesn't let this happen. He or she sees that the ball is in play and grabs it before anyone else: "Hey, it's my job to move this along. I'll call so and so, get a list of who should be there, schedule it, and write up an agenda." The good peddler realizes that after everyone leaves the meeting and gets involved in their regular work, it's unlikely that setting up the next meeting will be their top priority. If the peddler doesn't step up to the plate, he or she will be stuck waiting on the prospect rather than able to move forward.

You must be vigilant about not letting any chance to exert your influence elude your grasp. I mean absolutely nothing. It is paramount to grab anything and everything that can help you move your deal forward. The tiniest, most seemingly insignificant things can halt the movement of a deal. That is why the peddler has to be aware of everything's that going on. Hey! I'm not a big detail freak. But when a deal starts to sprout some legs, you better put on your white gloves and pull out your magnifying glass.

PEDDLER'S PREROGATIVE #61

Peddling is about moving deals down the line. It is the peddler's prerogative to be ever vigilant about any detail, no matter how trivial, that could slow down a deal, and to make it his or her number one priority to exert his or her influence to keep the deal moving. It is also the peddler's prerogative to be anal retentive about every aspect of his or her deal. The devil is in the details.

Timing Is Everything

And everything is timing. The definition of luck is being in the right place at the right time and knowing what to do.

Here's a joke about timing. A guy jumps off the 120th floor of a building. As he is flying by the 33rd floor, he's says to a fellow on the balcony, "Hey! How am I doing?" to which the fellow replies, "So far so good!" Bada bing bada boom!

Timing is a strange element of every deal. It is either a blessing or a curse. As a quarter starts to cycle, deals inevitably start to move. Sometimes they slip out, in which case they roll over into the next quarter, and sometimes they get hot and need to get done. Often, the sense of timing and urgency is different person to person. The V.P. of a division may want to get a deal done fast, but the person he has assigned it to may be overloaded and doesn't have the bandwidth.

If the timing is within your sales goal window then, hey, the deal's on the plate! If it's out lots of months, then it's off the plate—until the time comes to put it back on. You must monitor the time frame of a deal. There is nothing worse then getting to the 75% mark and having a deal fall off the table because of timing.

The net-net: The peddler wrestles with timing 24/7.

STORY TIME

It's the early '80s, PCs are kicking in big time, and I am selling some hot system software. One of the biggest computer manufacturers is in my turf. It is a Fortune 100 company and the big elephant that everyone in my company wants to snag. The problem is it doesn't need our stuff; it is building its own in house. My job is to show them the folly of their ways and convince them to buy from us.

Over the course of three months, I meet scads of people in the PC division and am mapping and presenting my brains out. Finally, I get a meeting with Geoff, a guy who has been around, knows the industry cold, tracks all the deals, knows the pros and cons, and keeps score. He also reports to the guy who calls all the shots and signs off on all the deals in this PC division. These are the two dudes who can pull the trigger on a deal.

About three minutes into my carefully-planned pitch, Geoff hands me my lunch saying that the company is developing software just like mine in house, so this sale is not going to happen, but thanks for coming in. Then he gets up and walks out the door. This is a guy who doesn't mince words.

Stunned, I gather up my belongings and dejectedly head down the hall to the exit. I see Geoff talking to some folks and decide to wait for him. He sees me and comes over. "Anything you didn't understand?"

"Geoff, I am a new peddler in my company. Your company is the elephant everyone wants to bag, and you are one of the guys I need to have a relationship with. What would you do if you were me? Give me a break and help me understand how I might get started. Teach me about what you folks are doing. Let's see if we can find a way for me to help you."

"I am way too busy for that, but I do appreciate your candor," Geoff replies.

Off I go, but with an inkling that Geoff isn't as bad as he projects himself to be. On the ride back to the office, I make up my mind that little by little, I am going to sell Geoff.

(continued)

I devise a game plan and start pinging Geoff with new product info and press releases of deals we are doing with his competitors. I write up quick notes and suggestions of how we might start with something small, such as a consulting gig or some development work.

Late one night I am alone in my office and the phone rings. "What are you doing there at this hour?" It's Geoff. "Trying to figure out how to sell you something," I reply.

It turns out that Geoff has some needs after all, and he puts a few ideas on the table. More importantly, he starts acting like a nice guy.

Many months go by as Geoff and I try to put together a few small deals. I become the conduit to my company, and arrange some high-level meetings between Geoff and our executives. At the same time, Geoff decides he likes me (after all, I am quite amusing). I am not only calling and getting through, but Geoff begins to mentor me, teaching me the ropes of the PC space, and giving me some great leads.

Now, all the while I'm developing my relationship with Geoff, my boss's boss (the COO who runs the business) is reminding me how I'm not breaking the bank, and that I'm the wrong guy in the wrong job, because I am new to the PC industry and haven't got a clue. He's a real hard biz guy and I swear he enjoys making me miserable.

I tell Geoff that my COO thinks I am wasting my time because we haven't done even a small deal. One day after a particularly grueling hour of torture with the COO I call Geoff and say I am a goner. I appreciate all his help and mentoring, but after my meeting I think I am a dead man.

Geoff laughs and tells me that I am one of the luckiest sons of a gun on the planet. He just left a meeting in which his company decided to stop developing the system software in house and do a deal with us or our competitor. Sometimes life is good.

Fast-forward to the end-of-quarter, up-against-the-wall, no-holes-barred, gigantic round of negotiations. This is a huge, mul-

(continued)

timillion dollar deal, and pretty much means my company has wrapped up the market for its niche. Things are flying fast and furious when a week before the quarter ends, Geoff calls and breaks the news to me: They have chosen the competitor.

I thank him for the fun and ask if he knows where I might be able to find some work, only half jokingly. Needless to say, the COO doesn't take the news well, and I slip to the "does not exist" realm. Finding yourself here at the end of a quarter is not what I call a good thing. At least when I am tortured I know I am alive and in the company. Now I am floating in the dark, cold regions of nowheresville.

In the afternoon of the last day of the quarter, Geoff calls. He reiterates from a few calls ago that I am one of the luckiest sons of a gun on the planet. He tells me that he is in one of three limos along with their corporate lawyers and product folks. THEY ARE EN ROUTE TO MY COMPANY TO DO THE DEAL! Negotiations broke down with our competitor and the entire negotiating team will be pulling into our parking lot in 30 minutes and counting.

I run, or should I say fly to my COO's office, which is jammed with people doing end-of-quarter deals. I barge in: "Time out! Big news, Geoff is going to be here in 30 minutes with the lawyers and product folks to do the deal."

The COO gets up with a big smile, walks over to me, puts his arm around my shoulder, and walks me through the door and down the hall. "Denny, I knew from the first time I saw you that we were going to have a great relationship, and that you had what it takes to make it in this company." I look at him and say, "Drop dead Bob, you jerk." He replies with an ear-to-ear grin. "Anything you say, Denny." (One of only three folks in my entire life who called me Denny.)

Needless to say, we do the deal, I make a mint, I am a hero, and from that day on I officially report to the COO. We ink lots and lots of business together and I learn a lot from him and Geoff over the next year or so. I also learn a lot about TIMING.

When you bring in a deal and the timing's right, you go from goat to god.

Time and Your Top Ten

Use your time wisely. It is a known fact that if you spend a lot of time working your leads and converting them to prospects, and you do it right, you will succeed.

I work off a top-ten list. It consists of my ten most important leads and prospects. I am lord and master of my list. Most peddlers have some sort of list. In some cases, their list is controlled by a system or a list management application. In some cases, their list controls them. Ugh!

I write my top ten on a white board. Ten happens to be a good number for me. For each lead or prospect, I also write down my next action or task. Anytime anyone comes into my office I say, "Hey, here's my list and some ideas for getting to the next step. What do you think?" I don't care if they are my admin or the janitor, I get everybody's opinion.

I start every day reviewing my top-ten list, and either taking action or thinking about what I can do to move each lead or prospect along. To me, moving along means up or off the list.

Working through my top-ten list can take 20 minutes or all day. After I do all I can, I start to work on my secondary list—but only until the end of the day. The next morning, I start again at the top of my list with my number one deal, think about how I can move it along today, take whatever action I can, and then move down to number two. When something moves off my top-ten list, something on my secondary list gets promoted.

Here's the thing: The first thing most peddlers do is spend time on their least important prospects. What's worse is when they wind up spending their entire day on them. They get to 5:00 and haven't spent a minute on their top prospects. This makes no sense.

The way to make cash is to focus on the leads and prospects that matter most. Do it first, do it every day. It's an easy formula: first things first, and then on to what's next after that.

It is also a known fact that if you take time to think about what the flock you are doing, peddling gets a whole lot easier. Thinking is time well spent. Tune your Internet radio to the Celtics channel and just sit and think.

Here's a hint: Think about your strategies and tactics.

Strategy and Tactics

The bane of peddlers is that they don't stop to think. They like to take action. Make things happen. (The bane of corporate is that they think they know everything.)

Earlier I mentioned that developing prospects takes patience. It also takes a strategy. Before approaching leads and prospects, devise a game plan. Then, all the while you're doing a deal you should be anticipating the prospect's actions and your reactions, thinking three or four moves ahead.

It's probably obvious by now that a strategy I use often is turning prospects into friends and mentors. I find a way to be useful to prospects, all the while making sure to convey the message that I'm an honest, hard-working peddler, trying to make a living, and who can sometimes make him or her laugh. I have no problem letting prospects teach me about their market or company, and how to get a deal done. I know I'll repay the favor down the road.

For me, any strategy must include two things: the straightest path to a prospect, and after qualifying him or her, the straightest path to closing a deal. I spend a lot of time thinking about these two things, which winds up being the straightest line to cash in my pocket.

Once you have a strategy, then think about the tactics you're going to use to execute your strategy. Strategy has to be married to tactics.

Most peddlers spend a lot of time on tactics and none on strategy. They are also not sure when to use strategy and when to use tactics. Here's a tip: When things start ballooning, faulting, or wavering big time, revert to the strategic.

They're Alive!

Deals that are alive are fun. The game's underway and something's cooking. I have seen my fair share of deals and I can tell you one thing for certain: They are all the same and they are all different. Are we all clear on that? It's the Zen of Peddlery raising its head again. Best we move along now and close some deals.

CHAPTER 15

CLOSING

The secret of all victory lies in the organization of the nonobvious.

—Oswald Spengler

Now that we have wiggled our way down the pipe and are heading into the final stretch, we have officially entered the land of commitment. Commitment is when your prospect commits to you, and your boss takes that commitment to his boss, and on and on up the chain it goes. No matter how you slice it, commitment is a very serious word.

During the 10% stage when a lead shows a pulse and becomes a prospect, you are pretty much on your own. You talk with the lead, they articulate a need, you qualify them, and a dialogue begins. It's the same at 25% when you're developing a prospect and talking with the evaluators, befriending the navigator, and hoping to lay eyes on the recommenders.

But as soon as you reach 50% and surface a deal to your manager, the heat gets turned up in the corporate kitchen. At this point, it's a deal that could be thrown into the corporate mix if it's the difference between meeting quota or not. Some folks call such a deal upside, others call it potential or back-up. It's not quite ready for commitment, but don't kid yourself, there is a jaundice eye on your deal. The corporate folks know you could drag this business in the door with discounts, attractive payment terms, an extra something or other: "Mr. Prospect, we'd like to close your business this month. What do you think it would take?"

Once you move a deal into the 75% realm, it's time to make a commitment to the forecast. Getting a bunch of peddlers at a sales meeting to step up to the table and put their deals on the forecast is an endless source of amusement to sales managers, as most peddlers are commitment phobic. The fact that many of them are males probably has a lot to do with it! But so does the unpredictable nature of the peddler's reality. Even though peddlers have carefully nudged and nurtured their deals all the way to the 75% stage, they know they still have a long way to go. It's all too easy for a deal to die or just fall off a cliff.

Ya, the peddling life is uncertain. Ya, there's a lot of ground yet to cover before you close a deal. But I gotta tell you, at this point, the biggest obstacle between many a good peddler and a deal is the MYTH OF CLOSING.

Legend has it that there are peddlers who can close business like no one else. Somehow, some way, they get prospects to sign on the bottom line. How they do it is a mystery to the rest of us. We assume they know the secret, use special techniques, or are blessed with a sacred gift. We hear stories about how these folks can get business from a stone and turn prospects into customers before your eyes. They have that closing knack! Bah humbug!

Unfortunately, the myth has been perpetuated by certain peddler stereotypes. First, there's the consummate dealmaker: "This guy never walks away without a deal, no matter what he has to do!" Ya, who needs to make a profit anyway?

There's also the bad mofo closers: "We need people who can close, who go for the throat!" Now that's how you keep customers coming back for more!

Then there's the peddler who is extraordinarily persuasive: "This guy could sell snow to an Eskimo!" Yes, he could, but if he was a good peddler he wouldn't because he shouldn't.

The message is, if you don't fit the type, you're not a closer and you're going to have trouble finalizing your deals. What a crock! But unfortunately, this myth haunts the hallowed halls of corporate, thus messing with the heads of even good peddlers.

Here are the facts: Closing is simply the logical end to a logical process. You can do it without giving away the store or gouging your prospects, and you don't need any special powers.

Closing is a natural occurrence. From the beginning, you're asking questions and the prospect is asking questions. If each of you is providing the right answers, the relationship progresses to the next step, and the next one, and the one after that. When you've both asked all your questions and received satisfactory answers, you're done. The deal is CLOSED. It is NO BIG DEAL.

PEDDLER'S PREROGATIVE #62

It is the peddler's prerogative not to be intimidated by the closing myth. Closing is simply the end of the selling process. When the last question is answered, you are done and the deal is closed.

One for You, One for Me . . .

I have a rule that I live by when closing business: It has to be good for the prospect and good for my company. Each side should give a little and get a little, and both should walk away feeling that they made a fair and decent deal. If that is not the case, then I as a peddler should fix it, even if it means not doing the deal.

As always in the land of the peddler, the question is, What is good for the prospect or customer? Selling someone something they don't need is an awful thing to do. Getting someone to buy something that sits on their shelf is a shame. Inflating deals with fluff is a hideous practice. Take heed, my fellow peddlers: If you do anything other than a good deal, it will always surface down the road, it will always come back to you one way or another, it will always haunt you.

PEDDLER'S PREROGATIVE #63

It is the peddler's prerogative to make sure that as a deal gets done, it is a good and fair deal for folks on both sides of the table. Bad deals always come back to haunt the perpetrating party. This is the karma of peddlery. Don't mess with it!

On the other hand, prospects can be unscrupulous. If they realize that they have you over a barrel, they might use their advantage to get you to overcommit. You have to remember there are good prospects and bad prospects, and some are experts at taking advantage of peddlers. Some have black belts in body slamming peddlers and their companies just for grins. Some folks on the other side of the table make a good living being the bad cops. Anytime you find a jerk like this ditch the deal. It can work both ways: bad peddlers, bad prospects.

Make sure that the folks you are working with are cool. That each side knows they will make some concessions and both sides will leave the table feeling that the deal is OK from everyone's perspective. I make a point to say this throughout the selling process and up front at the closing stage to make sure that everyone knows this is going to be done in a good way, and if there are any henchmen in the wings this homey ain't playing that game.

PEDDLER'S PREROGATIVE #64

As a peddler, it is your prerogative to choose only good deals and then set the tone for getting them done. You can let it be known that to do business with you, a prospect must be COOL!

STORY TIME

It is the early '90s, and I am CEO of a company that sells a great software tool. It saves the folks who use it time, money, and resources. We have an awesome sales force—they literally sell the

(continued)

product over the phone. We identify a project, give out a free evaluation, let the techies use the tool, and when the prospect is ready to deploy it, they cut us a purchase order. All and all, it is a great business model with a solid price point. We are growing at 20% per quarter, and have been for 12 straight quarters, which is pretty darn good for a bootstrapped company.

One day I get a call from a customer. He is paying down his extended payment terms and is not happy; his company is not using the product. It turns out the project for which he bought our software has been canceled, and now the product is sitting on a shelf.

There are plenty of ways to deal with a situation like this, but I know what is right for my customer.

"Don't give it a second thought," I say. "I don't want your money if you are not using the product. Forget about the future payments, and if you do need to use our product again, call me and we'll start the payments back up, same terms."

The customer then asks if he can get a full refund.

"I understand your project was canceled and you never used the product," I tell him, "but my company put in a lot of time training your folks and doing preliminary work for the project. In addition, canceling your future payments means de-booking that revenue, which is not good for me at all. So I think this is a fair deal. I give, you give, and we make it better. It's not perfect, but it's manageable for both of us."

He agrees. "I see your point, and I appreciate your helping me out."

When that customer is ready to do business again—whether it is at this company or when we bump into each other at future jobs—he will come to the new deal knowing that all will be fair and square. It will be easier to do the deal, because he knows first hand what kind of person I am and how I treat customers—before and *after* the deal is done.

What kind of peddler do you want to be? Choose to be one that prospects, customers, and fellow peddlers describe as real and honest. After all, there's really no reason to be hardnosed or a killer. The sales process is a natural cycle that has a beginning, a middle, and an end. The end is called the close. If you execute in the beginning and middle as you should, the close is easy. I mean easy peasy. You don't have to be a "closer." That's a myth!

Asking the Right Questions

Closing is all about continuing to ask the right questions at the right times to the right people. From finding through closing, there are hundreds of questions you should or could ask: Questions that qualify if a lead fits your profile, determine if your product's a fit, ascertain the budget, map the folks involved, and so on. Knowing which questions to ask when and to whom is the art of being a good peddler.

When you become a great peddler, asking questions will come naturally. In the meantime, find a super peddler or two, go on the road with them, and watch them do a few deals from beginning to end. Write down the questions the peddlers ask. One thing I have learned is that no matter what the product is, no matter whether it is an easy or complex sell, there is ALWAYS a basic suite of twenty or so key product questions that can get you a long way down the pipe. They are easy to round up if you are an astute observer with open ears.

Also note when—during finding, selling, or closing—these great peddlers ask each question, and which questions they ask or rephrase at more than one phase. Certain questions, such as those that confirm the process, participants, and budget, you want to ask again and again, at least once at every stage.

Then, before your next meeting, write down your questions and put a check box beside each. As you talk with a prospect and get answers, check them off. Before you leave, make sure there are no open questions.

I don't mean to harp on the importance of questions, but they are one of your most powerful weapons. Asking questions that are simple and relevant, and then listening to the answers, can set up a sale and expedite a deal exponentially. At the same time, don't downplay the incredible value of open, seemingly innocuous questions. Ever! Some of my favorites are:

- So, how are we doing?
- What do you mean?
- Does this feel right to you?
- So, what's happening?
- Do you think we are doing OK?
- What can we do to help?
- Can we make this better?

And, of course, my personal favorite: Is there anybody you would like me to kill in your organization? Just kidding!

Unfortunately, many overzealous peddlers ask great questions and don't wait for an answer. This phenomenon drives me batty. It is indicative of another crazy dynamic of sales: too much desire to close, not enough desire to listen. Unbelievable, but nonetheless 100% true. If you take the time to ask a question, take the time to listen to the answer. What you hear may astonish you.

PEDDLER'S PREROGATIVE #65

If you take the time to ask all the key questions in each phase of the selling process, it is your prerogative to take the time to listen heartily to the answers. Don't ever ask a question and then tune out or interrupt the prospect as he or she is answering. Save that for your sales manager!

Simple world, simple questions, simple truths. Who knew? There's that Zen thing again.

Your M.O.

As with everything else in peddlery, your modus operandi heading into the 75% realm should be simply this: Be flexible. If you are a corporate type and reading this book, please don't have a hemorrhage here. Flexibility is a great mantra. It means you are willing to listen, willing to accommodate, willing to deal.

Many companies establish rules for doing business that work for them, but not for their prospects. They set up their manufacturing, delivery, support, and so forth, to meet their needs, not their prospects' and customers'.

Pricing is one huge area in which companies are inevitably inflexible. They insist that prospects buy all modules even if they only need one. They refuse to ship a product until they receive a deposit even though they are selling to a blue-chip prospect that desperately needs the product tomorrow. They enforce a tiered-pricing structure even though the prospect has only one additional user for the life of the license. They refuse to discount. The list goes on and on.

News flash: If you want to turn more prospects into customers, you need to understand how your prospects do business, assess their needs on a case-by-case basis, and then accommodate them. Some prospects may say they don't pay for training; it must be part of the package. Make it so! Others may require that maintenance not exceed a certain percentage of the total price. Work it out! Still others may require a discount that they don't deserve:

> *Ms. Prospect:* We need a 25% discount.
>
> *Peddler:* But the number of units you are ordering only qualifies you for a 10% discount, Ms. Prospect.
> Do you want to increase the quantity?
>
> *Ms. Prospect:* I don't have the budget to order more.
>
> *Peddler:* How about in the next budget cycle? Can you commit to buying 15 more units in 6 months?
>
> *Ms. Prospect:* No.
>
> *Peddler:* How about in 12 months?
>
> *Ms. Prospect:* No.
>
> *Peddler:* How about in 18 months?
>
> *Ms. Prospect:* Yes, I can do that.
>
> *Peddler:* Great! We'll write that into the contract.

Flexibility. It's not a euphemism for losing money; it's a recipe for making it. If you know your business, industry, and product well, you should be able to listen to what a prospect needs and figure out a way to make it happen—to benefit both of you!

Unfortunately, many corporate wizards blindly institute the rules of the road and then rigidly adhere to them. Corporate narcissism once again. These folks can't conceive of budging from their restrictive business model to help their own company sell more product. For the love of God, have they never heard of WORKING WITH THE PROSPECT?

Here's the skinny: You need to have enough flexibility to make deals work for your prospects. If your pricing models, discount scales, delivery schedules, and so on, aren't flexible, fix them. I know it is frustrating and takes time away from selling to fight in-house battles about issues that should be no-brainers, but it is necessary. And when you win, it is worth it.

Three Quarters and Counting: Seventy-Five Percent

You know you've moved from 50% land to the 75% realm when you get the verbal. It is one of the best parts of selling, because it's the first real indication you are going to close the deal. You got to love it when prospects tell you they are going to do business with you. I actually get more of a kick out of receiving a verbal than the signed P.O. Sometimes I keep it to myself for a while just for grins; my little secret that enables me to torture my colleagues and cohorts!

There are several things that typically happen in and around the verbal: the prospect confirms the budget, asks for a quote or final proposal, and hints at a meeting with Mr. Big. Another is that just before the verbal, it always seems like you can get affirmative answers to your assumptive-close questions.

The Assumptive Close

The assumptive close is when a peddler takes advantage of an opportune moment to pose a seemingly innocuous question, which elicits an answer that indicates whether or not he or she has the deal. Got it?

OK, here we go. Let's say all of a sudden the navigator takes over your meeting. He or she is explaining who you are, why you're here, what your product does, why it's a fit. You're nodding your head, agreeing with all the navigator is saying, and realizing that there must be a god because your prospect is selling you, your company, and your product. He or she is on the bandwagon, and pushing the deal forward. You jump in:

> "We can have an engineer here a week earlier and that would ensure you can meet your delivery date. Would you like for me to arrange that?"

Or, the navigator sees the fit for your product better then you do, so you say:

> "Geez, you know this stuff better then I do! So when did you first realize this was a go?"

Sometimes, the navigator may explain new and different ways to use the product, which is when you respond:

> "Whoa! I never thought of those angles. Amazing! I'll submit a revised proposal to you in a week that includes those points. Can we schedule a meeting with your boss for the following week?"

You get the gist. If the navigator responds positively and starts acting like a customer, you're on your way to a verbal. If he or she backs off, you still have work ahead of you; this puppy hasn't reached the 75% mark just yet.

If an opportune moment doesn't surface, you may have to create scenarios to find out where you stand, which you also can use to push prospects past the evaluation checklist and onto implementation issues. For example:

> "Ms. Prospect, assuming you're going to deploy our product, we should talk about training, because our classes are filling up. Should I set up a call with our training team to assure you a slot?"

And if all else fails:

"We're spending a lot of time and resources with you, Mr. Prospect, I sure hope it's worth it."

If he gives you some affirmation and says something like, "Yeah, yeah, don't worry, it's worth it," you're on the right track.

Peddlers collect a bunch of probing and affirming tricks, and keep them in their bags to work the assumptive close. Of course, a prospect may or may not realize what you are doing, and may or may not approve. So be ready to deal with the person who says, "Hey, not so fast!"

But when these types of questions start rolling in the affirmative, it's the prelude to a verbal. A verbal means you are squarely in 75% land. Once you get a verbal, you have a deal within reach and a good shot at getting it done. So good, in fact, that if you manage to get a verbal and then don't close the deal, well, that is one gray day in the neighborhood.

Sometimes verbals come out of the clear blue sky. Other times it is a matter of asking this question: So, are we going to do some business together?

Of course, you must ask this of the right person. The right person is one who has the power to say yes. When a peddler gets on the phone or face-to-face with an executive who says, "It's a go, pending contract negotiations," you got a verbal. You also have it if you receive it from someone who is a credible person. For example, a navigator may meet with his boss or his boss's boss and come back with a verbal. You know it's real when it comes from someone who is truly in the know.

You also must ask for the verbal at the right time. If a prospect is surprised or balks, you have asked too soon.

PEDDLER'S PREROGATIVE #66

It is your peddler's prerogative to get to the verbal as fast as you can. A verbal from a reliable source means you're in! Enjoy the verbal, as it usually means you are getting the business. It also means it is time to buckle down and put this puppy to bed.

Gimme Some Sugar! I Am Your Neighbor!: The Budget

The funny thing about budgets is that prospects often have one or want to set one before they really know what they want or need, before you advise them how best to fulfill their requirements, and before you price out the cost for your products, services, materials, training, and so on. Usually, the money discussion comes up at the 50% mark, but it can happen as early as the first meeting with a prospect. When this happens, peddlers' reactions run the gamut: They want this now? Will they hold me to this number? What's the right answer? And on and on. Not knowing what to do, peddlers hem and haw, try to beg the question, and risk their credibility.

Relax. Have a ballpark price ready and put it on the table. Nearly all the time, for one reason or another, you will come in way high or way low. But knowing whether you and your prospect are in the same ballpark is a good thing and the earlier the better. If a project is likely to cost $150,000 and a prospect expects it to cost $50,000, it's best you know that sooner rather than later. So don't be afraid to tackle the issue and give them a rough figure, just make sure they understand it is a ballpark price.

One of two things usually happens next. The prospect says it's out of their range and walks away from the table, or they don't. If they walk away, be glad. That's a bad prospect off your plate, leaving you free to pursue other good projects. If they remain at the table, you know there's potential to bridge the gap. From then on, you work to close it.

No matter what you do, however, the budget is the biggest gotcha that can surface in 75% land. It can be there one moment, get zapped and vanish the next. Disappearing or suddenly attacked and weakened budgets can be a drag. Prospects are famous for playing budget games: We have the funds. Money is no object. We did our homework. We have the cash. Knock, knock, um, Dennis, we have a small issue . . . um, it's the budget.

The budget means you're dealing with finance, a very strange beast indeed.

What you don't want to do at any point during the selling cycle is ignore a budget problem, cross your fingers, and hope it goes away. Get the issue back out on the table as soon as you see it:

> "You seem concerned about finding the money. Should we take something out of the requirements list? Should we take something out of the Statement of Work? Where else can we get the money?"

Typically, a budget problem doesn't kill a deal, but it can take time to expropriate the cash, which can foul you up—particularly at this stage when HQ is expecting you to bring it all home very soon.

Simple Pricing Models

I have worked for companies where some nutcase analytic devises pricing models and schemes that would give Einstein a headache. No one can understand the models never mind present them. The peddlers are lost. Management is lost. The prospects are lost.

PEDDLER'S PREROGATIVE #67

> Pricing models should be simple and easy to explain to anyone—and I do mean ANYONE. If your mother can't understand how much your products costs, then marketing has gone overboard once again. It is your peddler's prerogative to haul them back into the boat.

To be able to provide a price to a prospect, you must have simple pricing models—really simple. If you are in a company and can't easily understand the pricing—and I mean in 30 seconds—send the pricing maven a copy of *The Peddler's Prerogative* with this page marked and the following message highlighted:

> Dear Mr./Ms. Marketer:
>
> You are a knucklehead. You need to devise a simple pricing model so your peddlers can easily understand it and explain it to prospects. YES, SO PROSPECTS HAVE ABSOLUTELY NO PROBLEMS FIGURING OUT HOW MUCH IT COSTS TO DO BUSINESS WITH YOUR COMPANY.
>
> Dennis Ford
>
> P.S. You may be smart and creative, but you're a knucklehead when it comes to pricing. Stop being a knucklehead.

If they still are not open to simplifying their models, seriously consider bailing, as they are clueless and it's not worth your while to argue.

One other thing: Every company is in business to make money. Being able to make a reasonable profit is a good thing; being greedy is not. You can nickel and dime prospects or hide outrageous profits using complex pricing models, but you will crash and burn. Prospects won't buy either because they can't figure out the true cost, or because after dissecting your pricing, they realize you are not competitive. It's a no-win strategy.

The Proposal: Quotes, SOWs, and Ts & Cs

After you and your prospect have confirmed the budget, the next step usually is to revisit the proposal. The one you presented at the 50% stage outlined, in general, the prospect's requirements and requests, and how you could fulfill them. The proposal at the 75% mark is more specific. A prospect has refined their specifications, and your proposal includes a description of the specific products and services you will provide, a quote, a Statement of Work, and some terms and conditions.

No one is asking for a quote if they are not getting serious about purchasing something, although it might not be your product. A prospect might be getting a quote from you for comparison purposes. But typically you are a serious contender if they ask for an OFFICIAL, detailed quote.

A quote is usually based on the standard pricing of your product and services as well as any ancillary items, such as training, support, maintenance, and so on. It also covers any special requirements or requests that are part of the deal. For example, you may have agreed to customize your product or provide special training. It's important to keep in mind the difference between ballpark pricing and a quote: You live with a quote, although undoubtedly it will change from when you first deliver it until the contract is signed, as a prospect's requirements and specifications usually change.

It is important that a quote leaves no room for misunderstanding or misinterpretation. So when it comes to soft deliverables, such as services, training, customizations, and the like, you should also submit a document that describes in detail exactly what you and your prospect have agreed to and the delivery time. Make it painstakingly clear. These documents are called various things from Statements of Work (SOW) to punch lists, and they change as the deal moves toward closure. Nevertheless, it's vital to create one and keep it up-to-date as the deal progresses.

Once you submit your quote to a prospect, the negotiating begins, which has its own myth and mystery attached to it. Your job as a peddler is to make it a normal, straightforward process. Be frank, be open, be up front. It seems like the hardest thing about discussing pricing is actually having a discussion. Not dictating. Not getting caught up in some foolish negotiating drama. Just discussing.

PEDDLER'S PREROGATIVE #68

It is your peddler's prerogative not to turn pricing and negotiations into a full-fledged drama. Be cool, calm, straightforward, and logical. Pricing is just pricing. Nevertheless, make doubly and triply sure you COMPLETELY understand it before opening your yap!

My goal always is to have an honest dialogue so that I can understand how I should structure the deal. I let the prospect know that I want to find something that works for him or her. It is amazing what happens when you have a helpful, let's-work-it-out attitude: The prospect relaxes and opens up. A good peddler doesn't want to negotiate with a stressed prospect. A good peddler wants the prospect feeling like this guy cares and wants to work with me. I trust him!

Let's face it, there's no reason to do otherwise. If a prospect balks at a quote there are a hundred and one ways to skin the pricing cat. So don't worry how a prospect will respond—unless you're trying to gloss over an obvious price disconnect. That's a bad thing. The peddler has to keep in mind what the prospect is expecting to pay, and either make sure the quote jives or address the issue up front. If you gave a ballpark price of $150,000, don't try to slip by a quote for $300,000.

Assuming you are not sticking your head in the sand, however, there are plenty of ways to address a prospect's concerns. Discounting, extending payment terms, adding special terms and conditions—

the list goes on and on. The point is, when you start talking pricing, always use the words:

> We want to do the deal and we want it to be a good deal. Please let us know how we can make it work. We can be flexible within reason. We want to get our product to you and make you a happy customer.

The navigator usually knows how to work the company and where to get more money. So, never panic if you come in over budget. Let him or her work their magic.

That said, sometimes the prospect takes a hard line, and keeps negotiating the price down further and further. You keep trying to work it out when all of a sudden you realize you've given a lot, maybe even too much, and this is not a good deal anymore. At this point, I speak up: "This deal really isn't going well for me. My company has bent over backwards and given you such a bargain that the deal is beginning to feel one sided. Before we go any further, can you find any way to make it better?" Just be frank and up front. Get a constructive dialogue going while you are all still at the table. After all, why the hell not?

Sometimes things are flying fast and furious, and it isn't until the end of the day, after you add up their side and add up your side, that you see incongruity. Well, guess what? You need to go back the next day and fix it. You need to make it fair for both parties. Otherwise, it will never ever work!

Hello? Is Anybody Out There?

It is a well-known fact that at any stage of a deal, the dang thing can go dead. One moment you are talking with the prospect, exchanging e-mails, getting your calls returned, setting up meetings, and then, it is THE DEAD ZONE. When this happens, life gets weird. Usually, it is just because things happen: the prospect gets busy, goes on vacation, or gets diverted to an in-house crisis. But without knowing that, it is freaky and unnerving. One day all is great. Then, a day goes by, then another, and another, and it is a big black void. No contact. The wind is whipping you on the barren tundra and you realize, I have a sales meeting and I have to report on this deal. YIKES!

When a deal goes dead, pick the right moment and send an e-mail along these lines. Send it before your sales meeting so you have some-

thing to report rather than having to admit you've been sitting on your hands whistling.

Subject: It's OK to say no!

Dear Mr./Ms. Prospect,

It's OK to say no! It's OK to tell me that the deal that we have been working on isn't going to come to fruition, or that you've been side-tracked and had to move it off your priority list.

I have left messages and sent e-mail over the last umpteen days, but I haven't heard back. I realize how busy things can get, and I don't want to be a bother, or waste your time or mine if things aren't on track.

As a person who tries hard to be a good peddler, it's important to me that we have an open and honest dialogue about any potential business relationship. It's just as important to me not to try to engage you if it is no longer appropriate.

If I hear back from you with some ideas for proceeding, that will be great! If not, that is OK. I will *not* contact you again unless I hear from you.

I always get a positive reaction to this e-mail. The prospect tells me they have been very busy, but everything's fine. We need to keep moving. We need to this deal done! That's a good sign. However, if you do not get a response, then tell your boss to remove it from the forecast and move on.

Bringing in the Guns: Leveraging the Execs

For better or worse, good or bad, there is always the big-boy-to-big-boy, let's-put-it-to-bed, drag-in-the-execs scenario, which always adds some amusement to the show. Many prospects let a deal progress to a certain point and then march in Mr. Big. In this case, you have to roll out your guy—the one who deals with the Mr. Big types. Many times, that's me and I get a kick out of anticipating which flavor of Mr. Big I may run into. Will he be:

Mr. Grinder:	"This deal sucks. I am going to extract a pound of flesh from you or lop off your head."
Mr. Psycho:	"I'll blow this freaking building up and the deal along with it."
Mr. Intimidator:	"You wanna play with fire, boys, I am the bad-ass mofo in this neighborhood."
Mr. Aw Shucks:	"I am so happy to be here with you and your company. Bob's told me all about you and your great products. I sure wish I had a chance to meet with you sooner."
Mr. Schmuck:	"Gee, we love you guys and your products. What is it that you sell again?"

You have to deal with each in a different way. You can't cave to Mr. Grinder, blink with Mr. Psycho, or look scared with Mr. Intimidator. And Mr. Schmuck, well, what can I say? At least he's entertaining, in a schmucky sort of way.

STORY TIME

For six months, I am working on a nice deal with a nice company. We work through most of the major issues and today is the day that their new CEO is coming in to allegedly give the nod and his blessing.

I'm chatting with my navigator when Mr. Grinder comes strolling in. He is just off a plane from Europe and acting like a tired, spoiled, cranky, two-year-old (ring a bell?).

We give him the agenda, explain that we will give him a synopsis of the work we have done with his troops, and that there are only a few outstanding items to iron out before we can put the deal to bed.

"There isn't any deal until I say there's a deal!" he blurts out.

A second outburst soon follows, with him sputtering about how he is in charge and nobody is going tell him how to proceed.

Needless to say, his staff sits there shocked and embarrassed. I try to explain that we all have worked closely together and done a good job. I ask him to take a moment and let us give him a complete account of the deal.

This makes him bluster all the more. It seems Mr. Grinder feels compelled to be a complete jerk and show everyone that he is in charge, not to mention a treacherous egomaniac. I proceed to watch the unraveling of this CEO and my deal, and realize he is an idiot.

An hour or so later, I meet with my navigator and explain that I am sorry, but I won't do a deal with that nutcase. I vote with my feet and walk from what was once a good deal. But a deal is good only when it is good for both parties, and this guy wasn't about to give me and my company a good deal.

The moral: Know when to hold 'em, know when to fold 'em.

When it comes to Mr. Aw Shucks, you had better hold on to your wallet. He's a tricky son of a gun. He'll make some outlandish requests with his eye-to-eye, good-old-boy, ear-to-ear grin: "Aw shucks, I was thinking of a 65% discount on our first purchase and increasing after that." He may seem sincere and honest, but he's way off the playing field and he knows it. At times like this, just smile back earnestly and tell him that you don't do deep discounts without big commitments, by golly, gee willikers. Eventually, he'll hear you and things will get agreed upon.

The exec you'll probably meet most often, however, is Mr. Ego: "Before we get started, I'll take a few minutes to tell you about me, my big-company experience, and my impressive accomplishments."

Don your rain gear, zip up your boots, get a twinkle in your eye, summon your best smile, and hold onto your sanity. You are about to see the rare bird who roosts and thrives in corporate America. He's got to be bizarre. Think about the skill set he must have needed to get the special office: ace groveler, adroit head nodder, cheerleader extraordinaire. He's probably your classic can-do, sock-it-to-me, right-you-are-boss, I-love-this-company, we're-like-family, type-A overachiever.

In an earlier chapter, I mentioned that I was a social worker before I became a peddler. I worked in a prison for a while (the pay sucked and it was dangerous). I am still amazed at the similarities between sociopathic prison types and a few of your garden-variety corporate executives. Neither has any sense of remorse for what they greedily take to serve their self-centered wants and needs. OK, so I digress!

Mr. Ego is relatively easy to handle, you just have to listen, smile, and nod. All he really wants is to unload all his greatness on you. Mr. Ego usually rations 70% of a meeting to talk about himself and his achievements, saving maybe 30% of the scheduled time to get any business done.

Then there are the seasoned, decent execs who show up as well. These folks are awesome. They are a pleasure to meet and do business with, have a let's-get-it-done attitude, and are accomplishing way more than I could ever hope to.

I love to make fun of corporate executives, because I am a peddler and that's what we do. I also have met my fair share of the good, the bad, and the ugly. But to be fair, there are many execs who are staunch supporters and allies of peddlers. These folks are great!

No matter which executive you are dealing with, remember that in their world, it's the net-net (the bottom line of the bottom line, another Zen issue). So be ready to go. Have the navigator sitting beside you, and summarize the deal cleanly and succinctly. Look the executive straight in the eye and be firm, telling him or her where there is wiggle room for negotiation and where there is none. Lead him down the path. Typically they are too busy to get too deep. So if you talk straight, make sense, and go slow, they will read you right and give the nod, approving the deal points and structure.

Before the meeting wraps up, however, make sure you ask the exec how the process works from here on out (ya, it's one of those things you must map over and over). Suggest that the executive build some trigger points into the deal so that there is not only regular dialogue with the project team, but a check-in call from you or some other designate to the executive. This ensures that everyone stays in context as the deal moves into contract negotiations and, finally, implementation.

Then, during the official handshake, ask the executive if he is available to run interference for you if the deal hiccups. They always say yes and that is great, because if something happens (bet on it) you can call and remind him of his promise: "Hey, Mr. Big, remember me? I need your help!"

He Ain't Heavy, He's My Brother: References

We have a saying where I come from: a favor for a favor. It means you help me out, I help you out. You scratch my back, I scratch your back.

As a peddler, your personal goal should be to have every one of your customers willing to do you a favor and act as a reference. I mean every single one. If you make a list of your current and past customers, and not all are willing to recommend you and your company, then shame on you. From this day forward, ask every customer if you can use him or her as a reference. If they hesitate or say no, ask why. Then fix their problem. Some companies have policies against recommending suppliers; there's nothing you can do about it. But most customers will pitch in to help you if they are happy with you and your company.

What good references can do for you is monumental! They are the best sales folk in the world. They are credible because they are objective third parties who have bought your product and are using it.

They can take a slow sales process and expedite it. And if they actually like being one, well, then they are truly great references. There's no better help than that of a customer who likes getting calls from prospects and candidly answering the questions they know are lurking in their minds. It reinforces everything you are telling your prospect.

It is also great when you drop names and the prospect has heard of that company or person, and gets excited about chatting with them. This is why for any market I sell into, I develop as many highly-visible, well-known companies or people as I can. As soon as a prospect expresses an interest, I hook them up ASAP.

Story Time

I am working for a company and having a ton of success signing accounts with a particular profile. In fact, I have sold to all first-tier accounts in my turf except one. Try as I might, however, I just can't get in the door. I research the company and map the players, but I keep getting stonewalled.

One day, I am at a trade show manning my company's booth like a good hung-over peddler when I see my target guy, Joe, with Bill, one of my customers. I know Bill well and jump over with a big ear-to-ear grin, outstretched hand, and a happy feeling in my heart.

"Geesus, Bill, how the hell are you? Great to see you here!" Pats on the back, giggles and grins all around, and finally an introduction to Joe.

"Glad to meet ya," I say. "I've been hunting you down for a few months. I'm Dennis Ford from XYZ Corporation."

"I know the name, but I don't think we have a fit or the time to talk to you folks."

"Not a problem," I blurt out. "I'm just glad to say hello finally. Bill knows everything about me, my company, and my products. It took me a year to sell him. If you want to know anything about us, ask him."

Then I turn to Bill: "Where are we grabbing a beer after the show?" He smiles and says he'll come by later to get me. Handshakes, smiles, and off everyone goes. Two hours later Bill shows up.

(continued)

"Hey, we nabbed a limo. It's impossible to get cabs around here. We're out front."

"We? Who's we?" I ask.

"You owe me a piece of the commission, Dennis. I invited Joe along!"

"Sure thing, Billy. Usual deal? Brown paper bag, small denominations?" and we both laugh.

That night, we have a great dinner. I don't try to sell Joe a damn thing; I just get to know him. Then as we're leaving I say, "Joe, if you give me 20 minutes, I know we will do some business together."

"Call my admin next week," he replies, "and we will set up a meeting."

A few months later, we did a deal.

When a customer likes you and your company, and goes out of his or her way to help you, that is a good reference. And that's why the next time Bill calls, needs my products, and asks me to jump, my reply will be, how high? It's all about a favor for a favor.

All too often when a prospect asks a peddler for references, the peddler fires off names and numbers for the prospect to call. WRONG! This is not the way to keep control of your deal or maintain your sphere of influence.

I am not a control freak, but let's be realistic. Giving two people each other's numbers and hoping they connect is stupid. Your deal now hangs on two strangers finding time in their busy schedules to connect. Your fate is in the hands of two people who have no notion of forecasts, monthly goals, or quarterly quotas, and who are not on peddler time!

What you want to do is volunteer to coordinate their schedules, set up the call, and make sure the two connect. If this sounds too forward, let me ask you: Which call would you rather make?

"Ms. Prospect, I'm calling to check in with you (yet again) to see if you have had the time to talk with our references yet."

"Ms. Prospect, I have Mr. Reference on the other line."

In the first, you feel like a nag; in the second, you rightly feel like the attentive, proactive peddler you are. It's your deal; take control and move it along. Don't let yourself be put in the position of waiting and hoping. This is the difference between a good peddler and a bad peddler. A good peddler does everything he or she can to make sure they are getting the prospect through the process.

The Mystery Inside the Riddle: The Process

Every company has it's own process for doing a deal, and everyone is only too happy to tell you what they think it is. Then you get your meeting with the top exec and you get his opinion. In the end what you're looking for is the straightest path to sign-off. Sometimes the top exec provides that: "Let's get this done. Give it to me, I'll sign it." But if not, here again, your trusted navigator should be able to guide you through the process.

A big mistake is leaving it solely up to your navigator. You need to be in constant dialogue with him or her, talking to each other at work, driving home, after dinner. You better be on it! The devil is in the details, and this is where simple mistakes can wind up costing you commission dollars. Even the best navigator is sidetracked, forgets, must shift priorities, gets sick—even leaves the company, leaving you short of your quota. You need to shepherd your deal.

Every day, validate what happened the day before and get a current status. Every day, outline the steps you have to go through to get the order. Always confirm the folks involved; get names and numbers. The hard part is being proactive without being a pain in the arse. Good peddlers find a way to be vigilant but not overbearing.

The Key to the Deal

It's possible to get to the 75% stage and not know the real reason why a prospect went looking for your product to begin with, or why it has to get this deal done. Sometimes it's clear, but often the REAL reason isn't forthcoming. You have asked folks along the way, but perhaps the answers you received were different or didn't ring true. Heck, even if you got the same answers and they sounded right, there still is a chance that you don't know the REAL reason. It happens. Often, the folks you're dealing with don't really know.

Don't give up! There is a reason why every deal exists, it is known to at least one or two folks, and it's worth your while to find out. So keep digging and validating the reasons you find with the right folks. Around the time of the verbal, this information is easier to come by. Note that the real reason is different than why your product is a fit. Some common reasons for having to buy a product or do a deal are:

- It provides the prospect with a competitive advantage
- It levels the playing field; the prospect is no longer at a competitive disadvantage
- It helps a prospect make or save money
- It is the missing piece to a strategic initiative
- There is an imminent deliverable
- There is an important upcoming event
- It is needed to create a prototype or proof of concept
- It is a pet project of Mr. Big's
- It is the ante in—something the prospect has to have to be a player

But the number one real reason may not be something so logical or rational. It could be because the CEO wants it to keep up with his golfing buddies.

Knowing the real reason can affect how you shape a deal, give you creative ideas during budget discussions, or help you to hold your own during negotiations. If you know a prospect needs your product to win a big account, for example, then perhaps you don't need to entice the prospect with a big discount. If the prospect is planning to use your product to meet an impending deadline, then you know by when the deal must close. And if you know the bigwig who's behind the deal, then you know who to call if your deal starts to head south:

Peddler: Mr. V.P., I know you really want my product, so I thought I'd let you know that this deal is about to unravel.

Mr. V.P.: No way, this is not going to unravel. What do we have to do?

Don't Let Your Deal Go Down

Your job is the care and feed-ing of your deal. You are its babysitter and you can't let it out of your sight. You have to anticipate its next move so it never gets into trouble. You have to be wary of all strangers who pause to ad-mire it. And you have to keep your eye on the clock, so you put it to bed on time.

Your prospect may have a reason to move this deal along. But more often than not, a peddler has to provide some impetus to get a deal done. You need to create a sense of urgency. That doesn't mean whipping everyone into a burn-the-house-down frenzy. Rather, create some pressure points for the prospect and for your company that keeps everyone moving along. This is where a peddler's creative orchestration capabilities can shine. No hair-brained schemes. No operatic productions. Rather, a stealth-mode operation that finds subtle ways and creative ideas to move the deal down the pipe.

Deadlines are most effective. They may be real or artificial, but ei-ther way, they help move it along. One of the first dates you should create is the proposal date. Let's say you and your navigator decide on a due date that is one week from today. Back at your company, you can say, hey, I had a meeting with the prospect (true) and they are expecting our best proposal in one week (true), and so ladies and gen-tlemen of my company, here is what I need from all of you now (true). Just don't tell anyone you created the date with the prospect.

When you do deliver the proposal, you get to (drum roll, please) create yet another delivery date: the date by when the prospect will review the proposal. This in turn will spawn another date for the clos-ing meeting, which is when both companies come together at a meet-ing or on a conference call, review everything one last time, and ne-gotiate the contract.

I know I have hammered on this issue as I've talked about the nuances of being a great peddler, but it's important. You must condition yourself to look at a deal as a live entity with all the work and surprises that implies. If you let someone derail your deal, you are being irresponsible. Don't be irresponsible!

So here we are, at the end of the 75% stage, wrapping everything up and getting ready to go into the final round. The budget has been approved, the pricing, Statement of Work, and contract terms have been generally agreed upon, the prospect has checked the references, and the contracts are in process. Everyone is on the same page and in agreement as to what we are selling and what they are buying.

Ding! Ding! Ding! We Have a Winner!: One Hundred Percent

When closing time arrives, and you, your prospect, and all appropriate parties congregate in a room or on the phone for contract negotiations, there are several hard and fast rules to follow.

First, don't pretend you're a lawyer. I have no idea why anyone would pretend that they have legal knowledge that they don't possess, but they do. I have seen peddlers, sales managers, and executives all lean into the table and start negotiating terms and conditions that they have NOT A CLUE about. If you are negotiating a contract, there are basically two aspects: the legal stuff and the business stuff. Stick with the business stuff and have a lawyer with you to handle the legal stuff.

PEDDLER'S PREROGATIVE #69

When involved in contract negotiations, it is your prerogative not to think you are a lawyer and negotiate legal terms and conditions. Join the business bargaining, but keep your mouth closed during any legal wrangling. We all know you are blessed and wonderful, but you ain't a lawyer, bucko, so cool your jets.

More often than not, a prospect arrives at this meeting with a list of things that he or she needs, expects, or wants in the contract. The odds are that at least one item is a surprise: The prospect needs the product a week earlier, or must have a 12% discount rather than 10%, and so on. He or she also has a list of nice-to-haves and lucky-to-get items. Getting the prospect to put all of these things on the table up front is the second rule of negotiating.

For seasoned business folks, this usually isn't a big deal. They know what they want and what they can forego. They are reasonable. They want to do the deal and go home. If your prospect is not forth-coming, then you'll have to ask or draw them out. Whatever you do, don't let them pull out a requirement, negotiate it, pull out another one, negotiate it, and on and on. You will find yourself at a severe dis-advantage. Only start the negotiations with a map of the minefield in hand. Then start maneuvering your way through it.

The third rule is what I call the three-times rule. Whilst negotiat-ing, don't take a no as a no until you hear it three times. Most folks have a hard time saying no three times unless they really mean it. The first couple of nos can be posturing or testing, but the third no pret-ty much means no. Over the years, there have been plenty of times when all of a sudden I've gotten a yes after hearing a couple of nos. My point is, if you hear no a couple times, don't stop until you get the third no. Now, anywhere else in the world a no is a no. But in negotiating, you don't know what the flock a no is until you test it.

PEDDLER'S PREROGATIVE #70

During negotiations, never take no as an answer until you hear it three times. Folks who say no three times really mean it. Less than that, how-ever, and they may change their minds. It is your peddler's prerogative to follow the three-times rule and make sure no means no!

Finally, for the love of Pete, stop selling. You are at this meeting because the prospect has already committed to buying. You do not offer anything more unless they ask you to. Inevitably, peddlers, a manager—often someone at the highest level—gets caught up in the deal making or believes he or she knows how to get a deal done, and starts making unnecessary promises: We'll give you the extra module for free; we'll throw in the training; we'll devote whatever resources are necessary to get you up and running in a week. Stop! Just do the deal.

Discounts

Some folks believe that asking for a discount or a bigger discount is part of the protocol of closing a sale. The discount chat is easy for me, because my mantra is, "I am happy to give you whatever the industry standard is." The good news is most industries have discounting guidelines or standards. For example, generally in the computer industry, software companies give a 0–20% discount when they sell direct to customers, they give a 20–50% discount to VARs (value-added resellers), and a 50–70% discount to OEMs (original equipment manufacturers).

Sometimes a prospect asks for an insane discount that is not grounded in reality at all. In this case, you have to gingerly explain how discounting works and bring them back down to Earth:

> Mr. Prospect, in this business, discounts are based on unit volume or dollar volume. Here are our discount schedules. Based on the numbers we discussed, I gave you a 20% discount. However, if you are willing to make a bigger commitment, then I can give you a bigger discount.

If you take the time to dissect the crazy ideas folks have, and explain your discount structure, most folks understand they have to give to get. "The more money or commitment I receive from you, Mr. Prospect, the bigger the discount I can give you. Capisci?"

PEDDLER'S PREROGATIVE #71

During the last part of the closing cycle, keep everything grounded in reality. Prospects can lose perspective and believe they can get more than is fair. Keep their reality quotient at 42. Search me, it's that Zen thing again!

Ts & Cs

Of all the terms and conditions in a contract, payment terms are most frequently the sticking point. Typical terms are net 30, hard and fast. It is common for prospects to ask for extended payment terms, however, such as 45, 60, 90, 120, or even 180 days. Some may have legitimate issues, such as a cyclical business or a temporary cash flow problem; others may be bad payers. Before you go into this meeting, you have to find out what your company is willing to do and how you are going to handle this issue.

Generally, I try to avoid more than 90 days, although on occasion I have agreed to 120 days. No matter what terms the prospect requests, however, I take such opportunities to reconsider the payment plan as a whole. If a prospect wants extended terms, I may ask for a some money up front, so some money comes in faster, some slower. Or if the total amount is due in 30 days, I might agree to 50% in 30 days, and 50% in 60 days, or 33% in 30 days, 33% in 60 days, and 34% in 90 days.

Then, after the deal is done, I have no problem calling the customer before a payment date and reminding them that I gave them extended terms so they had better pay on time. After all, most companies pay peddlers their commissions *after* the customer pays.

These are a few common ways to extend payments terms, but there are plenty of others. And, of course, you can always ask them: "It doesn't seem you're happy with what I can do. What have other competitive vendors done for you? What do you think is reasonable? I'll take your suggestions back to my company and see what I can do."

Remember, however, the more creative you get, the more chance you have of making a bad deal or promising something you can't deliver. Understand the parameters of a normal deal and stay as close to them as possible. Sometimes you need to think outside of the box to get a deal done, but don't get carried away. Promise only what makes good business sense and what you can legitimately deliver.

Once You Sign, Get Out

If anything drives me whacky, and I do mean off-the-wall, jumpin' crazy, it is when a peddler gets a signature on a contract, and keeps on flappin' his yap and winds up talking himself into a jam.

This is one of those subtleties of peddling, so listen up! I don't know why (maybe it's an adrenaline rush), but often when peddlers get to the end of the deal, get it all tied up nice and purty, for some zany reason they just keep on selling. This is a peddler phenomenon that is true, I swear.

Some folks just can't turn it off. They can't just say great, thanks, and leave. They dig in and keep on selling, keep on talking, which creates a potential situation for a major slip up. There have been times when I have literally grabbed a peddler by the arm and escorted him, jaws flapping, out of a room.

When you reach the end of the pipe, you are supposed to leave. When they flash the lights at closing time, it's time to get out of the bar. The danger is that you say something wrong. You mention an issue that should have been taken care of but fell through the cracks, a pivotal point surfaces that has to be put to bed, or, god forbid, a showstopper emerges and you're a dead man. So let's get something straight: After you get a deal, leave as quickly as possible. Once you are done, be gone!

PEDDLER'S PREROGATIVE #72

It is the peddler's prerogative to know when the heck to close his or her yap and stop selling. It is hard to do. Selling is a peddler's natural state. But when you have the deal, for the love of Pete, remember to stop selling. Stop selling. STOP SELLING!

If by chance there is something that has to be corrected afterward, it's no big deal. Customers have an immense psychological commitment after the contracts are signed, the deal is booked, and they receive an invoice. They are in bed with you and more amenable to working things out. In addition, customers often have to amend the contract as well. They can't accept delivery when they thought, they can't allocate all the resources they promised, they need you to install the product at additional locations. Things change.

Receiving the P.O.

On we go to the land of the Purchase Order. I have said that each facet of the process can be a universe onto itself. When it comes to the P.O., nothing could be truer.

Some companies have elaborate systems for generating a P.O. that come to a dead stop for weeks on end, leaving you and your P.O. hanging. If you want to feel what it's like to have a ton of bricks dropped on your head, try waiting for a P.O. to make its way out of the maze called The Purchasing Department. It is pure terror. I have often said that it's the little things that get you. Waiting for a P.O. is one of those little things that will beat you to a sobbing heap of pulp.

The mistake many peddlers make is to assume that the customer will expedite the P.O.; that he or she is just as anxious to get it done as you are. The customer shakes the peddler's hand, thanks him for all his hard work, tells him he'll send the P.O., and the peddler is off to enjoy a beer and think about how to blow his commission.

Don't come off the field before the game is over. This is how you miss your numbers, your bosses miss their numbers—maybe even the company misses its numbers. Ladies and gentlemen, when the contracts are signed, your P.O. adventure has just begun!

PEDDLER'S PREROGATIVE #73

The deal isn't done until you have cashed your commission check. If you are not using that money to buy yourself a pizza and some beer, you can't allow yourself to think all is fine. You have to make triple sure that the P.O. is getting through the bureaucracy at the customer's company and then at yours. It's your responsibility no matter what anyone tries to tell you. Don't foul up!

Before you leave your customer, ask what he has to do to get the P.O.—what is his next step? Explain that you would like to understand the P.O. process. If he doesn't generate it, who does? Is that person in the office this week? Who receives it next? Who has to sign it? Do they know where to send it? How long does it typically take? Get names and numbers, and then follow through:

> "I'm calling to introduce myself, as I understand you are the purchasing agent who will generate the P.O. for my product and I am the peddler. I want to let you know that you should feel free to call me for any reason. Here is my name and number.
>
> "By the way, is everything OK? Is there anything I can do? You've already sent it on to Joe? Great! Is he in today to get it? Do you have his number?"

A 30-second dialogue is often all it takes to keep everybody in the loop and prevent the P.O. from sitting in someone's in-box. So make sure you do it!

Purchase orders have a way of getting lost or stuck about two days before the end of the month or quarter. You call, only to learn that the purchasing agent is out sick and didn't generate it before she left. So you call her boss, who says you'll have to wait until she is back. You call her boss's boss, who says the same thing. Now it's time to call Mr. V.P. and ask for the help he promised to give you. It's times like these when good preparation and hard work pay off and save your deal!

Feel free to remind him that the nice fat discount he was so happy to receive was based on booking the business by a certain date, and there are only 24 hours left until then. He'll get the point. Be nice, but don't be afraid to sound a tad desperate, as it imparts a sense of urgency that is needed in order to save your butt.

Scheduling Delivery and Implementation

Finally, we come to the last hell-raising detail: scheduling delivery and implementation. During the selling process, you make commitments to your prospect, you draw up a contract, and in the heat of negotiations, your colleagues probably make additional promises: Sure, we can deliver one week from today. Sure, we can have an installation team on site the day after. Sure, we can have the engineers working with your folks in two weeks.

Now it's time to deliver. Many peddlers believe this is not their responsibility. As a result, they don't know the folks who are scheduling delivery and implementation. They have no relationship with the folks who are going to be paying a visit to their customer shortly. They give the paperwork to someone in house and wash their hands of it; they are on to the next deal.

Here's a tip: If you want the delivery and implementation to go smoothly for your customer, if you hope to sell more product to that customer, if you want them to act as a referral, you need to be intimately involved.

Your company is no different than your prospect's. It has the same problems, only they threaten delivery and implementation instead of your deal: folks get sick, they have their own priorities, they wait for someone to get back to them, they forget, they take a new job. You need to make sure the paperwork gets signed and processed, the order is booked, the resources are allocated, and the delivery and implementation is done on time and to spec. You're not done until you've talked to the customer and he or she is happy: "Hey, everything you said you were going to do, you did! It's up and running. It works. You came in on time and on budget. You guys are incredible."

Ideally, you have a good relationship with the folks whose job it is to deliver as promised, so it's easy for you to monitor their progress, work with them to resolve any issues that come up, and feel comfortable with how your customer is being treated.

If your deal isn't proceeding as it should and your customer is in a long queue he wasn't supposed to be in, you cannot sit idly by and do nothing. This is what separates the men from the boys, what makes you discover who you really are: a great peddler or a schmuck. Now's the time to make your company live up to its promises or be perceived as a wham-bam, thank-you-ma'am peddler who works for a fly-by-night enterprise.

Rectifying this situation can mean resorting to some sneaky tactics. Dinner, drinks, or a pair of Red Sox tickets (plus the requisite pleading) can be all it takes to move your customer to the head of the class. However, other times, you may have to put it on the line any way you can. Many a time I have screamed, yelled, thrown temper tantrums, went

one-on-one with hardnosed corporate types, and threatened to quit—
actually QUIT—in order to make my company deliver on a deal.

I have been yelled at, beaten down, dragged about, and ordered to
back down, but I have NEVER. Nor will I ever. Call me crazy, but
when my company does a deal and commits to a schedule for delivery and implementation, it has not only signed a legal document, but
it has given its word.

When it comes to making your company hold up their end of the
bargain, your customer will never see how far you push or how hard
you fight on their behalf. Nevertheless, you must take your company
by the hand (or the collar) and show it how to be a great company,
one that is trustworthy, honest, and true to its word.

My company's word is my word. My word is my bond with my
customers. If my word is good, I have happy customers and repeat
customers. So ya, I'll fight to make sure I keep my word. You fine peddlers better fight as well, because if you are not a credible peddler you
have nothing to sell.

PEDDLER'S PREROGATIVE #74

> Your word is all you have. If your company makes a commitment,
> that is your commitment; its word is your word. It is your peddler's
> prerogative to fight tooth and nail to keep your word and your good
> standing. If prospects and customers can't trust your word, you are
> dead and so it will go with your company as well.

Last but not least, delivery and implementation are pretty much
resource allocation issues. The one who screams the loudest gets the
resources. It shouldn't have to be that way, but it is.

Peddler Extraordinaire

There are three facets of the selling process, finding, selling, and closing.
Knowing them well aids you immensely in getting business. PLEASE
DON'T KID YOURSELF. You need to be good at all three.

Some peddlers are terrific analytics, creating a profile, finding
good targets, and mapping companies. But they can't bear to make
that first cold call. Or, if they can make the call, they can't figure out
what to say. Others have no trouble cold calling, getting a top-ten list,

juggling the deals, and maintaining relationships, but they lose it when they have to take it to the next level and put the deal together. Still others are great at finding and selling, but freeze at closing; they feel they are pressuring prospects and wheedling money out of them.

This is what makes peddling hard. You have to be good at all three. You have to be an adroit finder, an adroit seller, and an adroit closer. It ain't easy! It takes hard work, smarts, and a lot of energy. But if you succeed, you will be a peddler extraordinaire.

THE PEDDLER'S MANIFESTO

Peddler's Prerogative #1

You know what's right and you know what's wrong, so call 'em as you see 'em and act accordingly.

Peddler's Prerogative #2

It is the peddler's prerogative to follow corporate processes and policies if they keep the deal moving forward. If corporate policies and procedures impede business, it is the peddler's prerogative to do whatever is necessary by any means possible to get the business. (You will be rewarded either with compassion or a new job.)

Peddler's Prerogative #3

If business is business, it's the peddler's prerogative to understand intimately how the business runs, and then figure out how to make it work for him.

Peddler's Prerogative #4

It is a peddler's prerogative to wake up every single morning knowing that a good attitude will change the world and a bad attitude will really kill your quarter.

Peddler's Prerogative #5

It is a peddler's prerogative to make it obvious through behavior and actions that he or she loves peddling and enjoys all things sales. Joy is contagious and makes everything better.

Peddler's Prerogative #6

Not everyone is wired to leave the safety of their foxholes, join the charge, and take the hill. It is your prerogative to shield your scary, Rambo peddler side from animals, children, and the elderly.

Peddler's Prerogative #7

It is your prerogative to take the time and figure out a selling process that works, that is nice and cozy. Then stay with your process when great things are happening and when thing are in slow mo. It is adhering to your process that will get you through the selling doldrums.

Peddler's Prerogative #8

It is a peddler's prerogative to create a solid process that works. It is also your prerogative to be careful when you hop on the process bandwagon and not let an act of self-help turn into self-mutilation.

Peddler's Prerogative #9

You better be a funny bastard if you want to be a good peddler. It is your prerogative to figure out how funny you want to be. Be as funny as you should be, less isn't enough, more is too much. It's all a riddle anyway!

Peddler's Prerogative #10

It is your peddler's prerogative to take a break guiltlessly. Rest, recharge, and come back swinging. It is essential not to let anyone but you determine when you need a breather and when you should take it.

Peddler's Prerogative #11

When you meet folks with bad 'tudes, make no mistake, THEY WILL WEAKEN YOU! It is absolutely your prerogative to remove them from your reality. SHUN THEM!

Peddler's Prerogative #12

Being a peddler is a career that often expands across decades. It takes years to develop close acquaintances and solid friendships. It is the peddler's prerogative to take the time to cultivate meaningful professional relationships, as they will carry you through the down times and happily share your success in the good times.

Peddler's Prerogative #13

A right of passage for any great peddler is being formally stripped of an account, thrown out of an account, or quitting an account verily. Good for you. Bravo!

Peddler's Prerogative #14

It is your peddler's prerogative to bail on a forced fit. Whenever you see one coming, quickly parse it. It is usually an overactive imagination, desperation, or stupidity. Whatever it is, you have to throw the flag and make the call. Sit the peddler down and bring them back to reality.

Peddler's Prerogative #15

It is your prerogative not to take anything that happens in the sales process PERSONALLY. When bad stuff happens, it is your prerogative to pick yourself up, dust yourself off, and straighten your clothes (doing your best Charlie Chaplin, of course). Proceed to go about your day.

Peddler's Prerogative #16

It is your prerogative to forget the spotlight and focus on the details of the deal. It is your prerogative to realize that that's the way to preempt rejection, and that your spectacular moment is when you have cashed your commission check and are buying pizza and beer!

Peddler's Prerogative #17

Repeat after me: It is OK to be a peddler. It is OK to sell for a living. It is OK to tell prospects and customers that you want to sell them your product for cash. It is OK to ask for an order. And, above all, it is OK to treat your prospects and customers right and be true. It is all OK. (Psst! You can fire your psychiatrist now. It's all okey-dokey!)

Peddler's Prerogative #18

You have chosen to be a peddler and it's your prerogative to enhance or detract from the general world view of your chosen profession. It is under your control, so don't be a featherhead.

Peddler's Prerogative #19

It is your peddler's prerogative to realize that you are never going to sell anything to the wrong company or the wrong person at the wrong time. It ain't ever gonna happen!

Peddler's Prerogative #20

It is your prerogative to be a peddler who prospects and customers can rely on to look out for them and their interests. Make it your business to know the score.

Peddler's Prerogative #21

The world of the peddler is an ongoing morality play and you are either a champion of the good side or the dark side. It's your prerogative to choose to champion the good. Remember, right is right!

Peddler's Prerogative #22

It is always a peddler's prerogative to avoid the dance of death. If you are associated with a company that is unscrupulous, immoral, or corrupt, DITCH!

Peddler's Prerogative #23

It is your peddler's prerogative to be a mystic of the corporate world!

Peddler's Prerogative #24

It is your prerogative to remind yourself and your management that selling isn't a chess match or a 12-step program. It's an ongoing dialogue, an easy straightforward conversation.

Peddler's Prerogative #25

It is the peddler's prerogative to think big and outside the box. To dream about taking a little local deal with a lot of goodness and turn it into a monster of global business. Think big! Really big! BIG, BIG, BIG!

Peddler's Prerogative #26

Marketing in most companies is a hit or miss proposition. It is your prerogative to listen politely to their spin and then figure out for yourself how to sell your product. There's no earthly reason for letting a bunch of marketeers hold a perfectly good product HOSTAGE!

Peddler's Prerogative #27

It is your peddler's prerogative to believe or ditch. Believing in you, your product, and your company is square one if you want to experience the magic of being a great peddler.

Peddler's Prerogative #28

It's your peddler's prerogative to believe that it's not IF you'll get the deal, but WHEN.

Peddler's Prerogative #29

When it's the end of the quarter and your peddler reality starts to twirl and whir, it is your prerogative to cease and desist, and be patient. It is better to be patient than to tick off a prospect or customer, or have the value sucked right out of your deal.

Peddler's Prerogative #30

It is your peddler's prerogative to learn to be patient and suffer gladly for your deals.

Peddler's Prerogative #31

It is the peddler's prerogative to map his or her company, and figure out who can get things done, who can't, who won't, and who always says nope.

Peddler's Prerogative #32

It is the peddler's prerogative to enthusiastically embrace anyone or anything that moves him or her closer to a sale, and to wholeheartedly ignore anyone or anything that doesn't.

Peddler's Prerogative #33

It is the peddler's prerogative to demand that the company makes it easy for peddlers to sell and easy for customers to buy.

Peddler's Prerogative #34

If folks frustrate you it is your prerogative to ignore them. If you can't ignore them, then it is your prerogative to hide your dismay and limit your exposure. If that doesn't work, it's your prerogative to get someone else to deal with them on your behalf. Forget about explaining or trying to make them see your point. That never works! It is your prerogative to stay away from the last resort, which is blowing up their universe. Stay away from this alternative at all cost. That is unless of course, you are really ready to take that long walk or are really in the mood.

Ladies and gentlemen please stand back . . .

Peddler's Prerogative #35

It is your prerogative to truly understand the paradox of using a bazooka to kill a mosquito. It's not the best use of a resource, but it sure as hell gets the job done. It is also your prerogative to share your high-impact weapons with your fellow peddlers.

Peddler's Prerogative #36

It is your prerogative to classify your executive group into the good, the bad, and the ugly, and to facilitate a good and meaningful relationship with the good executives. The relationships you create will spawn an awesome selling team when you need it.

Peddler's Prerogative #37

It is your prerogative to remember that in the world of the corporate executive, there are good execs who can keep companies alive and well, bad execs who can put companies on respirators, and ugly execs who can kill them!

Peddler's Prerogative #38

It is your prerogative to realize that you must verily, and I DO MEAN VERILY, respect and honor the administrators in your life. If you do, you have a shot at success. If you don't, you will take the longest of walks off the shortest of piers.

Peddler's Prerogative #39

If you are a hunter, it is your prerogative to make a mint and be the best individual contributor you can be. If a company can't handle that, it is your prerogative to mosey on down the road, find a better position, or start your own business and buy them!

Peddler's Prerogative #40

If you are a farmer, it is your prerogative to go as far as you wish up the corporate ladder. If you like, you can work your way right up to chairman and CEO.

Peddler's Prerogative #41

It is the peddler's prerogative to make sure management under-stands that he or she prefers to be paid rather than praised. It is your prerogative to suggest they save the money spent on recogni-tion meetings and sign some checks for the best peddlers.

Peddler's Prerogative #42

It is the peddler's prerogative to advise the marketer he deems rele-vant (the higher the better) that he will be taking him or her out to the field. It is also the peddler's prerogative to tell said marketer that resistance will be futile, as he will take him or her kicking and screaming out of the building by any means necessary. It is the ped-dler's prerogative to delight muchly as the customer reads the mar-keter the riot act.

Peddler's Prerogative #44

It is every peddler's prerogative to discover who knows the most about the product he or she is selling. It is also your prerogative to engage those folks in your deals, overtly or covertly.

Peddler's Prerogative #45

It is your prerogative to figure out how to bust out the cavalry from corporate. If you're going to be good at anything, be good at that! Be adroit, but never cavalier or wasteful. You'll screw it up for the rest of us.

Peddler's Prerogative #46

It is your prerogative to remember that every product has a product manager and you have a one in three chance of it being an enlightened and engaging one. It is also your prerogative to find out fast if you are blessed with a good one or in need of an alternate strategy.

Peddler's Prerogative #47

It is the peddler's prerogative to avoid getting stuck in *magical reality* and not to be led astray by unreasonable hope, quiet desperation, or fanciful, wishful thinking, as it is the quickest way to get your ass in a sling!

Peddler's Prerogative #48

There are two kinds of accounts: right accounts and wrong accounts. It is your prerogative to pursue right accounts until the cows come home. It is your unequivocal duty not to kid yourself and waste time on wrong accounts. Every peddler knows up from down and right from wrong. Stick with right accounts and ditch wrong accounts.

Peddler's Prerogative #49

When you find a right account, then it's just a question of strategy and timing before you hook them. If you pursue a wrong account, you will never get them. So stop. Don't go after wrong accounts. Peddlers have an incredible capacity to try and make wrong accounts right accounts. This is a frivolous act.

Peddler's Prerogative #50

It is your prerogative as a peddler to understand the entire history of the company, its products, and services. It's your prerogative to know why and how they were created. It is important to understand the historical perspective so that you become an authority and can chronicle the product inside your head. It is your absolute prerogative to get this information from the people in the know. It is not their prerogative to put you off, ever.

Peddler's Prerogative #51

When you find a target or prospect that's "right," it is absolutely your peddler's prerogative to immediately start to see and think of them as a customer, they just haven't realized it yet! So be it.

Peddler's Prerogative #52

When prospecting and finding deals it is your prerogative to never say never on any idea or presuppose that this or that will not work until you have actually tried it by picking up the phone or getting in front of and talking to the prospect. If you think you can't then you can't! This kind of predictive attitude is stupid. Says me!

Peddler's Prerogative #53

When it comes to deals, pipelines, and forecasts, it is the peddler's prerogative to understand the agreement between corporate and the field. What is a qualified prospect? When does a deal enter the pipeline? And when does a deal go on the forecast? If the answers seem fuzzy or look funny, the adroit peddler should adjust accordingly and vacate the premises.

Peddler's Prerogative #54

It is your peddler's prerogative to leave nothing to chance, be ever vigilant, monitor everything, and maintain a meaningful dialogue with all key players—inside your prospect's company and inside your company!

Peddler's Prerogative #55

Never, never, never try and be a techie with a techie. He or she knows you are not and will think you are a dope if you try.

Peddler's Prerogative #56

As a peddler with a qualified deal, it is your prerogative to first find the navigator and second, determine the reason or compelling scenario that creates a sense of urgency about doing the deal.

Peddler's Prerogative #57

It is the peddler's prerogative to summarize the product and opportunity to every new face that appears during a meeting. This revolving door lets you reinforce the fit among the other participants. Turn a negative into a positive whenever you can.

Peddler's Prerogative #58

It is your prerogative to meet with your counterparts at all of your competitors. It's an essential part of understanding and familiarizing yourself with the market. It's extending your web. It shows you are a smart peddler. It's OK to be friends with the peddlers you are competing against. Remember, it's a very small world.

Peddler's Prerogative #59

It is the peddler's prerogative to make sure the prospect understands the value propositions. Anything less than 100% will proportionately decrease your chances of closing the business.

Peddler's Prerogative #60

It is the peddler's prerogative to avoid fighting for control of a deal, and make a rational call, deal by deal, whether he or she or the prospect is going to run the deal. When the prospect leads the deal, the good peddler remains in the game, participating and influencing accordingly. The smart peddler makes sure he or she is always sitting at the table.

Peddler's Prerogative #61

Peddling is about moving deals down the line. It is the peddler's prerogative to be ever vigilant about any detail, no matter how trivial, that could slow down a deal, and to make it his or her number one priority to exert his or her influence to keep the deal moving. It is also the peddler's prerogative to be anal retentive about every aspect of his or her deal. The devil is in the details.

Peddler's Prerogative #62

It is the peddler's prerogative not to be intimidated by the closing myth. Closing is simply the end of the selling process. When the last question is answered, you are done and the deal is closed.

Peddler's Prerogative #63

It is the peddler's prerogative to make sure that as a deal gets done, it is a good and fair deal for folks on both sides of the table. Bad deals always come back to haunt the perpetrating party. This is the karma of peddlery. Don't mess with it!

Peddler's Prerogative #64

As a peddler, it is your prerogative to choose only good deals and then set the tone for getting them done. You can let it be known that to do business with you, a prospect must be COOL!

Peddler's Prerogative #65

If you take the time to ask all the key questions in each phase of the selling process, it is your prerogative to take the time to listen heartily to the answers. Don't ever ask a question and then tune out or interrupt the prospect as he or she is answering. Save that for your sales manager!

Peddler's Prerogative #66

It is your peddler's prerogative to get to the verbal as fast as you can. A verbal from a reliable source means you're in! Enjoy the verbal, as it usually means you are getting the business. It also means it is time to buckle down and put this puppy to bed.

Peddler's Prerogative #67

Pricing models should be simple and easy to explain to anyone—and I do mean ANYONE. If your mother can't understand how much your products costs, then marketing has gone overboard once again. It is your peddler's prerogative to haul them back into the boat.

Peddler's Prerogative #68

It is your peddler's prerogative not to turn pricing and negotiations into a full-fledged drama. Be cool, calm, straightforward, and logical. Pricing is just pricing. Nevertheless, make doubly and triply sure you COMPLETELY understand it before opening your yap!

Peddler's Prerogative #69

When involved in contract negotiations, it is your prerogative not to think you are a lawyer and negotiate legal terms and conditions. Join the business bargaining, but keep your mouth closed during any legal wrangling. We all know you are blessed and wonderful, but you ain't a lawyer, bucko, so cool your jets.

Peddler's Prerogative #70

During negotiations, never take no as an answer until you hear it three times. Folks who say no three times really mean it. Less than that, however, and they may change their minds. It is your peddler's prerogative to follow the three-times rule and make sure no means no!

Peddler's Prerogative #71

During the last part of the closing cycle, keep everything grounded in reality. Prospects can lose perspective and believe they can get more than is fair. Keep their reality quotient at 42. Search me, it's that Zen thing again!

Peddler's Prerogative #72

It is the peddler's prerogative to know when the heck to close his or her yap and stop selling. It is hard to do. Selling is a peddler's natural state. But when you have the deal, for the love of Pete, remember to stop selling. Stop selling. STOP SELLING!

Peddler's Prerogative #73

The deal isn't done until you have cashed your commission check. If you are not using that money to buy yourself a pizza and some beer, you can't allow yourself to think all is fine. You have to make triple sure that the P.O. is getting through the bureaucracy at the customer's company and then at yours. It's your responsibility no matter what anyone tries to tell you. Don't foul up!

Peddler's Prerogative #74

Your word is all you have. If your company makes a commitment, that is your commitment; its word is your word. It is your peddler's prerogative to fight tooth and nail to keep your word and your good standing. If prospects and customers can't trust your word, you are dead and so it will go with your company as well.

ABOUT THE AUTHOR

DENNIS FORD is the founder and principal of Next Phase Business Development, a company that helps businesses achieve high-revenue growth.

As an expert peddler and 25-year veteran of the high-tech industry, Dennis knows that for a company to achieve its growth potential, everyone has to be on the sales team. Corporate, management, marketing, engineering, manufacturing, distribution, operations—everyone must come together, have a meeting of the minds, and commit to increasing sales.

This is a radical concept for many folks, but Dennis has proven it works. He has successfully ramped up startups as well as expanded business for established companies by transforming them from disparate, autonomous departments into well-honed selling machines. The results are companies that focus first on selling or supporting those who do and, second, on making customers 100% satisfied so they, too, become part of the team, gladly recommending a company and its products to others.

Dennis relies on his philosophy of peddling that he has developed over the years working for large and small, domestic and international companies. Now that it's been sufficiently battle-tested, Dennis presents his philosophy in this book.

www.ingramcontent.com/pod-product-compliance
Lightning Source LLC
Chambersburg PA
CBHW031806190326
41518CB00006B/218